100 DAYS

100 DAYS

GABRIEL JOSIPOVICI

LITTLE ISLAND PRESS

in collaboration with Carcanet

First published in Great Britain in 2021 by
Little Island Press / Carcanet
Alliance House, 30 Cross Street
Manchester M2 7AQ
www.carcanet.co.uk

A CIP catalogue record for this book is
available from the British Library.

ISBN 978 1 80017 203 6

Book design by Andrew Latimer
Printed in Great Britain by SRP Ltd, Exeter, Devon

Supported using public funding by the National Lottery
through Arts Council England.

Contents

for Tamar

When I learned that we were going into lockdown I decided I mustn't fritter away the unexpected gift of a bracket round life which the virus had imposed on us. What I needed, I felt, was a project which would be absorbing yet not too demanding, partly because anything really demanding, like getting down to a novel or even a short story, would probably be impossible for me in a time of extreme anxiety and uncertainty; and partly because such a task, were I to attempt it, would, I knew from past experience, make me an extremely difficult companion to be with and I did not want to inflict this on my partner. I decided then that I would keep a diary for a hundred days and that I would follow this every day with a short thought or memory, one a day, connected to a person, place, concept or work of art that had played a role in my life. These could not, in the nature of it, be perfect little essays or perfectly rounded autobiographical fragments, but rather a way of talking to myself in order to arrive somewhere I could not have arrived at without the day's work. And a hundred days, I imagined, would probably take us to the end of, or perhaps a little past, the lockdown.

Vaguely recalling Tony Rudolf's delightful memoir of his early years, *The Alphabet of Memory*, I also decided that I would allow the alphabet to trigger these thoughts and memories. Despite the fact that as a constraint this was fairly weak, since I would get to choose what topics to write about under each letter, I thought it might push me to revisit areas I might not have thought of had I written either randomly or chronologically. It might also, I thought, be interesting to see what sorts of juxtapositions the alphabet would throw up. And this indeed proved to be the case. I would not have thought of writing about Agami, the little resort near Alexandria where as a child I had spent a happy fortnight, or *Zazie dans le métro*, had the alphabet not nudged me in those directions.

I also decided that I would not write about any topic I had covered at length elsewhere, so Ivy Compton-Burnett but not Proust, spirals but not touch. I had no idea if my alphabetical list of subjects would take me to the end of the hundred days I had allocated to myself but I felt I should leave this to chance. I scribbled down a provisional list of items and every afternoon when we returned from our daily walk on the Downs I would sit down with a cup of tea and look over the list and add or take away a topic here or there.

As it happened my alphabetical thoughts and memories came to an end with Zoos on 26 June, ninety-seven days after I had started. And around that time the Government announced that there would be an almost complete easing of the lockdown restrictions on 4 July even though none of its own criteria for doing so had been met, so my hundred days was a pretty accurate forecast of the length of the lockdown.

The days did not go quite according to plan. On several occasions I was not able to complete my account of a thought or memory in one day and had to let it spill over into two; and once or twice I felt unwell and unable to do more than jot something down for the diary. As, towards the end, I realised I was going to fall just short of my hundred days, I tried to think of a few additional topics to write about, but none of these fulfilled the criterion I had set myself of making each day's writing a genuine exploration. In the end there are 86 thoughts and memories for the hundred days of the diary and the whole is, I now realise, an attempt to come to terms with my life as I approach my eightieth birthday.

When I was three-quarters of the way through I took Tony Rudolf's book down from my shelves to have another look at it and discovered that it was called not *The Alphabet of Memory* but *The Arithmetic of Memory*. Such are the delightful tricks memory plays on one.

Lewes, 25.9.2020

22.3.2020

Just past the Spring Equinox. Tomorrow, 23 March, twenty-fourth anniversary of Sacha's death. And a week in to the moment the coronavirus pandemic really hit the UK. That was on Monday 16 March, when the Government began to announce measures which have, by today, more or less brought the country to a standstill, as all places of mass gatherings, pubs, restaurants, theatres, sports venues, etc. have been ordered to close as from tomorrow and all those 'at risk', those with chronic conditions, pregnant mothers, and over seventies, have been advised to 'self-isolate'. Strange to feel so fit and well and yet know one is well into the 'at risk' category, and this is no mild flu but at best, if one catches a severe version of it, an excruciating week or two, and at worst, an excruciating death, as doctors struggle to keep one breathing. And I am haunted by the thought that my grandmother died exactly a hundred years ago of typhoid during the typhoid epidemic that swept across Egypt in 1920.

I imagine this is what the Phony War of 1939–40 felt like: you wait for the enemy to strike and both can't quite believe he will and are filled with nameless dread in case he does. But of course even when 'he' does there will be none of the horror of bombs and bullets, but none of the solidarity either, since each of us has been told to retreat into our houses and only go out for essentials or for exercise. So T has come down here to Lewes, though she is concerned about her mother, a not so frail ninety-two. But John, her brother-in-law, as a doctor, has (wisely in my view) told her there would nothing she could do for her mother in London, that her sister and brother are there, and there are two doctors in the family – and that anyway there will be no policing of London's borders, so in a real crisis she could get into her car and drive up.

Since we are told that the worst will be upon us in the next twelve weeks, that this may well last six and even as much as twelve months, I have decided I need a project to settle down to every morning. Since, alas, the longer fiction I so much crave to be at work on is still very nebulous, I have decided to use the alphabet to trigger memories and thoughts and try and write a memory or thought every day; and I have decided to preface each session with a brief 'coronavirus diary', of which this is the first and necessarily the longest instalment. Longest just because it is the first and I need to bring myself up to date, so to speak.

Who would have guessed, as the parliamentary Brexit saga dragged to its painful and horrible conclusion in the last quarter of 2019, ending with the nightmare of an eighty-seat Conservative majority and the certainty that we would leave the EU and that we would have five years at least of a bragging and reckless government slowly turning the country into an English version of Hungary and Poland (gradual erosion of any opposition, be it in the media, the judiciary or the universities) – who would have guessed that in the last week we have become a kind of Leninist country, with the state in effect employing the workers to keep things running? Johnson and the Tories, who crushed the opposition and cowed and uplifted the country, depending on your point of view, with a vision of heroic Britain at war with Europe and going it alone, now find themselves in effect presiding over a country at war – but not with Europe or with any visible enemy, but with a virus that is rapidly spreading world-wide and promises to decimate the planet in a way not seen in peace-time since the great Spanish flu pandemic of 1918–26. It is likely to be with us for a long time to come, though in eighteen months or so there is a chance that a vaccine will have been developed and put into general circulation. But how effective will it be? We have seen with the common flu vaccines that they often don't work, and we are told that this is very different from the flu. What will the country, Europe, the world, be like then?

There are some positives. Already, only weeks after countries shut down travel, China, where the Covid-19 virus started to infect humans, is showing a marked decrease in its emissions of greenhouse gases, with the great cities visibly less polluted, and Venice, since the vaporetti no longer run and the vast cruise ships have stopped coming, is swiftly and miraculously returning to what it must once have been, with swans and herons on the canals and the water clear enough for one to spot seaweed waving in its depths.

And countries, cowed for so long by populists bent on destroying the fabric of the state and of communities, are beginning to see that there is some virtue in efficient governments which can organise their countries to deal with a world-wide emergency, where inter-country co-operation in the field of science and the production of medicines and hospital equipment is a vital necessity, and where – in Britain at any rate – the innate kindness of people and their spirit of caring for each other, long thought dead, is suddenly blossoming. Whether any of this will survive the pandemic is of course a moot point. It may be that, as after the financial crisis of 2008, things will soon get back to 'normal' – but I wonder if modern capitalism and its mantra of ever more progress will have taken such a beating that some things at least will change – fuelled by the desperation of the young for far swifter action on global warming.

For me, at this moment, the key thing about it is that, unlike the last fifty-plus years of my life, spent in relative comfort in England, where what made me uneasy was that there was nothing to push against, that the march of consumerism and Americanism, which I was deeply troubled by, seemed inevitable and unstoppable, rather like one's nightmares of being slowly suffocated by an octopus, now there is something to push against, something that is making us change our habits drastically, calling all this into question – as perhaps religion did in earlier centuries.

Enough of banalities. On with the alphabetical memories.

Aachen

Robert Browning wrote a rather bad poem in rollicking verse, 'How They Brought the Good News from Ghent to Aix', published in his 1845 collection, which I had to study for A-level. The poem leaves it deliberately vague as to what the news is that the three riders are bringing from one town to another, and in the days before the internet if nothing was said about it in the notes and the teacher did not think it important enough to highlight, one was left to make do as best one could. My mother had often talked to me of the years she and my father spent in Aix as young students coming from Egypt and enrolling in the philosophy department of the University of Aix-Marseille to study under the distinguished philosopher Philippe Segond, so I presumed this was the locus of Browning's poem. I had no very clear idea of the geography or history of Europe, so no idea what the good news might be or where Ghent was or what the distance was these riders would have had to travel. It was only much later, after several years in England and a growing understanding of the Middle Ages, that I discovered that the Aix in question was not Aix-en-Provence, where my parents had studied, but Aix-la-Chapelle, the town where from the 770s to his death in 814 Charlemagne had established his court and where he had built a cathedral which all the commentators described as one of the strangest in the world. The word *aix*, I discovered, is the French for the Roman *aqua* and merely signifies that both towns were spas, where the Romans had discovered springs from which healing waters gushed. Aachen is still called Bad Aachen in German. It is a mere 200 kilometres from Ghent to Aachen, and, since the latter remained the centre of the Holy Roman Empire (strategically placed between the Frankish and Germanic kingdoms) till as late as 1531, the place where all the Emperors were crowned kings of the Germans, it is perfectly easy to imagine that news (of an attack or uprising repulsed?) would have gone there as quickly as possible from an outlying town, and that this is what Browning's poem must be about. It doesn't make the poem any better, but I wonder how much of the content of one's mind at any one time is made up of this jumble of true and false facts, unwarranted suppositions and a kind of benign darkness. For we seem on the whole to manage perfectly well and we do this, as Wittgenstein was always at pains to point out, by constant correcting or jettisoning of what are discovered to be false assumptions.

Some years after my revelation about the many spas or Aixes dotted about France, on our way to the Dolomites, my mother and I stopped at Aachen to visit the strange cathedral, originally built on the model of S. Vitale in Ravenna but added to for the next six centuries, leaving a curious and unsatisfactory mixture of styles, though the Carolingian portions, Charlemagne's marble throne, and the circular fountain outside are still etched on my memory.

23.3.2020

Nothing has changed radically, though lockdown officially starts today. Phony War still on in Britain, though Spain, Italy, France and Germany, the first two especially, well in the grip of it. People point out that at this stage in the pandemic other countries, even Italy, had fewer deaths per infected cases than the UK. But the Public Health England officers point out that these are very unreliable statistics.

The threat of a complete shut-down, with no one allowed out even to walk, has been raised, but only if people continue to flout the advice and go out in groups, etc. Were this to come into force I think that for me it would change everything. At the moment I'm very happy working, walking and reading. But I need to walk.

Abraham

'And the Lord said to Abram: "Go forth from your land and your birthplace and your father's house to the land I will show you. And I will make you a great nation and I will bless you and make your name great and you shall be a blessing. And I will bless those who bless you, and those who damn you I will curse, and all the clans of the earth through you shall be blessed." And Abram went forth as the Lord had spoken to him and Lot went forth with him, Abram being seventy-five years old when he left Haran. And Abram took Sarai his wife and Lot his nephew and all the goods they had gotten and the folk they had bought in Haran, and they set out on the way to the land of Canaan, and they came to the land of Canaan. And Abram crossed through the land to the site of Schechem, to the Terebinth of the Oracle. The Canaanite was then in the land. And the Lord appeared to Abram and said: "To your seed I will give this land." And he built an altar to the Lord who had appeared to him. And he pulled up his stakes from there for the high country east of Bethel and pitched his tent with Bethel to the west and Ai to the east, and he built there an altar to the Lord, and he invoked the name of the Lord. And Abram journeyed onward by stages to the Negeb.'

(*Genesis* 12: 1-10)

Robert Alter, whose translation I have used, succinctly makes the point that many have of course made before him: 'Abram, a mere figure in a notation of genealogy and migration in the preceding passage becomes an individual character and begins the Patriarchal narratives, when he is here addressed by God.' But he of course begins more than that. Here we are at the origin of the Hebrew nation. And that origin consists not in identification with the land, as is the case with most (all?) foundation myths, but with a getting up and a going. In Jewish culture the *locus classicus* of this is the exodus from Egypt, repeated playfully and sacramentally every year in the celebration of Passover, but here is where it starts. The story feels very ancient and clearly belongs to a culture very different from our own. Alter points out that what he has translated as 'he pulled up his stakes', (AV 'and he removed from thence') is his rendering of the Hebrew *waya'ateq* a word that 'is meticulous in reflecting the procedures of nomadic life'. The term for 'journey' in the following verse, he goes on, 'also derives from another term for pulling up tent stakes'. And the whole narrative is driven by the Lord speaking to Abram, who later builds Him an altar, while elsewhere we are told of a 'Terebinth of the Oracle'. But though all this gives us the feeling of far-off times and places, the essence of the story – and this is true of so many of the stories in the Hebrew Bible – is one every Jew – and, alas, today, not only every Jew – can identify with: the voice comes, saying: 'Get up and go', *lekh lekha*, literally 'go you'. And Abram, who will later be shown not to be afraid to argue with God, simply 'went forth as the Lord had spoken to him'. I think of my mother, in 1956, deciding that the time had come to leave Egypt – where she had been born and to which she had returned with me after surviving the war in France – despite the advice of her sister and all her friends to at least keep some roots there – not sell the property which had been her inheritance and ferret the money out to Switzerland, losing two thirds of it in the process. No, my mother said, there's no future in Egypt for a non-Moslem, we are getting out. And this even though all we knew was that I had a place reserved as a day-boy in an English school and there was no certainty that she would be able to settle in England herself. She was forty-five.

And I think of Elly, T's mother, leaving Vienna at the age of ten with her parents and her brother and sister, in the immediate wake of the Anschluss, for a new life in England, a country whose language she did not speak and about which she knew nothing. 'It was the best thing that could have happened to me', she has said in a film made by her daughter-in-law about the exodus of the Jews of Vienna in 1938. 'It taught me to think for myself.'

I recently found myself on a panel during Jewish Book Week, with two distinguished speakers, one of whom, an Auschwitz survivor I greatly admired. I was therefore horrified to hear her saying: 'People have always found us Jews very strange, they have always been suspicious of us.' And, later on: 'Jews are exceptional. What other people has produced so many great men like Einstein and Freud?' Every people thinks it's exceptional: the Irish, the English, the French, the Germans, the Chinese – the list is interminable. All have felt misunderstood and have consoled themselves with the thought that they can number very many great men amongst their people. Such ideas are not only misguided, they are dangerous. Of course Jews are different, but not because they are 'special' but because so many of us have, like Abram (he is only later called Abraham), had to get up and go, and there is nothing like crossing borders to give one a sense of how complex life is and there is nothing like living amongst different nations to make one see that none of them has a monopoly on the truth or on righteousness.

But, it will be argued, this very passage that you have quoted tells us that God picked out Abram and informed him that if he did as he was told, He would make him 'a great nation'. Is that not proof that the Jews have been specially chosen, are, indeed, The Chosen People? I would answer that it all depends on how one understands 'chosen' and how one understands 'a great nation' and one that 'will be a blessing'. It seems to me that the passage implies that God did not choose Abraham because of some special virtue in him, though that is how the rabbis understood it, filling in the silence of the Bible as to Abram's earlier life with pious stories about how he fought the idol-worshippers around him and retained his faith in a God who has no image. But all the Bible tells us is that a man, Abram, received a sudden call from God, telling him to get up and go. I think we need to make the effort to see the radical contingency of that: *it could have been someone else, it happened to be Abram.* And with the call come obligations: if you are called, and if you answer, then... No more. No less. And if we are a people who grasp more clearly what life is about than those who have always lived in one place we should also know that all peoples are different and none has a monopoly on truth or on God.

Today, of course, instead of wanderers and refugees being a minority among the peoples of the world they are most probably the majority. Everyone is on the move. And I found it particularly obnoxious of my fellow panellist that day at King's Place to describe Angela Merkel's actions in opening the German borders as 'giving way to her heart rather than her head and letting in a tide from the Middle East'. A tide? However one feels about the wisdom or not of Merkel's actions in 2015, Jews of all people should not generalise in this way about migrants, for from the time of Abram that is what, in the main, they themselves have been.

The Government tightened the regulations still further yesterday in response to images of crowds on Hampstead Heath at the weekend and tubes packed with travellers: all but essential shops (food shops, chemists) to close, no one to go out except for essential shopping and once a day for exercise. That's what T and I were doing anyway. Downs a bit busier than usual on Sunday but quiet yesterday, a typical fine Monday. Some complain the Government has taken these decisions much too late and is horrendously behind with its provision of protective gear for medical staff, ventilators and testing equipment, that they had two months to prepare but somehow hoped it would all blow away. And the supermarket shelves are apparently still emptied, as if by locusts. My neighbour, a Greek from Crete, says: It's English individualism, it's not like that in Italy or Greece or even Germany. If he's right this can be traced back to the Reformation, but must that series of events itself not merely have thrust to the fore something deeply embedded in English culture? Perhaps, but I don't see it in Chaucer or Langland or *Beowulf* – those great 'English' poets and poems that are one with the rest of the Europe of their time. Or in Shakespeare, despite the attempts by successive waves of jingoists to turn him into a celebrant of 'true Englishness'.

Adjective (and Adverb)

'I've written it because I need to make some money,' Rosalind said to me once. 'There are two adjectives in every sentence, so it should go down well.'

Like me, she thinks adjectives and adverbs are the visible sign of all that is wrong with the novel. Here, from the first page of an Iris Murdoch novel, is an example of what we mean:

Hilda and Rupert Foster, celebrating their twentieth wedding anniversary with a bottle of *rather dry* champagne, were sitting in *the evening sun* in the garden of their house in Priory Grove, London, S.W.10. Hilda, a plumper angel now, *reclined limply*, exhibiting *shiny burnished* knees below *a short shrift dress* of *orangy yellow*.

Admittedly Murdoch carries this to extremes, but the principle is the same. Novelists like Murdoch, which means ninety-nine percent of all the novels published in the world since the war, see it as their task to tell a story, but, no longer in active dialogue with an audience as the traditional story-teller once was, feel they have to 'see their characters' and find the words to make the reader see them in turn. They have, they think, to persuade their readers that this is more than a story, it is life itself passing before them. They imagine that the more adjectives and adverbs they use the more the reader will forget he or she is reading a book and enter the world the writer has conjured up for them. What I find is that exactly the opposite happens to me: the more adjectives and adverbs are used the more I am aware of the writer using words and the less I believe in what he or she is saying.

We have an almost copy-book example of the transition from the storyteller to the novelist in the successive editions the Brothers Grimm put out between 1812 and 1857 of their *Kinder und Hausmärchen* – constantly rewriting them and expanding the collection. The first edition itself was based on a manuscript written in 1810. We can thus trace how what had started out as a collection of German tales, collected and transcribed by them as part of a project which we find replicated in many European countries throughout the nineteenth century to foster national self-awareness gradually turned into a hugely popular book of stories aimed at children.

Here is the start of the well-known tale which opens the collection. In the 1810 manuscript it reads: 'The king's youngest daughter went out into the forest and sat down by *a cool well*. Then she took a *golden ball* and was playing with it when it *suddenly* rolled down into the well.' In the manuscript, as Joyce Crick, whose excellent Penguin selection and translation I am using, explains, the stories 'were written down with little attention to style, often with abbreviated forms, insertions and minimal punctuation', which she has normalised. In the first sentence there is one adjective, *cool*, which is not a description of how the well looked, but how it felt to the little girl. One would not wish it absent, for in one short word it explains why the child was drawn to go there. In the second sentence, similarly, there is one adjective, *golden*, which again does not so much help one to see the ball as signal how precious it was to her. That sentence ends with the crucial verb, *rolled down*, which leads into the third sentence, which is full of verbs: 'She *watched* it *falling*... and *stood* at the well and *was* very sad.' Even the *was*, hardly an expressive verb, here acquires great force precisely through its passivity: all she can do is stand and *be sad*.

Here now is the version in the first, 1812, edition of their great collection:

> There was once a king's daughter who went out into the forest and sat down by *a cool well*. She had *a golden ball* which was *her favourite toy*; she would throw it up high and catch it again in the air, and enjoyed herself as she did this. One day the ball *had risen very high*, she had already stretched out her hand and curled her fingers ready to catch it when it bounced past onto the ground quite close to her and rolled straight into the water. [The German is better: *rollte und rollte und geradezu in das Wasser hinein*.]

Here the rot has started to set in. Why say that the ball was her favourite toy? The manuscript version knows it is and trusts the narrative to bring that out; the 1812 version feels it has to *explain* and so loses time and energy. In the same way there is no need for 'had risen very high' – what is important is that the ball gets away from her control and falls into the well. All that business of 'she had already stretched out her hand and curled her fingers ready to catch it' is redundant, as is 'rolled straight into the water' – it rolled into the water, that's enough.

And here, finally, are the first lines of the much longer 1856 version:

> Not far from the king's palace there lay *a big, dark forest*, and in the forest, beneath *an ancient linden* tree, there was a well. Now if it was *a very hot day* the king's daughter would go out into the forest and sit at the edge of *the cold well*; and if she was bored she would take *a golden ball* and throw it up high and catch it again; and that was *her favourite toy*.

Now the rot has well and truly set in. The collection, which had started out as an attempt by the brothers to record and publish ancient Germanic tales, is now firmly a children's book and this is what they believe children will respond to: atmosphere. So the forest is not just a forest but big and dark, and though we all imagine that if the well was in the forest she must have sat down under a tree, this is now spelled out and the tree described: ancient, linden. The girl does not just start to play with her ball, she does so because she is bored; and it is insisted upon that it is her favourite toy.

It is clear even from this that the brothers grew more and more self-conscious the longer they lived with the stories they had collected, and, as they saw it, refined and improved them, though some (me included) feel that instead they came close to ruining them. For children don't need atmosphere: the parent's voice is enough, what they want is *the story*.

Benjamin was right: the novelist, unhoused, exiled, no longer a story-teller telling his stories in public but a private individual writing alone in his study, feels, in his impoverishment, that he must hide this at all costs, that he must either disappear altogether or create a *persona*, as the Grimms do here or as Dickens does, which will somehow 'speak' to the growing and absent audience. And clearly, in spite of the puncturing of the assumptions that lie behind both the genial persona and the 'neutral' narrator by a Cervantes or a Sterne, they have proved right: the 'traditional' novel has brushed all literary competition aside and still reigns supreme, though more and more with a sense that it is fighting a rearguard action against film, television and online 'reality' entertainment.

For some of us, though, the whole thing feels like a sorry charade. I think of Duchamp's remark: 'It is demeaning to a painter to expect him to fill in the background.' A well-placed adjective, such as 'cool' for the well is fine, a playfully used adjective, as we get it in Chandler and Wodehouse ('The refined moon which served Blandings Castle and district, was nearly at its full, and the ancestral home of Clarence, ninth Earl of Emsworth, had for some hours now been flooded by its silver rays'), is also fine, but adjectives that aim to set the scene only get in the way.

But that of course is a personal view. The bulk of the book-reading public and the judges of literary prizes clearly think otherwise. But my body balks at the of use adjectives and adverbs, and I can't gainsay it. Aharon Appelfeld said to me once: 'My style I learned from the masters of clarity and simplicity, Kleist and Kafka, and above all the narratives of the Bible.' That's my man.

25.3.2020

Last night on the telly, Matt Hancock, sent out by Johnson, couldn't quite bring himself to say it, but kept implying that it was all right to keep working if what you were doing was essential, and blaming Sadiq Khan for reducing the number of trains in London. When asked why then Scotland had decided to shut down all building work except for hospitals and the like he wriggled and squirmed and just repeated what he had said. Again, clash between money and life will cost lives (mine possibly) and do nothing for the economy.

Agami

I think I only visited it twice but on each occasion it was at an important juncture in my life.

Agami in the 1950s has been described as 'a compound for the elite of Egypt'. In fact it consisted of a few fairly simple holiday villas built on the white sand of the Mediterranean some twelve miles west of Alexandria, with no running water, so that it could only be used by those with cars. We didn't have a car but the parents of my friend Ronnie Sullam did, and one summer I was invited to spend a week with Ronnie, his younger brother and his parents in their villa. Did they rent it or own it? I have no idea. At twelve one doesn't ask questions like that.

I had never much liked Alexandria so had no great expectations, but I looked forward to the novelty of a car journey through the desert and then to a week away from the routines of home life. I had not expected the sheer unbelievable gloriousness of Agami. The sand was nothing like that in Alexandria but purer, whiter, deeper, softer, the sea was a blue I had never seen and, in the sand between the villas fig trees in full fruit grew in abundance.

As if that wasn't enough a girl inhabited one of the villas, a creature whose name and even whose appearance I can, alas, no longer recall, but whose swimsuited body filled our night-time dreams, our daydreams and our waking desires (though plucking ripe figs from the trees and eating them in our bathing suits as we waded in the shallow waters also figured and was a desire more easily satisfied). I think we spoke to her once or twice, she may even have swum with us, but we never really got to know her. Did she have friends with her? Siblings? I can only remember the intense rivalry that developed between Ronnie and me, never I think spoken about, for the favours of this nymph, though what we meant by 'favours' consisted, I suspect, of a laugh and a smile and perhaps the toss of her glowing curls.

The Agami I returned to three years later was still just as beautiful, just as unspoilt, but the times had changed and the nymph had gone. My mother and I were on our way out of Egypt. We had said goodbye to my aunt, my uncle, my cousins and the two dogs we had left with them, and taken the train to Alexandria with just the two suitcases my mother had decided would constitute our worldly possessions in this new stage in our lives. In Alexandria we stayed with Joe Tilche and his wife and it was they, with some friends, who took us out to Agami on the day before our boat was due to sail, a boat we were not sure we would in fact be sailing on, for if the authorities had found out we were leaving for good we would be taken in and asked to account for the money my mother had received on the sale of the house and, since it was (we hoped) now in a Swiss bank, who knows what we would be charged with, and we might well, I thought, end up in jail.

So the bathing and sunbathing in Agami, though as delightful as I had remembered it, was tinged with anxiety and foreboding, as well as with the huge weight of sadness I felt at leaving my friends and especially my dogs behind.

The next day we boarded the boat without trouble but the anxiety we felt at the possibility of being stopped did not abate till the boat finally sailed and from the deck we saw Alexandria and its harbour slowly disappearing in the haze of an Egyptian summer's day.

26.3.2020

Weather continues beautiful and Downs walks more and more enjoyable. Spring in the air and newborn lambs and blackthorn in the fields at Landport Bottom. But everywhere that strange sense of a phony war, waiting for the April Offensive. Yesterday the Government under pressure again for doing too little too late – still only 8,500 ventilating machines say the NHS though Hancock boasts of 12,000, a figure repeated by Johnson. But what worked for Brexit, when lies and reality happily intermixed in Government announcements, does not work when the NHS provides cold statistics, frontline staff still not given the protective clothing they need and the experts all insisting testing in the quantities needed will not be available for weeks – as with the ventilators, probably long after the peak of the epidemic has passed.

Albert

My uncle, the husband of mother's sister, Monika and Anna's father. The only Catholic in the group of Jewish *lycéens* to which my mother and aunt belonged in their twenties in Egypt, where they grew up, he was the one Chickie fell in love with. She determined not only to marry him but to convert. However, she had doubts, not about her love for him but about whether that love trumped her love of God. Should I marry

Albert or should I become a nun? she asked the priest who was instructing her. Marry Albert, he said, you are not cut out to be a nun. He was a wise man. No one was less suited to be a nun than my wilful and impulsive aunt, though the idea of one great renunciation which would make her life meaningful never left her and in later life she came to England and did try, with the help of her friend Manya Harari, Anna's godmother, to become a nun. She lasted barely three months.

A serious, calm, blonde man, the son of a Cairo jeweller, with a sister who had become a nun, Albert worked all his life as a clerk in a Cairo firm which made typewriters. His real life was elsewhere: at the Maadi Sporting Club, where he became librarian and at one time ran a regular music evening for members, playing records of his favourite classical music and, I am told, speaking knowledgeably about them; where in the summer he was to be seen in immaculate whites, playing bowls; and where, after the virtual breakdown of his marriage (though he and Chickie continued to share the same house), he flirted with the many bored and beautiful women, married and unmarried, who made up a fair proportion of the membership.

His day was probably typical of that of many middle-class men in Mediterranean countries at the time: he got up at 5.30, had a cold shower, breakfasted, caught the train to Cairo (15 minutes), worked in the office from seven to one, came home, showered, changed, had a leisurely lunch followed by a siesta, dressed and went out to the club, where he stayed till dinnertime at around eight-thirty or nine, or sometimes, if he had one of his musical evenings, ate at the club and was not home till eleven.

I remember him as a kind but reserved man. Part of the trouble was that my aunt loved animals and at one time had as many as forty cats, plus a few dogs, in the house, while he, though I don't think averse to the odd pet, loathed the all-pervasive smell of so many cats and of the meals my aunt was constantly having to cook to feed them all. It was a rule in their house that no cat should come into his room or into the dining room. I remember Sunday lunches there. The dining room was very large, with two French windows opening out onto a terrace and the garden and a raised dais at the end furthest from the door, where the large dining table stood. At one time a favourite cat of my aunt's had learned how to leap up to the door handle and hang on to it as it opened. We would be in the middle of a meal when the door would suddenly open, with Pazouki (why was he called that?) still clinging to the handle while the other cats, who had obviously lined up behind him, would stream in, my uncle would utter a stifled *Ah mais non alors!*, and my aunt and cousins would rush down to try and reverse the tide. Eventually all the cats would be bundled out of the room, the door shut again (and locked?) and we would settle down once more to our meal.

I can't remember Albert ever talking to me. Not that he was stand-offish, it just never (in my memory at least) happened. He was, however, a great raconteur and teller of jokes, always with a very straight face, *pince-sans-rire* the French called it. He would read out, or pretend to read out, adverts from the paper. '*Restaurant cherche petit vieux avec la tremblotte pour sucrer les fraises.*' [Restaurant seeks little old man with the shakes to sugar the strawberries] is one I particularly remember.

Though he sometimes conversed in Italian with my aunt and my cousins the language we all spoke together was French, though my aunt, like my mother, was bilingual in French and English, the result of having had an English nanny when they were small, and the girls, like me, had been to English schools. My aunt in fact preferred English to French literature and talked to me at length about her favourite books, Keats's *Letters* and de Quincey's *Confessions of an English Opium Eater*, and was happy to recite Donne's 'The Good Morrow', especially its opening, 'Busy old fool, unruly sun' (very apposite in that country ruled by the blazing sun) at every opportunity. I don't know if Albert ever read any English (or indeed Italian) books, but the Club library over which he presided was largely French.

I recall him coming out onto the terrace where we were sitting one day and telling us that the club library had just received a book, the text of a play that was all the rage in Paris, written by an Irishman living in France, *En Attendent Godot*. That would have been in 1953.

My aunt fell in love with an Italian builder/engineer, and, though he had a wife and daughter, he and his daughter were often at the house. I understood nothing of all this at the time of course. But eventually Albert took up with a much younger woman, a friend of his daughters. By that time the engineer had returned to Italy with his family and Chickie found Albert's new passion very hard to bear and decided to leave him and come to England. In her Buddhist way she imagined she could earn her living cleaning for people and thus keep her mind and spirit unsullied. She had not realised how hard and exhausting cleaning was, though she found some compensation when one of her employers thrust a sheaf of typewritten pages into her hand as she was leaving for the day and asked if she would be so kind as to read her poems and give her an opinion of them. After an abortive attempt to become a nun she returned to Egypt. They had forfeited the mortgage on their house (she was a terrible spendthrift and her animals had cost a small fortune) and settled into a small flat with a monkey and two dogs who had to be kept apart or they would fly at one another. The monkey found this great fun and when he could, would open the doors my aunt had carefully shut to keep the dogs apart. We saw them when we visited Egypt in 1984, twenty-eight years after we had left, and Albert seemed unchanged to me. His girlfriend had married and moved to New York and the club had changed as well, and had no further use for him, but he endured everything with his usual equanimity. He died the following year.

Weather continues wonderful. Number of known infections and deaths in the UK rises and though London hospitals are already starting to say they are reaching full capacity, the sudden sharp rise we have seen in other countries is not yet upon us. Chancellor Rishi Sunak goes on forking out, this time to the newly unemployed.

Alexandria

'Ah, you come from Alexandria!' 'No, Cairo.' 'Oh.'

Unlike Cairo, Alexandria is a city all in the West can dream about. It has been made into the equivalent of a technicolour film by Laurence Durrell and written about with empathy by Forster. It is where Cavafy, one of the great twentieth-century poets, lived, loved and worked. But though in the early years of my mother's return to Egypt with me after the war we spent some of most summers there, staying with my mother's half-sister Charlotte and her daughter Nell, my memory of the place is fragmentary and thin: breaking my arm when I jumped off a low wall; the banyan tree in Joe (Carlo) and Nadine Suares' wonderful garden (there was also one of those giant cactuses whose spikes, my mother told me, were once used as gramophone needles – was that true?); diving off Alexandre Naglovsky's boat in the Bay of Alexandria (I learned later that one reason we went to Alexandria was because he and my mother had an affair, only ended when he decided to go to

South America and she felt she couldn't uproot me again and follow him there, though he very much wanted to marry her); sitting upstairs with my mother in the double-decker tram that went round the perimeter of the city, with its exotically named stations, French, Greek, German, Arabic, English, evidence of Alexandria's cosmopolitan history: Sarwat, San Stefano, Zizinia, Mazloum, Glymenopoulos, Saba Pasha, Bulkley, Roushdy, Mustafa Pasha, Sidi Gaber, Cleopatra, Sporting, Ibrahimieh, Camp de César, Chatby, Mazarita, Ramleh. The whole journey to the terminus and back took at least two hours and I can still hear the sound of the ticket collector's horn as the next station was announced.

But, unlike André Aciman, who was born and brought up in Alexandria before his Jewish family finally left, long after most Europeans, in 1964, and whose *Out of Egypt* is the best evocation of that city at the height of its cosmopolitan glory, it does not resonate in my memory, suggesting that I never really liked Alexandria or felt at home there. And in those early years after the war, between the ages of five and ten, I think I was still a bit shell-shocked by the war years and the abrupt move when the war was over to a country where the indigenous inhabitants spoke a language I did not understand and rich and poor – the middle-class town of Maadi where we lived and the Arab village half a mile away where my mother occasionally shopped – seemed to belong to different worlds. I think I felt the same sense of shock, followed by a shutting off of any deep feeling, when, after eleven years in Egypt we uprooted ourselves again and arrived in England.

Whatever the reason, the Alexandria of Cavafy and Forster, let alone of Durrell, remains as foreign a land as the Blandings Castle of P.G. Wodehouse.

Ravelli, the Italian physicist, on *Newsnight* last night. Said the reason the West had been so much less efficient than the Far East in dealing with this pandemic was hubris, a sense that it was superior, knew better. Maybe a bit of that but I also think it's part of the DNA of Western democracies that if a situation arises in which there are two possible sets of actions, both with disastrous consequences that can be foreseen, they tend to put off the decision, hoping it will all go away; and so of course when they do finally have to choose they have a lot of leeway to make up. As with confronting Hitler in the '30s, or the dithering over climate change, or, now, Covid-19, where shutting down will bring the economy to a halt and lead eventually to huge job losses, and not shutting down will lead to the rapid spread of the pandemic.

Animals

How did we acquire our first dog? Lala was his name. A mongrel (*baladi*, 'from the village', was the Egyptian term), like all our dogs, he became part of our life when we lived in Road 9, between the railway line and a busy road, but where, from the terrace we could see, beyond the railway, great fields of maize and, in the far distance, on clear days, the sails of the *feluccas* moving in stately fashion on the Nile. It was our first flat in Maadi (we had lived with Chickie, Albert and my two cousins, Anna and Monica when we first arrived from France in October '45), and there is a beautiful set of photos taken by Alexandre Naglovski of me with Lala on the banks of the canal that ran through the town. But all I really remember about him is my mother waking me up one morning, kneeling by the bed and saying: 'Lala is dead.' He had been run over by a car, she explained, holding me as the news sank in. It was my first direct experience of death and it was terrible.

After Lala there was Rex, who left the Egyptian family he was with because he decided he preferred being with us. One day, taking him for a walk on the outskirts of the town, a woman came out of a house and, pointing to him, said he was hers and had been missing for a while. But when she tried to pull him into the house he dragged himself away and rubbed up against our legs. You see, we said, he's ours. She became aggressive and said we had no right to steal her dog. Eventually we had to buy him off her. Then there was Judy the little epileptic bitch who drowned one day in a shallow puddle during a fit; Paavo, a woolly, gentle little dog, named after the great Finnish runner Paavo Nurmi, one of my heroes at the time, who had the knack of sleeping on his stomach with his hind legs out behind him like a frog; and Sambo, the beautiful and impossible mixture of black Labrador and setter, who was incensed by anyone in a *galabieh*, a constant worry to my mother though she loved him for his fiery spirit and splendid looks; and, in England, Bimbo and Pilic, our English dogs, about whom I have written in *A Life*. My mother was known in Maadi as *omm-el-kilab* or mother of the dogs, and her sister as *omm-el-ottat* or mother of the cats. But we had cats too. In Egypt there was Batly or, to give him his full name, Batleymous, the Egyptian king known as Ptolemy in the West, a name which, to our ears, was both pompous and funny, and somehow suited him. He liked to sleep on his back in the bidet in which my mother put the dirty laundry prior to washing with his legs in the air. In England, Ginger, the large neutered Tom we inherited, who was the inspiration behind the only children's novel I have ever written, *Mr Isosceles the King*; Miss Black, another animal who adopted us, this time in Woodstock, and who would bring in live shrews from Blenheim Park, for her kittens to play with, something that both fascinated and repelled us; and Nimrod in Lewes, given that name because we hoped, in vain, that it would stop him from being a mighty hunter, although his main prey was slugs which he would lay down carefully on my bed or my mother's as a gift-offering. All the Egyptian dogs died, run over by cars or, in Judy's case, drowning in the course of a fit – except for two, Rex and Paavo, whom we had to leave behind with Chickie when we left Egypt in the summer of 1956. But what happened to Batly? He must have died but I have no memory of it. Why?

Summer time. But the UK is hardy celebrating. Yesterday the highest number of deaths in one day was recorded, and one of the medical people was on TV to say that if we kept the number below the 20,000 mark we would have triumphed. We are at the beginning of the upward curve, following Italy by about a fortnight, as all the pundits predicted.

America now has the highest number of recorded infections anywhere in the world and even Trump is having to admit there is an emergency.

Animals (cont.)

I wrote about our dogs in *A Life*, but I did not pause to reflect on what it means to love dogs (and even cats) in the way I still do, though it is a long time since I had one. I suppose being with T, who is terrified of them and would not dream of having one, has made me realise that to love them and want to have them in the house is not a given. So what is it?

In my case at any rate there is a powerful sense, if one is rescuing a dog (as we always were in Egypt), that here is a creature who is suffering as I can imagine myself suffering. Empathy I suppose. Cf. Raskolnikov's dream of seeing the horse being beaten to death by men who treat it as an object there to serve them, and of course our sense as readers that this dream is produced by his repression of his killing of the old pawnbroker and her saintly sister, for whom, as he did the deed, he had pushed all empathy out of his mind. And Bonnard's identification at the end of his life with the circus horse whose head he so powerfully paints (his ghostly presence on the right, palette in hand, suggests a self-portrait). Sentimentality, some might say, self-pity. But it isn't, of that I'm convinced. It is an awareness, which clearly some people have more than others, that all living creatures are interconnected, that what is done to an animal is done to me. That is why, Rowan Williams remarks in his wise book on Dostoevsky, Sonya presses Raskolnikov to 'kiss the earth and confess your crime'. By kissing the earth you accept that we are all part of something bigger than ourselves, says Williams, part of nature as well as the human race, and no confession is possible without that.

It is well known that the Nazis drilled it into their killing troops, the *Einsatzgruppen* that Jews and Slavs were inhuman, vermin, and so desensitised them and made the killing possible. My heart goes out to an animal. I could not kill it, though I have taken dogs to the vet and held them while the vet injected them so as to put them out of suffering that could never be alleviated. I wonder, if the need arose if I could do that to another human being? (But I would not know how.)

But where are the limits? I'm not a Buddhist. I kill a mosquito without compunction (but not a spider; though I feel nothing but horror at the sight of a spider, I try to put it in a glass and throw it outside). And I always have scruples about killing moths or ants, though in the end I often do.

Timothy Sprigge claimed he felt empathy for everything with eyes and was a strict vegetarian. I'm not so clear on where the boundaries are. Once, walking along the jetty at Newhaven with Sacha, we watched as a boy caught a fish on his line and then watched it expire on land, struggling for breath. I decided then and there never to eat fish again, but now I do. I have to repress something, though, as with free-range chicken, which I also eat. Perhaps if I was a better cook I wouldn't need to? I could make delicious vegetarian dishes? (I have the time, so why don't I become one?)

But having a dog or a cat is the result of more than empathy. Just as you can see the fear in a dog's eyes when it is afraid so you can see the pleasure a dog takes in running free, a pleasure I again can identify with, though humans, after the age of about three are never able to show it as dogs do. And cats, in a different way, not by running free but by lying in the sun, rolling on their backs. Such sensual delight. A joy to behold. (In the mountains above Kabis we have seen horses and foals do it on the grassy meadows.)

That is why one is not sentimental if one responds with pleasure to Christopher Smart's *Jubilate Agno* and especially to the long string of verses on 'My cat Jeoffrey', so often anthologised separately. The simplicity of the structure, the iteration without any attempt to join up or subordinate, catches beautifully the moment-by-moment nature of a cat's life and the innocence of its expressions of pleasure and of pain.

Certainly my dogs and cats have given me many happy moments, many moments which no human being could give, not even the people I have been in love with or very close to. And consequently their deaths have in many cases been every bit as painful as those of any human being close to me.

The death of Lala when I was six or seven and the death of so many other pets has certainly helped me cope with the deaths of friends. (Sacha's was different, for all the reasons I explored in *A Life*.) That is one reason why I feel it is so good for children to have pets, even goldfish or guinea-pigs – they are part of creation too, and if they are our pets we feel responsible for them and grow used to them being part of our lives, so that their deaths are painful, and the closer we have been to them of course the more painful.

30.3.2020

Now with Johnson, Hancock and the Chief Medical Officer all down with the virus we get daily briefings from the ever more sinister Gove, who still sounds as though he's trying to sell us how wonderful the Tory vision of Brexit is; or from junior ministers, flanked by the admirable Jenny Harries, the Deputy Chief Medical Officer. Yesterday she was telling the nation that they ('we'!) must be prepared for six months of this regime or more. On the airwaves the skirmishes go on between those who keep asking us to think ahead and ask if it's wise for the economy to shut down in this way and even, in the more extreme cases, try and make out that 'more people will die from a recession than from the virus', a repugnant Malthusian doctrine that I suppose has never really gone away, and those who insist that saving lives is the most important thing and we must cross bridges when we come to them. A few even dare to hope that the crisis will force the world to rethink its priorities and cease to see Growth as the be-all and end-all. I am of course one of those, but not very hopeful, unless this gets much worse.

Anonymous

Much of the art I love best is anonymous: The biblical narratives, Homer, *Sir Gawain and the Green Knight* and *Pearl*, the Border Ballads; the bulk of medieval visual art; plainchant and traditional folk songs. And what is Shakespeare if not anonymous, as Borges pointed out in 'Everything and Nothing'? The modern artists I love, too, have on the whole been as anonymous as they could be: Pessoa, Beckett, Robbe-Grillet, Klee, Morandi, Stravinsky. Of course there are plenty of artists who have developed by creating dazzling personae: Yeats, the patriot and then the wild old man; Rilke, the solitary, the lover; Valéry, the sleepless intellect; Giacometti, the bohemian; Stockhausen, the mage from planet Sirius. But this was a way of hiding as well as revealing. Eliot, when asked what he thought of Hugh Kenner's book about him, *The Invisible Poet*, with Eliotic deflection replied: 'I like the title.'

At the root of it is not so much the desire to hide as the feeling that you only exist as you work. There is a passage in one of the poems of Samuel Hanagid, a Jewish poet who lived in Spain at the turn of the eleventh century, which runs:

> She said: 'Rejoice, for God has brought you to your fiftieth year in the world!' But she had no inkling that, for my part, there is no difference at all between my own days, which have gone by, and the distant days of Noah about which I have heard. I have nothing in the world but the hour in which I am: it pauses for a moment, and then, like a cloud, moves on.

This must have meant a great deal to me in my forties, for I used it as an epigraph in my 1984 novel, *Conversations in Another Room* and again in an autobiographical piece I wrote at around that time for an American publication, *Contemporary Authors*. Since then I have of course written *A Life*, which, though about my mother, is inevitably also about me; have explored the genesis of various works of mine in a long online interview with Victoria Best; and have plundered episodes in my life to illustrate the intertwining of memory and forgetting, the desire to remember and the need to forget, in my recent book, *Forgetting*. Elly said to me after reading that: 'You don't seem to be afraid of revealing a great deal about yourself.' But I don't think I feel it that way. I can 'reveal' precisely because it does not seem to be part of me, it seems to belong to someone else, a writer I have lived with, an immigrant I have known. That the writer and the immigrant are me is difficult for me to comprehend. This disconnect is I think experienced by everyone, even those who cling most forcefully to the notion that they have 'a biography', as they move from middle age to the next stage of life – beautifully expressed by a tiny poem of George Oppen's which I remember Tony Rudolf sending me as one of his Mencards. The title is 'Old Age' and the poem consists of just one line:

'What a strange thing to happen to a little boy.'

So while I admire Beckett's resolute shunning of interviews and refusal to talk, except to his intimates, about himself, I find this almost verges on the paranoid. To my mind one can talk about the work and, strangely, even the life, while preserving anonymity – 'not me, gov.' Borges again:

The other one, the one called Borges, is the one things happen to... I know of Borges from the mail and see his name on a list of professors or in a biographical dictionary... It would be an exaggeration to say that ours is a hostile relationship; I live, let myself go on living, so that Borges may contrive his literature, and this literature justifies me. It is no effort for me to confess that he has achieved some valid pages, but those pages cannot save me, perhaps because what is good belongs to no one, not even to him, but rather to the language and to tradition. Besides,

I am destined to perish, definitively, and only some instant of myself can survive in him. Little by little, I am giving over everything to him, though I am quite aware of his perverse custom of falsifying and magnifying things... Years ago I tried to free myself of him and went from the mythologizing of the suburbs to games with time and infinity, but those games belong to Borges now and I shall have to imagine other things. Thus my life is a flight and I lose everything and everything belongs to oblivion, or to him.

I do not know which of us has written this page.

31.3.2020

Yesterday Raab as Foreign Secretary was on TV, saying that £75 million was being spent on getting stranded Britons home and much had already been done (long list). But when journalists track down some of these stranded Britons, whether in Peru or Pakistan, they all say nothing has been done and they have no information, while other nationalities fare far better.

After a bright early morning the skies are now grey, but what wonderful weather we've been having. Good walks in the direction of Mt Harry every day since T arrived, over a week now.

Art and 'the arts'

In adolescence, I remember, I was much exercised about whether one could talk of 'the arts' as one thing, 'Art'. I think there was a book by Herbert Read on the subject. I soon lost interest in it, feeling it was an issue for philosophers of art but not of much concern to me. Nevertheless it has remained a basic conviction, almost a matter of common sense that the arts have much in common. Surely Beethoven, Wordsworth and Caspar David Friedrich throw light on one another, as do Schoenberg, Kafka and Munch. What excited me so much when I first read Heller and Blanchot while at Oxford was that they went deep into the questions post-Romantic artists were struggling with, that they brought out, even when dealing with some very specific writer or even single work, such as Musil's *The Man Without Qualities* or Kafka's *Metamorphosis*, what all the arts and, by implication, all of us, had in common. But attempts to explain what artists of a particular time have in common too often come unstuck as critics/sociologists/historians of ideas reach for obvious links, such as industrialisation or the First World War. No doubt the Eiffel Tower or the rise of supermarkets can be linked to the art of the time, and in quite interesting ways, but with such talk we remain on the surface of things.

That, anyway, is my feeling about the matter, and always has been, which perhaps led Rachel Trickett to say to me, when I was her third-year student at Oxford, that I was the only French intellectual she had ever taught – which said as much about the Oxford perception of French intellectuals as about me. But if it's taken to mean 'not your usual English undergraduate', she was right, I now see. My intelligent and delightful fellow-tutee, John Davies, was hoping to go on and do a B.Litt on Jane Austen and eighteenth-century education, while I was starting to think about a problem that had begun to bother me, which was whether there was more to the often remarked-on parallels between Rabelais and Joyce, especially *Ulysses*, than mere love of and playfulness with language.

I refined that, when I got a good enough degree to be given a grant and a place at Oxford to continue there, into something on Erasmus, Rabelais, Sterne and their creation of anti-novels before the novel was born. Much too large and vague, my supervisor John Bamborough told me, a B.Litt title should look very precise but actually be very vague. So I came up with 'Swift's *A Tale of a Tub* in Relation to Renaissance Fictional Forms'. But I was not cut out to be a scholar, as Helen Gardner, examining an end-of-year paper I had written, informed me. I was not in the least upset by her comment because by that time I had begun to feel that I was not cut out to be a scholar either and knew in my heart of hearts that I would never write the B.Litt. Since I had only started the thing because I felt ill-equipped to do anything else except be an academic and really only wanted to write, fondly imagining that being an academic would both pay the bills and allow me to do so, the realisation that that career looked to be closed to me filled me with dread. I was saved by Providence in the form of the new universities that were springing up in the early sixties, just as I was coming to this sobering conclusion. First off the mark was the University of Sussex, and when I examined its syllabus I knew at once that if it would have me it was the place for me. Look, I said to John Mepham, who had sat down beside me at one of Edgar Wind's weekly art historical lectures in the Playhouse, Sussex has just sent me its syllabus. It seems one can teach everything from Homer to Robbe-Grillet, and there is provision to teach courses with philosophers, historians and art and music scholars.

I had had interviews for Junior Research Fellowships at Oxford and for a Junior Lectureship at York, none of which I got, but the Sussex interview was totally different. I came out feeling it had been an exciting and interesting conversation rather than an interview for a job. David Daiches, the Professor of English, the son of the former Chief Rabbi of Edinburgh, had written a book on sixteenth-century English translations of the Bible and as attitudes to the Bible seemed to me one of the issues connected with the work I was doing on Rabelais and Erasmus and Sterne, we had much to talk about. Then they asked me to devise on the spot a Renaissance course similar to the course taught to all students in the Schools of English and American and European Studies, called 'The Modern European Mind', and though I panicked at first I found the problem sufficiently intriguing to give myself over to it completely, with a few promptings from the other two members of the interview panel.

Fortunately I got the job, and at a dinner to welcome the new faculty Daiches took me aside and asked me how the thesis was going. Not that well, I had to admit, I don't think I'm cut out for that kind of thing. Do you think there's a book there somewhere? he asked. I said I thought there might be. That's fine, he said, I wouldn't worry about the thesis, you'll have plenty to do preparing for the courses you'll be teaching here. As a result of this wise counsel, inconceivable today, where you need not just a PhD but probably a book as well under your belt before a university will offer you even a temporary post, I was able, several years later, to publish *The World and the Book*, which incorporated many of the ideas I had been struggling with in the B.Litt, but was much the better for my being that bit older and having a good deal of teaching and conversations with colleagues at Sussex under my belt. It has not been out of print since it was first published in 1972, testimony to the sagacity of both Daiches and the new University of Sussex.

This has not been a digression. What I wanted to say was that at Sussex I found an institution ready to welcome a 'French intellectual' who believed in the unity not just of the arts but of all the component parts of a culture and was prepared to think through how such a holistic view could best be taught to undergraduates. And though Thatcher destroyed that vision, along with English universities in general, and a smaller, meaner, jobs-driven concept of higher education emerged from her reforms and that of subsequent governments, both Labour and Conservative, I still meet students from those days who confess to me that Sussex changed their lives.

Even at Oxford I felt that I had more in common with composers and painters than with other novelists. Though I published stories in *Oxford Opinion*, a student literary magazine at one time edited by Ian Hamilton, and made friends with one or two Oxford writers, in particular with Gabriel Chanan, I felt it was Gordon Crosse, the music scholar at Teddy Hall, with whose ideas I felt most in sympathy and with whom (as with John Mepham, then reading bio-chemistry but who later joined me at Sussex as a philosopher before moving into literary criticism and publishing a wonderful book on Virginia Woolf) I could talk about art and the possibilities open to artists today.

When I first got to know him, in my first term as an undergraduate, Gordon had a huge one-page score, a beautiful thing, hanging up on his wall. He explained to me that it was a piano piece by the young German avant-garde composer, Karlheinz Stockhausen, and that the pianist could start at any point and move through the work in any direction he chose. I suddenly felt, as I later did at Sussex, that I had, by great good fortune, come to just the place where I wanted to be.

1.4.2020
First of April

The Government is coming under pressure from commentators over their attempts to 're-assure' the public that they are doing everything in their power to get more PPE and more ventilators and roll out much more testing. It seems though that Germany in particular has kept deaths right down precisely because it had foresight and got in stockpiles of tests and Britain is way behind every other country not because they are very careful that the tests should prove accurate (their excuse) but because they didn't start early enough – in fact when the outbreak was first revealed in Wuhan.

Reading again André Aciman's *Out of Egypt* I realise I have been hard on him, especially taking against the first chapter, about his Uncle Vili (Mr Jumping Levi as we called him when we saw him in Maadi, because of his peculiar way of walking). In fact it's brilliant. I'm full of admiration. But for all the strangeness in his family, especially having a mother who was deaf and dumb, his is a picture we can easily label as 'Egyptian Jewry'. Reading his book made me even more aware than I had been how weird, how unlike any other was my family and my upbringing. I think that's why I now keep coming back to it – as though to make myself understand that it really was like that. To start with a family very like the great Egyptian Jewish families whose ancestors had no doubt been pedlars but who had long since left that behind and become bankers and lawyers and doctors. Now add to the mix my grandfather from Odessa, bringing into this Sephardi family something utterly different, and add to that the death of my grandfather when Sacha and Chickie were five and six and of my grandmother (from typhoid) when they were ten and eleven; the tug of war between their Syrian, non-Jewish stepfather Max and their grandparents for custody of them; and then add to that Chickie's conversion to Catholicism and marrying Albert, Monika's conversion to Islam and marrying Medhat, and Sacha's own odyssey to France and then back to Egypt with me, and our leaving Egypt not after but before Suez – and there is no group I can really identify with – with their ways of being, as it were, their habits and habitus. I see that with Jimmy and Nicolette, with Martine and Donald and Claudia. They are 'Egyptian Jews', *un point c'est tout*. Transplanted, it is true, to England at various ages, but still, Egypt and Italy mark them. Not so for us. For me. That is why writing Sacha's 'story' was so critical. How to talk about that feeling I have always had that others *come from somewhere*, have a solid base, as it were, to spring out from, whereas I feel I have nothing to look back to – not France, not Egypt, and I'm certainly not English. Al I can say is that I have a British passport. And a unique life I shared with Sacha for many years.

Art and 'the arts' (cont.)

At Cheltenham my kindly English master invited me to join him to hear a piano recital in the Town Hall. This was my introduction to live classical music and I was bored stiff, couldn't wait for it to end. When we moved to London at the end of the school year we stayed at first with Stella, my father's cousin, who had introduced my parents to each other, and her husband, Didi. They lived in the downstairs flat at 52 Clarendon Road in Holland Park, while Tante Hélène, Stella's mother and my grandfather's sister, occupied the upstairs flat. Kindly and dull, they did their best to make us feel at ease. Imitation wood paper covered many surfaces and Didi was the proud owner of an up-to-date hi-fi set. He would put a record of a Brahms symphony on the gramophone and conduct it as it went. I sat and listened and tried to see what he obviously saw in it, but to no avail. I would make my excuses and go for a walk in Holland Park.

When we moved to a rented flat in Putney and bought a radio we would sometimes listen to concerts in the evening and always on Sunday afternoons to Anthony Hopkins talking about a work to be broadcast the following week. 'Talking about Music' the programme was called. Hopkins had an infectious tone and he made you feel that the music really mattered to him. One day the work he discussed was Bartok's *Second Piano Concerto*. Bartok, he explained, treats the piano not as a lyrical and expressive instrument but as a percussive one. Inspired by Hungarian folk music, he returns us to the primal impulse of music, which is bodily, not spiritual, dance, not dream or contemplation. And indeed, with the very first chords my heart started to beat faster and I felt that I had crossed a threshold: I suddenly knew what music could do. Having left the strings, the staple of the Romantic orchestra, entirely out of the first movement, Hopkins went on, Bartok then wrote a second movement where the strings take over completely, but not so much to drive the themes forward as to take us into an eerie, desert or even galactic atmosphere, a world beyond the human, inhabited perhaps only by cicadas, into which, eventually, the piano intrudes, but quietly now, mysteriously, almost underneath our consciousness. And where in Beethoven, say, such an opening would be a simple prelude, leading to the piano finally emerging triumphant, here time stands still and the piano hovers as time itself seems to hover, and then the movement comes to an end.

When I was thirteen a much older friend had given me a little Worlds Classics edition of Shelley's poetry, and I had turned the pages with a beating heart, conscious that this was *poetry* I was reading. Eventually I had to admit to myself that I did not find any of it very interesting, and lost any appetite I might have had for poetry. Then, at Stella's, I found a copy of Michael Roberts' *Faber Book of Modern Verse*. I began to read *The Waste Land* and at once I knew what poetry was. I am not sure if the hairs on the back of my neck stood on end, but the experience was certainly more physical than mental. And now I felt the same with the Bartok *Second Piano Concerto*. Whatever it was, it was something I wanted more of.

So while the question: What is art? ceased to concern me, poetry, music, and the visual arts (though there I cannot remember a similar *eureka* moment to the one I had had with poetry and music) have continued to nourish me and a life without them would be bleak indeed. But another *eureka* experience, and one that would decisively qualify that last sentence, awaited me in that crucial year between school and University: the discovery of Proust. While trying to write a novel in the mornings and feeling more and more unhappy with it, I also began, with the help of the magnificent Putney and Wandsworth public libraries, to read my way through the major fiction writers of the world: Tolstoy, Dostoevsky, Flaubert, Stendhal, Dickens, George Eliot. I had noticed the ten or twelve NRF volumes of Proust on the shelves, but volume one was always missing. I waited for it to be returned before plunging into Proust, but as time went by and it remained missing I decided I would simply have to do without it and so began with *Un Amour de Swann*, rather than *Combray*. And by the time, months later, I had got to the end of *Le Temps retrouvé*, the slow French reader who had borrowed it had finished or abandoned volume one and there it was, back on the shelves. In a way, since the novel ends with Marcel ready to begin writing the book we have been reading, it matters less than with most books where we start. But in another sense it matters more than in almost any other book (the exception is Dante's *Commedia*, which has precisely the same structure as *À la recherche*), because the seed of the whole is sown in its opening paragraphs. But books come to us in many ways and this was the way *À la recherche* came to me, and, as with *The Waste Land* and the Bartok piano concerto, I knew at once that *this was it*.

Other novels I had been reading were perhaps more profound, more heart-rending, funnier (though Proust is up there with them on all three counts), but none, I felt, was more *true*. This is strange because on the face of it neither Marcel's childhood nor his adolescence and certainly not his mature years were anything like mine; his snobbery, his obsession with sexual deviance and his denigration of friendship were none of them things I could readily identify with. So why the feeling that it was *true* in ways other novels weren't?

Perhaps it was the details, such as his description of the joy the memory of a freshly laundered childhood pillow evoked in the adult; perhaps it was in the constant sense that failure was not something that either destroyed you or was there to be overcome, but was rather a feature of life, to be accepted and learned from. When Marcel, unable to put into words his feelings of joy as he walks by the river one day strikes the ground in frustration and can only say 'Zut! Zut! Zut!' my heart quickened, as it had when I read in *The Waste Land*:

On Margate Sands
I can connect
Nothing with nothing
The broken finger-nails of dirty hands

So they too were feeling what I so often felt, I thought, and yet they came out of it and produced *À la recherche*, *The Waste Land*! I was energised and wanted to read on. And what I read, scattered throughout the giant novel as well as encapsulated in Proust's great early essay, 'Journées de lecture', which is in so many ways a dry run for the novel, was the profound thought that while art can give us what nothing else can, we must never fetishise it, never worship it. The work of art can lead us to the threshold; it is up to us to enter the house if we wish.

2.4.2020

Grey this morning, which is quite a surprise as the last ten or twelve days have been bright sunshine. Reminds one of what England is like for much of the time.

Despite a century of advance in medicine, in virology, in epidemiology, etc. no one seems to know at this stage how to deal with this new virus. I suppose I have always had an exaggerated view of what advances in medicine have achieved.

Robert Peston, in the press briefing two days ago, raised the question of when hospitals should discharge patients back to die with their families rather than struggling to keep them alive. And Joan Bakewell very sensible on Radio 4 yesterday, asking us to think hard about all this and asking the Government to give clear guidelines, so that it won't be left to individual decisions, very hard for doctors. The worse thing that can happen is for people to die alone, she said, and indeed, I'd rather die at home with family around me than by myself, even if that means losing a year or two of life. Rather like Marianne and Giglia both in their eighties and recently widowed, deciding, when they learned they had cancer, not to go down the chemotherapy route but to let the disease run its course.

Baboon

Historians of art these days often talk about Duchamp's *Urinal* as being the distinctive artwork of the twentieth century. And perhaps if one is thinking of influence that is the case. It was the first piece of conceptual art and conceptual art appears to have swept all before it. And unlike most conceptual art it certainly makes one think, and laugh – a speciality of Duchamp's and the mark of his genius. Others talk of the *Demoiselles d'Avignon* as being the key work. If I had to choose one work it would indeed be a Picasso, but it would be his *Baboon and Young*, made in Vallauris in 1951. It's not my favourite Picasso by any means and certainly not my favourite art work of the modern era, but the combination of wit (to see the baboon in the toy car), skill (it's made so roughly and yet with such total assurance), and empathy (it catches the protectiveness of the mother and the trust and dependence of the child so well), all I hold most dear in art, means that it has a special place in my heart. I think of those lovely twelfth- and thirteenth-century wooden-seated Mother and Child sculptures in the museum in Bressanone, and in the great medieval museum in Nuremberg, sculptures that in their directness and tenderness are moving beyond words, and feel the Picasso can live with them, though he had no tradition to work in and with, only instinct and imagination.

Interesting, too, that while he rarely produces anything that isn't a joy to the eye, he is only truly moving when he himself is really stirred, when his own vulnerability in the face of the world is given free rein, and he seems to have been stirred by three things: children, animals and death. The RA exhibition that was on when the pandemic hit us, *Picasso and Paper,* but which I managed to see twice before lockdown, opens with, among other things, the sketches for the circus family (*Les Saltimbanques)* that Rilke found so moving and meditated upon in the fifth of his *Duino Elegies.* Here we can see Picasso exploring both the overall composition and individual details. In the corner of one he draws two children playing, tiny figures worthy of Brueghel's *Children's Games,* brought to instant life with a few deft lines, though the only features visible are a single eye, a mouth and a cleft buttock. Like Brueghel, what fascinates him is not what the children *look like* but what they *are* in the fullness of their young lives. The exhibition, among so many riches, goes on to include both the *Baboon and Young* and the *Man Carrying a Goat,* monumental figures brilliantly placed at the end of one of the Royal Academy's vast imposing rooms. Right at the end of the show we come across a self-portrait, drawn at the age of ninety-one, after more than eighty years of extraordinary work, more a skull than a face, but a skull with those penetrating eyes we have always identified with him, except that now they seem to stare out in terror.

Like the two sculptures this is both monumental and intimate, profoundly moving, and not the least bit sentimental.

Hancock yesterday at the press briefing, obviously recovered from his bout of Cv. 'I totally get it.' 'We made mistakes.' Etc. Promised 50,000 tests a day 'by the end of the month' and much else besides. But a doctor from Manchester on the radio made the point I'd been hurling at the TV set as he talked: 'This is just warm words. We've had enough of those. Let's see some action.'

Berio

The only composer of the post-war generation to be guided first by his ear and then by his mind. Too facile to say that's because he was Italian? After all, perhaps the most 'pure' of post-war composers, Nono (despite the 'political' titles of some of his pieces) was also Italian. What I mean is that no matter how complex the writing, all Berio's music is pleasing to the ear. Stockhausen was of course the great showman, the twentieth-century Wagner, but, like Wagner, the showmanship was based on a profound belief in himself as uniquely in touch with the spirit of music and the spirit of the time. And many of Stockhausen's pieces overwhelm you with their musical power and invention – *Mantra, Stimmung, Trans* – but one can feel, as one listens, the structure underlying it, being made manifest, as it were, by the music. With Berio one can enjoy each moment as a pure audial experience and not, I think, do the music an injustice. And he is a master of the use of the human voice. Where Nono married Schoenberg's daughter, Berio married an Armenian-American singer, Cathy Berberian, for whom he wrote the *Folk Songs*, or rather orchestrated and brought together folk songs from all over the world, letting go his invention in the sure knowledge that Cathy would not only be able to do what he asked but would relish the challenge. Like his friend Calvino with his great collection of the folk-tales of Italy, here Berio reminds us of the close links between the anonymous folk art of the past and the concerns of modernism.

Cathy Berberian may have helped Berio realise his gift and it survived their separation. I remember a question and answer session before a Prom in which one of his works was being performed, when he was asked why he composed so much. Stockhausen would have talked of the God calling him, or perhaps the World Spirit; Boulez would have rightly seen the question as ironic and defended his limited output and compulsive need to return to old scores and emend or develop them as driven by the Mallarmean drive for perfection. Berio answered: 'I have had many wives, so I have much alimony to pay. I need to write all the time to pay the alimony, you understand?' Implying that he would much rather have been tending to his olive groves in Tuscany. Projecting a persona? Perhaps, though it felt genuine as he uttered it, a cry torn from the heart. And anyway a persona is a projection of the self, one aspect, but a prominent one.

His greatest vocal works, in any case, were not written for Cathy Berberian but for and with the poet Edouardo Sanguinetti and for The Swingle Singers. I have heard other, remarkable, groups perform *Sinfonia*, but only The Swingle Singers, it seems to me, had the total confidence in the music and in their ability that would allow them to sound so free, so improvised. And *Sinfonia* needs both, with its extraordinary collage of quotations from Mayakovsky, Levi-Strauss, Beckett's *The Unnamable*, graffiti from Paris '68, to Berio's own witty bridging passages, such as the sudden cry 'I have a present for you', followed by a passage from Boulez's 'Don', the first movement of his *Pli selon pli*.

There may be extremely complex structures underlying the work but what it feels like is Berio using his ear and his instinct to bring these disparate elements together. There is no musical reason, for example, for the use of the scherzo from Mahler's *Second Symphony* as the central ship, as he describes it, which brings gifts to the island of the goddess of love (he calls the movement 'Voyage to Cythera'); the 'reason' lies in his obvious love for the piece, his sense that today (1968–9) it is no longer quite viable, and his feeling that it can 'carry' the crazy collage of quotations with which he loads it.

The other work is *Laborintus 2*, his homage to Dante, with a 'libretto' by Sanguinetti (and Sanguinetti himself reading/performing it at the premiere and on the recording I have). It opens with the poet declaiming the first lines of the *Vita Nuova*, but cut up and repeated for greater emphasis: '*In quella parte. In quella parte del libro de la mia memoria. In quella parte del libro.*' Hearing it one wonders why composers have been so tardy in using the speaking voice and simply reinforcing the words and rhythms with an accompaniment. It is utterly mesmerising. And Berio so writes the work that he can move effortlessly from Dante to Pound's great *Usura* canto and never allow the power of Dante's verse to overwhelm his own very personal work. And once again jazz rhythms, echoes of the Romantic music he loved, and the sound of the spoken language (here Berio's beloved Italian) happily intermingle.

I have always thought that the best introduction to modern music would be to play Stravinsky's *Petrushka* followed by Berio's *Folk Songs* – if that doesn't dent people's prejudice against modern music nothing will. And Berio will for me always be associated with the marvellous performances of the London Sinfonietta of a range of his works in the 1960s and '70s and by my friend and one-time colleague David Osmond-Smith, whose enthusiasm for the composer and ability to convey in words the richness and complexity of his music in private conversations, seminars and lectures, is etched on my memory.

4.4.2020

Many more deaths, including doctors and nurses, further fuelling anger that the Government has failed to provide them with the right protective equipment. Things have started to get like Italy and Spain in the past few weeks, though we have so far been spared the sights of army trucks carrying corpses to makeshift morgues. This has driven out news of what is happening in the rest of the world. We do hear about the rapid spread of the pandemic in America and how at every step Trump's interventions, verbal and practical, only serve to make things worse; and about how in Hungary, Orban has used emergency powers to turn the country into even more of a dictatorship, mirroring Russia.

Bicycles

I seem to have spent a good part of my youthful life in the saddle. Not of horses, of course, but of bicycles. Maadi, 5 miles south of Cairo, where I grew up in the forties and fifties, was made for them. Apart from a few main arteries the roads, though pavemented, were untarmacked and there was very little traffic. So we children of the bourgeoisie lived with and by our bicycles. I cycled to the Club, to school, whether the little primary school by the canal or Victoria College just beyond the flood ditch, and round the town with my friends.

We had slow bicycle races, where the winner was the one who crossed the line last without putting his foot on the ground. It was all boys – girls were to be talked about, sometimes obsessed over, but only mingled with on an equal footing at swimming training and competitions.

I learned to ride almost as soon as we came to live in Maadi, that is, as soon as we arrived in Egypt after the war. The owner of the bicycle sales and repair shop was my teacher, as he was of all my friends, of my mother, who had driven a car in France but had never had a bicycle, and of my aunt, who had never had a car or a bicycle. He would get onto his bicycle and tell you to get on yours, then tell you to relax, put your feet on the pedals, and start pedalling when he told you. Then, holding the back of the saddle, he would half push and half pull you forward until you were both bowling along the street. At some point he would take his hand off the saddle and you would go happily on till you realised you were on your own and then probably lose confidence and slide gently to the ground. After several more trials you would find that you didn't fall and that you could even slow down and turn and return triumphantly to where he was waiting. After that he sold you a bicycle and off you went.

But some mastered cycling more quickly than others. I remember a bicycle ride in the desert with my mother and my aunt. I was cycling ahead of them and we came to a slope. I was happily freewheeling down it when I heard a cry of *watch out!* I moved to the side of the dirt road and Chickie came crashing into me, sending us both to the ground. Luckily neither of us was hurt. In later life she preferred to walk, but my mother still cycled to the shops and, in the mornings, before breakfast, would take the dogs out for a run in the desert before stopping at the town oven, where she would buy those delightful rolls called Kaiser, made up of a large round bottom with a small round head on top, for our breakfast.

In Cheltenham, where we lived for a year after leaving

Egypt so that I could do my last year of school there, after a horrible month boarding with one of the teachers, we moved to a little cottage in the grounds of a manor house on the top of Battledown Hill. I remember that hill well, because I cycled up it (as well as down of course) every school day of that strange year where I was working hard and trying to come to terms with a new county and with leaving Egypt and my friends and animals behind. Most bikes in those days only had three gears, so the hill was a test of stamina and fitness which I did not always pass. Sacha, returning from the shops with her front basket laden, would walk the last part.

But when one got to the top one was richly rewarded. There was an old horse called Denmark, who had, the owner of the big house told us proudly, once been an award-winning steeplechaser. Now he took life easy, roaming the extensive grounds, nosing in Sacha's basket or my school satchel for the apple he was sure we had brought for him, and sometimes, when we had the kitchen/dining-room window open, sweeping the books off the window-sill to remind us he was there and looking forward to food and good conversation.

I have a photo of Mrs Tanner, the owner, and her granddaughter, holding a pet rabbit, Denmark, Sacha and me and my cousin Anna, who had come from Egypt to stay for a while after a terrible car accident in which her fiancé was killed. I wonder who took it, for Mrs Tanner lived alone, though some of the house, as well as the cottage where we lived, was let – so perhaps it was the flight lieutenant who lived with his family in one of the flats.

We brought the bicycles with us when we moved to London at the end of the school year, and in those days, the late fifties, cycling in London was not the terrifying experience it is now. From the Putney flat we would cycle to the Wandsworth Public Library along the Upper Richmond Road, and even as far as Richmond Park. Did we park the bicycles in the entrance hall to the little flat in Carlton Drive? I suppose so, but I have no memory of that, only of sailing along London roads in single file, though I cannot recall either if Sacha was behind or in front of me.

And Oxford, of course, was a city of bicycles. After a term in college I could stand it no longer and got permission to move into digs on the excuse that my room, in an old building the Hall has long since pulled down and replaced, was bisected by pipes which gurgled into life whenever anyone anywhere in the building turned on a tap, making my nights a torture and rendering me unfit to work or think. The rules stipulated that undergraduates must keep within a three-mile radius of the city centre, so I acquired a map, and with ruler and compass drew that three-mile radius and set about finding digs as near to the perimeter as possible. I ended up on another hill, Hinksey Hill to the South of Oxford, in the home of a mild and absent-minded Professor of English at Westfield College, University of London, and his rather more hard-headed wife. Not quite as steep as Battledown, it led on to Boars Hill, where Matthew Arnold lived for a while. Having digs so far out always made it a wrench to leave my friends in Oxford and set out on my bike – in winter – into the dark. But once there I felt I was expanding, escaping from the comfort blanket of Oxford and – very slowly – returning to somewhere where I felt more alive. From my room I could look down on the city and I could also walk out into the woods and try to feel my way into whatever story I was trying to write at the time.

When Sacha left London and we moved in together first into a rented flat off the Iffley Road and then to the cottage in Woodstock, we both took our bicycles with us. In Woodstock Sacha would cycle down on Monday mornings to her work at Parker's bookshop, use the bike for shopping during the week, and cycle back on the Friday evening. At weekends we would cycle out into the Oxfordshire countryside and the Cotswolds, sometimes as far as Banbury. With bicycles one could go so much further than on foot but it was always easy to stop and have a look at an intriguing church we might not have noticed in a car.

My getting the job at Sussex changed all that. The prevalence of the Downs means that there are fewer roads and thus that there is much more traffic on them, and then the hilly nature of the country means that old fashioned three-gear bikes are nearly always more hard work than fun to ride. I would occasionally walk over the Downs to the University but never cycled, even when a cycle lane was established on the A27. I had two short periods in Oxford, at St Anne's for a term in 1996 and then for two terms at All Souls in 1999. For the first I rented a bike but rarely used it as I was living in college; for the second I bought a bike, as I was lodged in Iffley and the cycle ride along the river was always a joy. But though I tried to go out on it when I returned to Lewes I found I preferred to walk for pleasure and use the car for longer distances. T keeps talking of getting good bikes and fixing a bike-rack on the car, memories of her days in flat Suffolk never far from her mind, but I doubt if we ever will. The bicycle enriched my life immeasurably but I feel I have done with it.

5.4.2020

The curve of known infected cases and of deaths gets steeper, precisely as in Italy. More and more doctors and nurses are dying. Yesterday a doctor refused to perform unless he had the right protective gear.

India and the US are now raging centres of the epidemic, while Tokyo (Japan seemed to have been miraculously spared) has suddenly flared up. The world is waiting for the virus to really hit Africa and South America, where health care systems are poor. Here the sun goes on shining and yesterday was the most perfect and the warmest this year. This is a headache for the government for it inevitably brings people out in droves, but lovely for us in Lewes so close to the Downs, which did not seem noticeably busier.

But, as Tim said on the phone yesterday when I rang to thank him and Judith for a gift of cheese and cake they had had delivered to us, it's all a bit of a lottery. Except for doctors and nurses.

Body

I recently read Brian O'Shaughnessy's huge book, *The Will*, for the essay I'm trying to write on act and action. Though O'Shaughnessy worked (he died in 2010) in the English tradition and certain chapters are full of the signs and symbols of formal logic that I cannot decipher, it is a deeply thoughtful and humane work, equally at ease in dialogue with Schopenhauer and Sartre as with Quine and Davidson. What he wants to do is put to bed once and for all both a mechanistic and an ideological concept of will. He wants to show that when I raise my arm to open a door, say, I am doing something other than responding to stimulus, that it is quite different from having an electric prod compel me to raise my arm; at the same time he wants to show that raising my arm is quite different from merely imagining that I am raising my arm. Gesture, movement, introduce something new and will always do so, though in retrospect it may seem that the action was inevitable.

What is it that is new here? Babies kick their legs out in reflex action, but that is quite different from what happens when they reach out for their mother's breast. That movement, says O'Sh., links the baby to the simplest animal life, which

63

acts and moves to do two things, to protect itself from predators and to feed itself. Because we have bodies we have wills, and in that we are like all other animals. If in later life I learn to drive a car or kill the lover who has jilted me, these are merely sophisticated developments of the basic principle. Action is performed in order to fulfil a need, whether it is my taking cold water out of the fridge or waiting on the stairs like Proust's Marcel for his mother to come to bed.

I have always felt that my writing fulfilled a need that was almost (?) physical. When I hit on the right way of moving forward with a story or novel I feel it in my groin, not my head. When I fail to do so I want to hit my head against the wall – and in earlier days would indeed bruise my knuckles as I made do with my fist. And nothing made me happier than when, back in th '80s, a lady with very severe ME (she was for a while in a wheel chair), asked if she could write about my work because reading me, she felt, actually helped her body cope with its terrible affliction. The book she eventually wrote tried to trace in detail how this effect worked in practice. I had hoped, on the back of interest in the work Oliver Sacks was doing at the interface between body and culture, that it might get published, but, sadly, she never found a willing publisher.

Everything we do bears the stamp of our bodies. Not just bodies, of course, as O'Shaughnessy makes clear. I know that I play tennis, tidy up and write, all in the same way. That is, if I try to go slowly, carefully and deliberately forward I simply stall. The only way I know to get something done is to rush forward, trusting in my ability, and then return to the task again and again. In tennis I was a great admirer of Borg and couldn't stand the petulant McEnroe, yet I found myself playing more like the latter than the former. If I tried to rally from the baseline and slowly wear my opponent down, as Borg did, moving him further and further out of court before delivering the killer blow, I would find myself turning passive and eventually being outplayed. My only hope was to keep coming forward, even if I left my opponent with a few easy passing shots. The idea was to pressure him into making mistakes. Sometimes it worked and sometimes it didn't. In tidying up I tend to rush at the task, get enough sorted to leave myself with an easy task next time. I know it would be better to take everything out, make big strategic decisions, then go for it – but I can't work like that. If a picture needs to be put up or a wall repainted, T will prevaricate for months, if not years, then make exactly the right choice – of position, of colour. I tend to feel that even if I waited for years I might still not get it right, so I do it quickly – and sometimes it works.

It's the same with writing. I would love to be able to work like Thomas Mann – spend months on a chapter but know that when that chapter was done it was really done. This must give the writer a sense that more and more of the book is there as they work and even a few bad weeks cannot wreck it. I, on the other hand, once I've got a sense of the parameters of the book and its rhythm and ending, have to go at it full pelt – and sometimes find that after several months' work I have nothing at all to show for it. If all goes well I rush to the end, then return to the start and have another rush at it, and so on until I am satisfied. Not a comfortable way to work but I have discovered over the years that it is my way and I cannot change it.

Body, then, or something else? Body, I'd say, but body in the sense of what I ask my body to do, or what my body does best, rather than what in itself my body is. It is always a matter of action, and, as O'Shaughnessy so brilliantly demonstrates, that action is anything but mechanical or part of learned behaviour, but a product of the self, whatever that is, while also contributing to the *formation* of the self, for the self is constantly evolving. Not being a philosopher I'm happy to let the mystery remain.

An extraordinary spring day yesterday, and we walked the big racecourse in reverse and then climbed to the millennial Beacon on Mt Harry before turning back to Lewes. Strangely, a walk I had never done. Difficult to think of the pandemic in such circumstances. Terrible to be in a big city on a day like that, even more if in a high-rise block. Let's hope the few who continue to flout the rules understand why the rules are there or we will all face a complete lockdown, as has happened in Italy, France and Spain.

Boris Johnson still not recovered and now in hospital. Ironic that the thing he craved all his life, to be Prime Minister, has landed him there and when he recovers he will have to go on presiding over this nightmare with only his shambolic government, picked solely for their ideological commitment to Brexit, to help him. Beyond irony really that in the same month as he achieved his goal and won his huge electoral majority coronavirus was already appearing in Wuhan, on the other side of the world.

Border Ballads

As soon as I began to read the so-called Border Ballads, those anonymous poems which we can trace back to the late Middle Ages and the border country between Scotland and England but which must stretch back much further in time and be much more widely dispersed than this suggests, I was smitten. As happens in such cases one reads on and returns to one's favourites and it is only later that one starts to wonder what it is about a work of art that has such a powerful effect on one.

I think it was Chickie who first introduced me to them,

reciting 'Sir Patrick Spens' (I have lost her voice, as I have, more mysteriously, Sacha's) in the garden of the Club one summer evening:

> The king sits in Dumferling toune,
>   Drinking the blode-red wine:
> 'O whar will I get a guid sailor
>   To sail this ship of mine?'

The harsh unEnglish sounds that nevertheless produced comprehensible words; the simple but powerful rhythm, accentuated by the many consonants; above all I now think, the speed of it, the way it dispenses with connective passages and is nevertheless perfectly comprehensible – no need to say: 'He spoke', 'he said', 'he cried out'. Just the king at his revels and his question, which will set the whole tragedy rolling – all this made me an instant convert.

The passion stayed with me. At one point I thought of writing my B.Litt thesis on the Border Ballads and even went to see Catherine Ings, whose excellent lectures on the subject I had attended as an undergraduate. But I soon realised that I lacked the Scottish background and the anthropological know-how, which I came to feel would be essential. But their mysterious power has never lost its hold on me, and in a way they form the unspoken Other of *The World and the Book*.

A courtier suggests that Sir Patrick Spens is the best sailor he has, and the king writes 'a braid letter', which he personally signs and sends to Sir Patrick, who receives it while 'walking on the strand'. What follows ratchets up the tension, though again not by telling us how he felt but, as in the narratives of the Hebrew Bible, by simply telling us what he did and said:

> The first line that Sir Patrick red
>   A loud lauch lauched he:

The next line that Sir Patrick red,
  The teir blinded his ee.

'O wha is this has don this deid,
  This ill ded don to me,
To send me out this time o' the year,
  To sail upon the se!'

'Mak haste, mak haste, my mirry men all,
  Our guid schip sails the morne';
'O say na sae, my master deir,
  For I feir a deadlie storme.

'Late late yestreen I saw the new moone,
  Wi the auld moone in hir arme,
And I feir, I feir, my deir master,
  That we will come to harme.'

Is Sir Patrick Spens' laugh when he starts to read the letter
a bitter and derisive one, and are we to understand that as
he reads on the façade cracks and he is reduced to tears? Or
is it that the laugh is one of pleasure at receiving a signed
letter from the king and it is only as he reads on that its
real significance comes home to him? We will never know.
What is clear is that by the end of his reading he has grasped
two things: that someone in the king's court has done him
a bad turn, either intentionally or unintentionally; and that
there is no getting out of it. To his men he lets show no
sign of his anguish; he addresses them as 'my mirry men all'
and reminds them that his ship is 'guid'. But – again, no
transition, no information about this man – one of his men,
we presume an old sailor with much experience of the sea
and the portents of the heavens pipes up in protest: he has
seen an omen of danger, ironically the seemingly comforting

image of the new moon with the old moon 'in its arms', and he is afraid.

We are not given the luxury of a debate, because whatever the captain and crew feel the king's command has to be obeyed. We are not even given the comfort of a narrative about how as they sail a storm comes up. No – and I love the ballads for this – we cut straight to a scene that could be ironic and almost comic were it not so tragic – no, a scene that is so tragic precisely because it is comic and satiric:

> O our Scots nobles were richt laith [loath, reluctant]
>   To weet their cork-heild schoone [shoes]:
> But lang owre a' the play were playd
>   Their hats they swam aboone [floated above them].

Instead of describing the cries of terror of the crew the poet chooses to present us, in two lines, with the scene of the noblemen who were accompanying Sir Patrick (on a mission to France or Germany to find a bride for the king perhaps), finding the water rising in the ship, hopping from foot to foot on deck to protect their elegant shoes from getting wet. The next couplet, picking up from the old sailor's prediction of doom, looks at the event from a position well above the fray: long before the play was played, we are told, and the poet himself plays with 'play' as a kind of game the courtiers are playing, a sort of desperate hopscotch, and with 'play' as the game of life – *les jeux sont faits, messieurs-dames*, as the croupiers in nineteenth-century novels about gambling call out. But when the game is over all that is left of the ship and the elegant nobles is their hats – 'swimming aboone', a particularly ghoulish way of describing them floating, assigning to the hats the power to survive in water that their owners sadly lacked.

And then, as in Deborah's great song of triumph in the biblical Book of Judges, we cut to the courtiers' wives, sitting waiting for them to return, 'with their fans into their hands'. And the poet then once again stands back and gives us the facts, though here too, in his description of Sir Patrick as 'guid' and of the nobles 'at his feet', we are made to do more than register a marine disaster and to focus instead on a social and human tragedy:

Half owre, half owre to Aberdour,
  It's fiftie fadom deip,
And their lies guid Sir Patrick Spens,
  Wi'the Sots lords at his feit.

Of course there are many very different kinds of Border Ballads: ballads about the human properties of the seals with whom the people of the coast and islands shared their lives, such as 'The Lailey Worm and the Machrel of the Sea'; supernatural ballads and ballads about love and death, such as 'The Unquiet Grave' or 'The Wife of Usher's Well'; ballads of the revenge of the dead, such as 'Edward'; ballads about cattle rustling in the border country; and many others. Few are as great as 'Sir Patrick Spens', but all share its qualities of sparseness, unflinching honesty, an often ruthless wit and irony, and an ability to convey the sense of doom through prolepsis and other devices designed to crack the fabric of time as simply one damned minute after another.

It is this which has made them such favourites with modern novelists like Carson McCullers (*The Ballad of the Sad Café*), Gabriel Garcia Marquez (*Chronicle of a Death Foretold*) and above all, Muriel Spark, who is the only one I know to catch in her spiky novels (and not just in *The Ballad of Peckham Rye*) the combination of black humour, human truth and clear-eyed realism one finds in the Border Ballads. But then she prided herself on the fact that she belonged to the same world as they did.

In Italy and Spain the rise in cases and deaths seems to have slowed, the curve flattened in the new virology-speak. But shooting up in Japan and Germany. Experts here go on the air to explain that mere social distancing will not eradicate the epidemic, merely suppress it. To eradicate it you need to test and control and the Government clearly doesn't have the capacity or the will to do either.

Borges

I think it was in *Encounter*, in 1959, that I first came across Borges. They published two stories by him, I can't remember which, I think 'Tlön, Uqbar, Orbis Tertius' and 'The Library of Babel'. Although they are not now among my favourites, a world opened up for me that day, a sense of immense possibilities. Soon I had found a couple of his books in French in the old Parker's in the Broad, down in the basement, those yellow Gallimard volumes in a series of Spanish South American writers edited by Roger Caillois, and begun to deepen my understanding of him. I found I loved the more realistic stories, such as his very first, 'South', about a man who travels south from Buenos Aires for I can't recall what purpose and there meets his end, and 'The Waiting', about a man hiding from a criminal gang he has betrayed and knowing that sooner or later they will get him.

I loved the reason he gave for writing only stories, that he did not have the stamina to write books and so would write the summaries of the books he might have written. I loved his remarks that Argentinian literature, having no real roots, should not seek false ones in romantic tales of gauchos and the South, but should on the contrary, just as the Jews had always done, celebrate its rootlessness and thus its ability to cross borders with ease. I loved all this because it spoke to my condition as a writer as I was starting to understand it: without a country to call my own, without a language to call my own, not inward with any culture, incapable of and uninterested in writing the kinds of novels I saw being written all around me. Like Eliot, Proust and Kafka, Borges was confirming me in my instincts. And all he said, in stories and parables and essays, rang true and went on ringing true the longer I lived and the more I understood about myself and about the possibilities of a genuine art in a world where art seemingly has no place. Whether it was 'Pierre Menard, Author of the *Quixote*' or 'Borges and I', his short pieces went on reverberating in my mind and heart long after they had been read, never quite giving up their secrets but always yielding new insights, like the greatest art.

Borges is not interested in infinite libraries and the wilder shores of idealistic philosophy for their own sakes, as lazy commentators have gone on telling us; he is interested in imagining them in order to free us of the hold the imagination has on us and in order to return us to our common humanity. That is why the narrator of 'Tlön, Uqbar, Orbis Tertius' ends his account of the gradual encroachment upon our world of another, more perfectly organised, more rational yet deadly world by retreating to a quiet Argentinian port town and there attempting to complete his 'Quevedian' translation of Sir Thomas Browne's *Urne Burial*. The story was written in the early 1940s, as the Nazis threatened to overrun the world.

Is this book in a sense the record of my 'Quevedian translation' in the face of the encroaching catastrophe?

Because the stories are so compressed a summary cannot do them justice, one must follow every twist and turn of the half dozen pages, as one must follow one of Webern's minute piano pieces, for any lapse in concentration and one risks losing everything. In 'Sur' ('The South'), the first story he felt truly reflected what he was trying to do, the narrator, running to catch his train, brushes an open shutter on the stairway of his building and on emerging feels a dampness on his cheek and ear and, putting up his hand and then bringing it before his eyes, sees that it is covered with red paint, no doubt from the newly painted shutter. At the end of the story, as he is drawn against his will, into a duel with a youth in the café of the strangely empty place in the South at which he has arrived, he hears the shot of the other's pistol and feels a wetness on his cheek. He puts his hand up to it and then brings it down before his eyes: it is red with blood.

After that initial encounter with him in the pages of *Encounter* Borges became part of my life. And unlike Kafka and Proust, he was alive. His books appeared in English translation at regular intervals and were universally admired, though, as I have suggested, usually for the wrong reasons. One could still buy more of him in French than in English and I regularly stocked up on him whenever I went to France. He even came to England and gave lectures and answered questions. I remember only one, at the ICA. 'Mr Borges,' the questioner asked, 'you write very rarely about women. Do you never think about them?' 'On the contrary,' replied the blind Borges, holding his stick between his knees, his kindly leathery face held out to the footlights, 'I think about them all the time. In fact I write to stop myself thinking about them.'

8.4.2020

Passover tonight. T and family are planning various Zoom sessions, one at 5 where T will talk to all the different children, from Jesse (11) to Nina's Julie and Ludwig (7 & 9) and Zoe's Sol (3), along with Nina and Zoe, about Passover. Then we will all read the Haggadah separately, to 'meet' again at 9.30 to 'discuss' it. Let's see what it yields.

La Bourboule

When I wrote *A Life* I described how Sacha and I had revisited La Bourboule on one of our European car holidays and how she noted the difference between the benign feel of the place then and how she remembered it – high mountains on either side, gloom, depression – obviously the result of the circumstances: locked there for the duration of the war with a young child, having just lost a second child. But when T and I drove there from Bernard's house in the Drome three years ago I had no memory at all of either our first sojourn there in 1943–45 or my visit with Sacha in the '70s.

It was a long drive and the last couple of hours over the dreary mountain moors of the Massif Central seemed unending. But eventually we reached La Bourboule and the hotel where we had booked a room for the night. This turned out to be outside the town, at the top of a mountain in a kind of chalet which obviously catered for walkers and holiday makers. We asked about a meal and were informed there was only a set menu, and that included no option apart from meat. So, tired though we were, we drove the twenty minutes down the mountain into town, parked and walked along the main street, which seemed to consist almost entirely of run-down hotels and trinket shops. We eventually found a hotel that seemed a little less dilapidated than the rest and where the dining room, visible from the street, seemed actually to be quite welcoming. Yes, they said, we were in time for a meal and there were plenty of free tables.

It was one of the best meals of our lives, true old *France profonde* in all its culinary glory. Nothing fancy, but a great bowl of vegetable soup left on the table for us to help ourselves to as many platefuls as we wanted after the waiter had helped us to the first portion. This was followed by a perfect escalope for T and a perfect *sole meunière* for me.

As we relaxed and tucked in we looked round. It was the kind of hotel, we realised, where people booked in for the season. The other clients seemed to be nearly all long-time residents, with their napkins and opened bottles of wine waiting for them on their tables. And suddenly it hit me that this was exactly the kind of place my mother and I had spent the war in, that it might indeed be the very place. I racked my brains to try and remember if Sacha had ever mentioned the name but nothing came.

After a desert of *crème caramel*, as good as Sacha ever made it, we stepped out into the street and continued, in the gathering dark, to make our way up the main street. More hotels. More trinket shops. And then, on the opposite side, the grand Baths which had given the town its reputation in the late nineteenth century, when health spas began to be all the rage with the European bourgeoisie. We determined to go in the next day and have a go at 'taking the waters' – only to discover, when we tried to do so, that you had to have a medical chit before they would allow you in.

La Bourboule and the Mont D'Or at the top of the mountain were both spas, the latter catering for adults, the former for children with chest conditions. During the war there was of course no call for cures, the hotels remained empty during 'the season', and as a result both towns became a magnet for those fleeing the front lines, whether in the East, the South or the North. It was there that Ida Bourdet, who had saved us from being rounded up by the Germans when Italy fell in early September 1943 and the Germans moved in, insisted we go. The Germans would not come looking for Jews there, she explained, and food would be more plentiful than in the arid South. As it happened she had friends, for whom she had also procured false papers, who would be making the long train journey to the Mont D'Or the following day. We were to join them and get off at La Bourboule. Which Sacha, with me, not quite three, and heavily pregnant with a second child by then, duly did.

At first we lodged with a family, but after Sacha had given birth and the baby had died of malnutrition (or *her* malnutrition, she explained to me many years later) after only a few days, we moved to a hotel where we stayed for the duration of the war. I will say more about the hotel and its inhabitants a little later.

I recalled Sacha talking about the Ferme de la Fosse, where she would walk with me to fetch milk and butter to add to the meagre rations we were allowed (I would barter a dictionary for a pat of butter, she told me later, it was all a question of need), and where she would exchange the shoes and clothes I was outgrowing for bigger ones, since the farmer's family had many children, some younger and some older than me. So I asked at the hotel whether they knew of such a farm and, if so, where it might be. No, they said, they'd never heard of it. But in bed that evening, studying a map of the area, I suddenly came across the name – nowhere else but off the road up to the hotel from the town. So the next morning, on our way down to the town, we looked out for a sign and indeed, there it was, clear as anything, the people at the hotel must have passed it every day but it never registered.

We drove for a short distance along a track and eventually saw the farmhouse We parked the car and got out. A dog started barking in the yard. I'm staying here, T said, you go. So I walked towards the house, stopped a little way from it, and looked. No memory stirred in my mind. But at least I had seen it and could, as we descended, gage the distance to the town and so try to imagine the route my mother and I would so frequently have taken seventy years before.

We had decided to go into the town, park the car and walk to the Mont d'Or. This would stretch our legs after much driving the previous day and I would have the chance to retrace a route I would have taken with my mother when I was three and four. For in among the family photos there is one of me in the snow on the way up, and Sacha told me she had once turned round on one of these hikes to see where I was and seen nothing but my head – I had stumbled into a snowdrift.

I'm amazed though that I could even do it. The Mont d'Or is about five kilometres away from La Bourboule and the ascent, through pine-woods, while beautiful, is also fairly taxing for an adult, so what it must have been like for a child of that age I cannot imagine. Yet I have nothing but pleasant memories of our walks there, usually with friends of Sacha's, though who these were I have no idea. Her later accounts of the two years we spent in La Bourboule were of the two of us thrown together by a hostile environment and of her terrible loneliness. She did talk of a Russian woman, a refugee from Alsace, with whom she had forged a bond and who committed suicide a few months after arriving at the hotel.

T and I eventually, exhausted by our efforts and the summer heat, left the woods behind and continued up a steep winding road into the town, considerably smaller than La Bourboule, equally proud of its mosaic-covered Baths, and just as run-down. It – and indeed La Bourboule – reminded me, I suddenly realised, of Buxton, the Derbyshire spa town which also gives out this air of having once, long ago, been a fine and bustling place, now only a distant memory.

After eating a sandwich on the terrace of the café attached to the baths we went back down. I remember only the end of that walk, along the flat into the town, with the sun right in our eyes, exhausted by the heat. But eventually we were in the town, found a café and cooled off with tea and an ice cream, before our abortive attempt to partake of the medicinal baths. Turned away there we wandered the back streets of the town for a while, as I tried to determine if the hotel where we had dined was indeed the one Sacha and I had lived in during the war. But no memories emerged. All I could think was that though now and again I had managed to stir up dim memories of my childhood in La Bourboule, I had absolutely no memory of having visited this place with Sacha thirty or forty years previously. That visit, though I knew it had taken place, had been totally erased. I could only wonder at my having recalled, when writing *A Life*, that Sacha had been surprised at how different the town was from how it had remained in her mind since the war, and that I had found it a charming and cheerful place. Now it struck both me and T as a deeply depressing and sinister place and I could perfectly well understand how Sacha had felt about it. We left early the next morning, relieved to put it behind us, though I was glad to have seen it; for the first time since I had lived there during the war I felt I had understood what Sacha must have gone through in the two years we lived there. Why though I had no memory whatever of that first return visit remains a mystery.

9.4.2020

Passover last night. Earlier, T on Zoom with the various children in the family, going through the songs with them. And after our quick run-through of the Haggadah and lovely meal, more Zoom with the three girls and their partners. Strange but touching.

Boris's situation unchanged – still in intensive care but not deteriorating. Ridiculous claim on Tuesday by Raab that he would 'pull through' because he's 'got incredible willpower' – as though the thousands who've succumbed lacked it. Horrible.

La Bourboule (cont.)

There is a coda. Two years ago, while in Paris for Nina's fiftieth birthday party, and staying not far from her and her family in Peter and Sian's tiny apartment next to the Botanical Gardens, we were walking along the ridge that separates the two flats, and decided, since we passed right next to it, to look in on the bookshop in the rue Mouffetard where a few months' previously I had done a reading for Pascal of *In a Hotel Garden*, which he had just published in French. As soon as we entered the young owners recognised us, rushed up and greeted us, and one of them said: 'We have something for you.' Intrigued, we waited as he disappeared into the office. He returned with a large envelope. As I was opening it he explained: 'A lady dropped it in shortly after your talk here. She had seen the poster and wondered if you were the son of Jean Josipovici. I wrote to Pascal asking for your address but he never replied.' 'I think he's been a bit overwhelmed by personal problems and by the death of Bernard,' I said, as I pulled a bulky typescript out of the envelope. Attached was a letter. 'Cher Monsieur,' it read, 'Si vous êtes le fils de Jean Josipovici, voici un manuscrit d'une pièce qu'il avait écrit et qui traine chez moi depuis des années. P.S. Je suis la petite fille avec qui vous jouez a l'hotel à La Barboule pendant les dernières années de la guerre.' I looked again at the top: there was a phone number.

I rang the number but there was no reply. She must have gone on holiday, we thought. It was Nina's party that evening and we were leaving the next day, but I tried again in the morning and this time someone picked up the phone. 'This is Gabriel,' I said, 'the little boy you played with in the hotel in La Bourboule.

I've just been given the parcel you left with the bookshop and your letter. I'd very much like to see you.' 'Le petit Gabriel!' she said. There was a pause. Then: 'I'm afraid I'm leaving for the country tomorrow,' she said. 'We're going back to England this afternoon,' I said, 'but we could see you now. Where do you live?' 'Right by the bookshop,' she said. 'Could we not drop by?' 'I suppose you could,' she said, and gave us instructions.

Twenty minutes later we rang her bell. An elderly but smart French lady opened. We looked at each other, not sure how to greet each other. I introduced T. 'Come in', she said, and, pointing to the suitcases waiting in a corner: 'I'm leaving for the country tomorrow.'

She ushered us into a large living room with windows giving on to a splendid communal garden/courtyard and went off to make coffee. We glanced about us, waiting impatiently for her to return.

'You see,' she said, when she had poured us our coffee and sat down, 'I have had this typescript for many years and I didn't know how to get it to you.' (Clearly she was not *au fait* with the internet.) 'My son is not interested in such things and had he found it among my things after my death he would have thrown it away. It's a play your father wrote and which I performed in. You may find it somewhat old-fashioned but it was a great success at the time. It was performed at the Théatre du Vieux Colombier.'

I had no idea my father had ever had a play put on at a prestigious Parisian theatre. But while she wanted to talk about the play I wanted her to talk about him. 'I don't understand,' I said. 'How did you know my father?' For in my understanding of what had happened between my mother and father, he had left her in Nice, pregnant and with me, and gone off to Paris with another woman, in the middle of the war. He had returned to La Bourboule after the death of my sister for a few days, then left again, never to return.

'It's a long story,' she said. 'Your father was a very great man. He was a philosopher. A genius.' 'But how did you get to know him?' I asked. 'And why were you in La Bourboule during the war?'

Since I had first opened the parcel in the bookshop I had had at the back of my mind a photograph, which I reproduced in *A Life*, of a large armchair in which a girl of about fourteen is sitting holding an open book, with me, aged three or four, sitting beside her. She seems to be reading or perhaps trying to teach me to read. My mother had explained that this was a teenage girl who was living in the hotel and had taken to playing with me. That was all.

'My mother,' the old lady explained, 'ran a factory in Normandy, but she felt this was a dangerous area to be in and sent me to La Bourboule to be out of harm's way.' 'By yourself?' 'By myself.' 'But how did you come to know my father?' 'Oh, he lived with us.' 'Lived with you? Why?' 'Oh,' she said again, suddenly looking embarrassed, 'that's a long story.'

I waited.

'I was very fond of your mother,' she said. 'Always knitting you things to wear. I taught you to ride a child's bicycle, you know. Along the corridors of the hotel.'

'Yes,' I said, 'but about my father...?'

'My mother was a very beautiful woman,' she said. 'Very beautiful. When she came down to see me she got to know your father and then he went back with her to Paris and lived with us. He was with us for many years after the war. He was a philosopher, you know, as well as a writer. He would give talks in my mother's salon. Many distinguished people came to hear him.'

She didn't realise the effect this was having on me. 'But how did he survive in Paris as a Jew during the war?' I asked.

This did not seem to have occurred to her. 'Oh,' she said, 'he knew many important people.'

'But he couldn't have lived with you after the war,' I said, 'He got married to Viviane Romance.'

'Ah,' she said. 'That's another story. You should have seen my mother. She was out of her mind when he left her for Viviane Romance. It was a terrible blow.'

'But you went on seeing him? You were an actress?'

'Briefly. I was a pretty girl and I thought I had talent. I had a small part in this play. Your father was very good to me. He taught me a great deal about literature and philosophy. This play,' she went on, 'it may not be fashionable any more, it may feel a little old-fashioned, but I'm sure you could get it performed.'

An awkward silence ensued. I looked at T and she nodded. 'I think we ought to be going,' I said. 'I could send you a photo I have of the two of us together in a chair in that hotel.'

'I go to Ibiza every summer,' she said. 'I have a house there. But first I'm going to my house in Normandy. I'm going tomorrow. As you can see, my bags are packed.'

She saw us to the door. We shook hands.

Out in the street T said: 'You look shaken.'

It was difficult to tell how much of what she had told us was true and how much had altered in her memory. I don't think she realised for a moment what her revelations were doing to me. As far as she was concerned she was telling the son about how wonderful his father had been, how much he had done for her and what a great man he was. What I heard was that my father was a womaniser on the make, taking up with her mother because she had money and looks, then leaving her when something better turned up in the form of a famous film actress of the thirties intent on reviving her reputation, which had been seriously dented by hints of collaboration during the war, and hoping this handsome young Egyptian screenwriter would help her achieve that aim. What she had told me about his being in the hotel in La Bourboule and then leaving with her mother didn't fit in with what I had understood from my mother, that he had left for Paris 'with another woman' when we were still in the South. But what the truth of that was I would clearly never know.

I have still not been able to bring myself to read the play.

10.4.2020

The number of deaths keeps on rising throughout the world and in the UK. And the virus has not really hit Africa and South America, though it's beginning to do so – Venezuela on the news last night. *The Guardian* keeps publishing dispiriting articles about the impotence of the WHO and the EU as countries become more introverted and nationalist in the face of the virus just when everyone can see that the only solutions have to be world-wide. But with Trump in the White House the entire world hurtles downhill faster than it would otherwise have done. Feels more and more like the '30s and who knows how things will look as we emerge from the pandemic – if we ever do.

More and more museums and concert venues are opening their doors online – no doubt a wonderful opportunity, but I just don't seem to have the time or inclination for any of it.

Breakfast

Always the best meal of the day for me. To come into the kitchen to prepare breakfast and then sit down to it fills me with joy. The light in the summer on the bowl of fruit on the table. The sense of the potential of the day – that is a pleasure like no other.

The breakfasts of my childhood are terrace or verandah breakfasts. The terrace in our first flat in Maadi, in Road 9, with its view across the maize fields beyond which lay the Nile and where the tops of the high masts of the *felluccas* could be seen moving with stately dignity against the always cloudless sky. The verandah of the villa by the Club, overlooking the canal, which ran round three sides, and where Sacha would lay out breakfast when she returned from her bicycle run in the desert with the dogs. And then, in England, the second Putney flat, with the little circular wall-table sitting at which one looks straight down on the river. (Though evenings, when the light seems to come up off the river even when it has practically disappeared from the sky, are perhaps the best time in Putney.) And here in Lewes the round table in the kitchen with the bowl of fruit in the middle, a joy even when there was only the window facing towards the next-door house, and even more so now T has masterminded the transformation of the kitchen, with a big window at the end looking South to the garden and the trees beyond, filling the room with light.

The sense of the world new-made. That is what gives breakfasts their special quality. The daily miracle.

11.4.2020

Three weeks since T came down. Bright blue skies ever since – but the weather has changed from wintery to summery – with temperatures of 25 degrees forecast for Easter Sunday, tomorrow. All this adds to the sense of unreality that pervades the country, the world.

Horrible press briefing by Matt Hancock yesterday – called PPE a 'precious resource' and asked (?) those in need of them to use it 'sparingly' and only in case of 'absolute need', even suggesting one piece could be used throughout the day, before going on to 'explain' shortage as due to world-wide 'difficulties of procurement'. Thus threw front-line staff under the bus and then added that the steering of the bus might be erratic but it wasn't his or the government's fault. Unbelievable.

Finton O'Toole excellent in this morning's *Guardian*, showing how the nonsense about English exceptionalism has contributed heavily to the Government's late and confused response to the pandemic, which looks likely to make Britain the country with one of the highest death-rates in the world. Johnson's own brush with death will no doubt be treated by the right-wing press as a further example of the 'plucky English spirit' instead of the sad truth that all that is a nonsense and a dangerous nonsense, that the C-19 virus is not impressed by the myth of English exceptionalism.

Bressanone

I wrote about it so extensively in *A Life* that I hesitate to come back to it here. But it is changing and I want to say something about that and try to understand what I now feel about the place.

The Goldener Adler where Sacha and I spent so many holidays, with its quiet single rooms with their double doors (which I have only ever found elsewhere in old Oxford colleges), and where the sound of the gently flowing Isarco gurgling beneath the windows is a constant presence, and where, when you open the shutters you look out onto the Plose and the little villages dotted about its slopes – that is now a 5 star hotel, expensive and pretentious. The Gasser and the Grüner Baum have amalgamated. The town is packed with holiday-makers and queues of cars clog every road. That though probably due in large part to the fact that for the past few years, because of T's teaching commitments, we have had to be there in July or August, the high season. We now go straight to Kabis in S. Pietro and come down to Bressanone for a wander and a look at the cloisters and the shops. And even those visits are getting rarer as T is not over-fond of the mountains and I wonder whether I am up to the walks and climbs I used to take in my stride.

Yet as I talk about all this I feel its hold over me. This, after all, is the place where Sacha and I comforted each other after Robin's suicide and where I began to think through the memorial story, 'He', I wrote in the wake of that to ease my pain; this is where we met up with Rosalind one summer and where we brought Anna; this is where I had that incredibly powerful dream of writing a marvellous essay on Wallace Stevens and woke up with only the memory of the title remaining, 'The Great Clock that Tells the Time', an essay I still find myself incapable of writing and a title still in search of a body; this, I now see, is where so much of my interior life seems to have occurred that it is little wonder it is still such a presence in my life.

I don't feel that about Cheltenham or Oxford but I do about Putney and Woodstock. Perhaps it has to do with the fact that during my year working for my A-levels in Cheltenham and my three years as an undergraduate at Oxford I was simply too busy to feel or think very much, that it is only when there is a period of leisure in a place, as in my gap year in Putney or our holidays in Bressanone, when I have taken innumerable long ruminative walks and had the leisure to scribble away, that the memory persists so powerfully. But it is more than that with Bressanone. It is something I felt when Sacha and I first drove there from where we were staying in Bolzano, Sacha almost reluctant, when it came to it, to show me a town and countryside she had so loved in her youth. What I felt was that this was paradise, my *locus amoenus*, that the combination of small but architecturally rich and varied town, the two rivers running through it to come together at its heart, the generosity of the wide valley in which it sits and the imposing but not overwhelming mountains all around – that all this did indeed make it a magical place, a place surpassing in all ways anything I might have dreamed of, perpetually surprising, perpetually revealing new riches – what else could paradise be? For a non-believer like me this, even today, even with the changes wrought by the 'onward march of progress', this is indeed paradise.

'Why do you keep on going back to the same place, year after year?' people used to say to me. 'When you've found the perfect place, the place that instantly lifts your spirits, why would you go anywhere else?' I would reply. I hope I have the chance to return.

12.4.2020

Growing unease at the Government's failure to supply PPEs to those on the front line. Ministers bluster about world-wide demand but this can't hide their woeful unpreparedness, even though we had ample warning from Italy. Laughable if it wasn't so tragic. (It also happens to be Easter Sunday.)

The experts warn that the 'spike' might not yet have occurred. I know that when it does we will have solemn words about this being a serious matter but that it was all predictable and not to worry, they have it under control. Even a child can see that there's plenty to worry about.

Burial

'Now we need to have a serious talk,' said Jeff, the rabbi friend who had rushed down on the Saturday afternoon after I had left a message with his wife to say my mother was dying. As it was he arrived too late and caught up with me at the house of Andrew Robinson, who, with Stephen, had come to visit her in the hospital in Brighton and found me there that morning. As we talked and the nurses made her bed one of them came out and told us my mother had just died. She drew back the curtains and I said a last goodbye and then Andrew took me back to have lunch with him and Judy at their house in Falmer and this is where Jeff turned up, a few hours later.

I knew what the talk would be about.

'We have to talk about the funeral,' Jeff said.

In the days leading up to my mother's death, when I sensed that it was approaching, I had dreaded more perhaps even than the death itself all the paraphernalia of a funeral neither she nor I wished for.

'Do we have to?' I asked.

'Yes,' Jeff said.

He was good at telling the truth and then not breaking any ensuing silence.

'Why is it,' I said, 'that in the worst moment of one's life one has to think of things like that? Why can't we just be left in peace?'

'I'm afraid we really have to,' Jeff said.

'All right,' I said. 'But I know Sacha would have been totally indifferent. She never dug graves for the many pets we lost and laughed at members of her family who quarrelled over who would get to lie in the family tomb in Cairo or Alexandria.'

'We are not talking about Sacha,' Jeff said. 'We are talking about you.'

I had never thought of it like that.

'What do you think of cremation?' he asked.

'I suppose there's something purifying about fire,' I said. Then, after thinking about it. 'But I don't like it. I prefer the idea of burial.'

'Cremation is not really recognised in Judaism,' Jeff said. 'But of course a lot of Jews get cremated.'

'I don't like it,' I said, realising I felt quite strongly about it.

'So you would like Sacha to be buried?'

'I suppose so,' I said.

'Wait a moment,' he said.

He came back a few minutes later. 'I've found a plot in the Jewish cemetery in Hove,' he said.

'I didn't know there was a Jewish cemetery in Hove.'

'It gives onto the sea.'

Suddenly a ray of light broke into what had been unrelieved blackness. 'Sacha loved Valéry's *Le Cimetière Marin*,' I said. 'She would like to be buried there.'

And so it came to pass. Jeff took the service in the utterly simplified form I had asked for. Present were only Anna, Stephen and Andrew, who had been with me when she died, and Jess, who had been to see her more than anyone else when she was in the main hospital in Brighton.

Not only had the day been less horrific than I had feared, it had actually been a big step in the long process of healing and recovery, which I suppose still goes on and will never stop until I myself die.

I realised that I had so dreaded the very idea of a funeral because in my mind funerals were associated with the Christian ones which were the only kind I had ever attended, and which seemed to me profoundly false because they talked of an afterlife in which few of the participants believed and even, in certain cases, of the joys of heaven to which the dead person had at last been granted access, which people believed in even less. Jewish funerals, by contrast, Sacha's and those I have since attended with T, including those for her father and aunt, seem immensely helpful in their acknowledgement that the loss is an intolerable one for the bereaved to bear, that we all come to it in the end and that we have to console ourselves by the thought of what the dead person meant to us in life and will go on meaning to us after their death.

No doubt this is a doubly biased view, unfair to Christian

burials partly because I do not believe what Christians do and partly because not all Christian funerals are as I have described them. Certainly when I read accounts, in books on peasant communities in Europe in the last century, or of the Christian burials of the Middle Ages and earlier, there is more stress on the anguish of bereavement and less on the salvific power of Jesus Christ and the idea of a blissful life in heaven for the righteous dead. And this brings them into line with other cultures, probably the majority in the world, which bury their dead. For burial seems to have been a universal practice since time immemorial and the superstition has always existed that to leave someone unburied is to risk the hauntings of their restless ghost – a topic that figures in both the *Odyssey* and the *Aeneid*. Of course there are many cultures, such as the Hindu, which insist on cremation, or the Tibetan Buddhist and the Zoroastrian, where the dead are laid out on the mountainside to be devoured by birds until nothing but the clean bones remain. But even there what is important is the ceremony which brings about the final separation of the living and the dead. 'I will go to him but he will not come back to me,' as King David says on learning of the death of the baby Bathsheba has borne him – that is perhaps the only certainty in life.

13.4.2020

The number of deaths in Britain continues to rise. More doctors, nurses, bus drivers and people in care homes dying for lack of PPE. College of nurses telling its members not to go to work if they don't have PPE.

First Zoom Hebrew Bible session. Death of Ahab. Jonathan, just recovered from some bad illness (without testing impossible to say if C-19, but likely), very interesting as always – this time on the strange kind of heroism of Ahab at the last. (Maybe like some of Dante's damned.)

Today the weather has suddenly changed. Grey skies, wind, temperature down from 20 to 10 or 11. In a way quite a relief. The perfect blue skies, sunshine, etc. of the past 21 days only added to the unreality, though enjoyable enough. At least today, Easter Bank Holiday Monday, no one will be tempted to sunbathe in parks.

Cairo

I'm not a city boy. I've only gradually got to understand what the word 'streetwise' means. It means having an instinct for the life of city streets, knowing when to steer clear and when to bluff, when to saunter and when to run, when to take something at face value and when not. I have none of that. Brought up in small towns till I was fifteen, I have settled in another small town and made my life there. I know the thrill of walking the streets of a big city, whether it be London, Paris or Berlin, but I don't instinctively know how to deal with it; in a city I am an innocent and know I am, not streetwise as Tim and T are, both Londoners born and bred.

Cairo was where I went with my mother if she had shopping to do that couldn't be done in Maadi and if I had saved enough pocket-money to buy a book or to add an item to my carpentry set. We would take the little train that ran from Helwan to Cairo, stopped at Maadi and went on past St.George (Mari Girgis), where the Coptic cathedral (and, I discovered on a later visit to Egypt, the old Cairo synagogue) was located, went on through the run-down areas of Saida Zeinayb to arrive at Bab-el-Luk. Now this is only the first part of an electrified line that goes underground as one enters the city and continues into the centre of Cairo, but in those days one got out at Bab-el-Luk and walked into the old European centre. 'Hold my hand,' my mother would say as we got off the train, for at Bab-el-Luk the crowds were so dense, there was such a noise, such a sense of different currents swirling this way and that, that it seemed only too easy to get swept away and I had no idea where we were going or how to get back should we lose each other.

As we left the area the crowds thinned a little, but I was still afraid of losing her. Then, suddenly, we were in the European quarter. We would enter various shops, including the English bookshop where I, nursing my Egyptian equivalent of six shillings and sixpence, would spend a long time trying to decide which of the myriads of Worlds Classics or Everyman Library books I would buy. In a scene that has only changed with the arrival of internet shopping I would agonise over this as if it was a matter of life or death, when actually, once I got home with my precious parcel, I might find what I had bought too difficult or too boring and give up after only a few pages. I remember one occasion when I had whittled the choice down to two: the *Meditations of Marcus Aurelius* and Scott's *Waverley*. I've no idea why just those two caught my fancy, but suddenly it seemed as if my future happiness entirely depended on them. And I just could not make up my mind which I wanted to read more. They both looked and smelled so good in their small format and trim hard covers which, once opened, seemed to hold out the promise of so many unimagined riches, so many worlds to be explored. I held each in my hand, trying to decide between them. Then, finally, with a wrench, I left one behind and went determinedly up to the counter with the other, only, at the last minute, to change my mind and hurry back, put it down and pick up the other. Finally my mother, taking pity on me or perhaps thinking that we really needed to move on, said: 'You buy one with your pocket-money and I'll buy the other for you.' I couldn't believe it, now I could have both! My joy was boundless. Sadly, though, I don't think I finished either and have not done so since.

After the bookshop, if my mother had made her purchases, we would go to Groppi's, for an ice-dream or a milk-shake if it was morning, tea and hot buttered toast if it was the afternoon. There were two Groppis, one in a great garden, where a tree grew through the glass roof of the building from which the *suffraguis* came with the orders, and which was my favourite, and the other, on the ground floor of a large modern building, which was delightfully air-conditioned and hushed and where the milkshakes were better but the toast less good. In the garden Groppi it came in a round metal dish with a cover. One lifted the thick round top slice, into which the butter had already melted, put it on one's plate and put the lid back on to keep the lower slice warm. I don't recall it arriving in such a dish in the other tearoom and I have never seen such a toast container since. Indeed, were I to find it I would be disappointed, for it belongs only there, in the Groppi garden of my childhood.

Groppi had been founded by a Swiss at the turn of the twentieth century, when Cairo was at the height of its European glory, and in the 1950s it was still where 'everybody' went. I recall my mother meeting a friend of hers going in once as we were leaving and introducing me to him. 'Ah, you're studying at Victoria College,' he said. 'And what is your favourite subject?' I said history and he said: 'Then you must read the greatest history book ever written. It's by Arnold Toynbee and it's called *The Study of History*. It deals with the entirety of world history from ancient civilisations to the present and is in many volumes, but there is an abridgement in one volume and that is what you should read. It will change your life.' For some reason I did not trust him, and as we walked back to Bab-el-Luk my mother rather confirmed this by saying that he was a great show-off, but cultured in his way and at heart a kind man.

But though the encounter has remained in my memory and even his excited manner of speaking as he talked about Arnold Toynbee, *The Study of History* has joined the innumerable books I have wanted to read but never got round to.

At fourteen my English teacher suggested I join the British Council library in Cairo, and at that point I started going to Cairo on my own. I knew my way from Bab-el-Luk to Tahrir Square, later famous of course as the place where the abortive revolution to oust Mubarek took root, but then a dusty Cairene square dominated by the huge government Home Office building (the Mogamma) where we later went, day after day, in the heat of the stifling Cairo summer of 1956, to try to get exit visas to leave Egypt for ever. On an upstairs floor of the British Council close by stood the open shelf library, from which it was possible to borrow up to three books at a time. That was when I moved from Biggles and Gimlet, which I would buy at the Maadi bookstore, to Conrad, returning on the little train clutching my copy of *The Secret Agent* or *Under Western Eyes* and proud of myself for having ventured into the great city and returned unscathed. For where more adventurous adolescents would have gone on to explore the city I was too timid to do so. Perhaps the fact that we had managed to survive the war in France, not been picked up by the Nazis or their French collaborators, but nevertheless always aware of danger, had led to my feeling of insecurity, exacerbated by coming to a country whose language I hardly knew and whose people, especially the common people, though likeable enough, seemed ineradicably alien and, speaking an alien language, people I could never hope to understand – all this fed into my sense that the great city was something to be visited with trepidation, but it may simply have been that I am fearful by nature, surprised sometimes, even now, that I have got through a day there without mishap.

When I returned to Egypt in 1976, twenty years after leaving it, I was introduced by my aunt to George Scanlon, a brilliant, exuberant, opinionated American Islamic archaeologist, who had worked with the great K.A.C. Creswell, the historian of Egyptian Islamic monuments, and excavated Fustat, the first capital of Islamic Egypt and the seed from which Cairo blossomed. George, the most generous of men, offered to show me round the old medieval Cairo and what better guide could I have had? The ancient buildings and monuments are thick on the ground, for almost every Sultan would build a mosque, partly out of piety and partly to perpetuate his name, and then next to the mosque, naturally, a *madrassa* or Islamic school, and next to that, quite possibly, a *hammam* or bath. The brother or son who deposed (and frequently murdered) him would naturally wish to build a bigger mosque, a bigger *madrassah*, a more elaborate *hammam*, and when he in his turn was murdered by a brother or son, the new ruler would build in his turn. Thus it is that Old Cairo boasts more great buildings per square mile than almost anywhere in the world (the Ankor Wat temple complex in Cambodia may come first but it is not in the middle of a huge modern city). We started at one of the gates of the Old City, Bab Zuwayla, which he had spent years excavating (being an archaeologist is a bit like being a theatre director, this most theatrical of men told me, you have to guide, motivate and keep everyone in the team happy), and followed up, in the course of several outings in the baking heat of an Egyptian May, by visiting the best of the city's ancient buildings. It was then I realised that while ancient Egypt and its much-vaunted art on the whole left me cold, the Islamic art of medieval Egypt thrilled me quite as much as did the cathedrals of Europe. Years later I visited Cairo with a friend and we sat for an hour or more contemplating the lovely courtyard of the mosque of Ibn Tulun, the oldest of Cairo's mosques to survive intact. Like the plays of Aeschylus it is utterly simple in its overall conception and unbelievably rich in detail.

The city of Cairo as a whole, however, remains alien and frightening. But then, though to a much lesser extent, so does London, in which I've lived and some parts of which I know fairly well and whose inhabitants on the whole speak my language. Only Paris of the cities I know seems utterly benign.

14.4.2020

The death toll continues at Italian rates – around the seven to nine thousand per day. The medical and scientific advisors may talk of plateauing, but we all remember the horror with which we watched scenes of the havoc caused by the virus in Italy – three weeks before it hit Britain, three weeks' grace squandered by the Government.

Last night T alerted me to a programme on *aphantasia*, in which Sue Armstrong talked to Professor Adam Zeman, a neurologist at Exeter, who a few years ago 'discovered' and then named this 'condition', which consists of not having a 'mind's eye', not being able to call up *visual* memories. Armstrong and Zeman seemed to see this as a *lack* – certain people *do not have* this faculty, and Zeman even talked of a possible genetic cause, since apparently the 'condition' is often found in families. The artists and others they talked to on the programme, especially the visual artist Michael Chance, did not see it that way. They felt it was not something they missed and might even be an advantage in their work.

I would want to go further. For a long time I have been aware of the fact that unlike many writers I have no strong visual memory, perhaps no visual memory at all. But I have a memory of people, places and events, quite enough to write the memoir of my mother and essays on art for example. In fact I have always felt vaguely superior to those who talk of a 'mind's eye', believing that they live in a static universe, full of images, while I live in a dynamic universe where what I call up are powerful feelings which are not located in the head but which I would describe as bodily. That is why reading Proust at seventeen was a defining experience for me, for that is exactly what Proust describes. As someone remarked, you could make a dress from Thomas Mann's descriptions but never from Proust's, even though he talked at such length about the dresses of Odette and the Princesse de Guermantes. At times I have wondered whether people really do have a stack of visual images 'in' their heads. Are they not perhaps simply persuaded that they do by all they've read and heard? What I suspect they really have. What I suspect they *really* have is a feeling, a feeling that requires work (Proust is very good on this) to bring it out into the open. Unable to do this work, they fall back on the cliché of a 'mind's eye'. I may be wrong on this and the programme suggested that most people do indeed have such images in their heads and that I am part of a minority who don't (Zeman put it at two percent if I remember rightly).

In my writing I have always eschewed visual descriptions, perhaps because I don't have a strong visual memory myself, but actually it is because reading such descriptions in other people's novels I am instantly bored and feel it is so much dead wood. T thinks I am merely talking about bad writing, but whether you call it bad writing or 'the classic novel', there is no doubt that if someone enters a room in a novel or a new character is introduced this is often followed by a description of what the room or the character 'looked like'. But when, in life, one enters a room one immediately takes it all in, whereas a description in words on a page is inevitably linear and time-bound, however fast one reads, so that these elaborate descriptions, which are meant to make you experience the world the novel inhabits, in fact push you away from it. I see this as a clumsy attempt by naïve artists to compensate for the disappearance of a living audience such as the traditional story-teller enjoyed and the fact that the novelist is writing by him or herself in a closed room, reaching out to readers they don't know, feeling they must 'draw them in' to the story they are telling. But this was not true of Cervantes or Sterne, who held their readers precisely by questioning the very assumptions made by the other kind of novelist, whose way of working gained prominence in the nineteenth century, and who still dominates today. The tradition I warm to and that I would seek to be a part of, on the other hand, the tradition that runs from Rabelais to Perec, from Cervantes to Kundera, and that includes Kafka, early Faulkner, Duras, Muriel Spark and Aharon Appelfeld, on the whole eschews description. (As do the wonderful Biblical narratives I so warm to.) It may be that all these writers suffered from aphantasia. A question I will leave to Zeman and his colleagues.

Cars

In my childhood cars belonged to other people. To Ronnie's parents, for example, who took me with them to their chalet among the dunes in Agami. Or to the young Egyptian men who drove Anna to the various swimming galas I took part in, while I took the coach with the rest of the team.

Strangely, one of my abiding memories of the Maadi years is waiting with my mother in front of Goma's grocery store by the level crossing next to the station to see if any of her friends with cars was going in to Cairo. If after fifteen or so minutes no one came by we would make our way up to the platform and wait for the next train, which was never long as there were three or four trains an hour. But often a car would draw up and the driver would lean across, open the passenger door and invite us to join him. The car would then speed over the railway tracks and (at least in my last years in Maadi) keep going till we reached the river and the yacht club, where we would turn right and go along the newly built corniche. Before the corniche was built we would take a route that led through the Arab villages and townships on the southern edge of Cairo, so that our entry into the city was almost imperceptible. And one advantage of the lift was that we would be dropped in the centre rather than having to walk in from the station at Bab-el-Luk.

I can't put a face to the many men (were they never women?) who gave us lifts, though some of them must have been people I had seen either at Chickie's or at the club. They invariably spoke French and they never addressed me as I sat at the back. That was fine by me. A car ride was a treat and it was good not to have to make conversation.

I acquired my first car shortly after I got the job at Sussex. I remember driving Gordon, John and my mother to Coventry to see Basil Spence's new cathedral. I was taking driving lessons in Oxford, but an hour a week, I realised, would never get me through my test, so I bought a third or fourth hand mini and stuck an L plate on it and got John or Gordon, who both had licences, to accompany me on various outings. On the way back from Coventry John, who was sitting in the front with me, suddenly said, 'Here's the turning!' and I swerved too abruptly and the car ended up on a grass verge on the side of the road, all of us rather shaken. I think John took over the driving for the rest of the trip, but it gave me a strong sense of how quickly a car travels even though, sitting inside, one does not realise it – quite different from the scooter I had been used to, where you were always conscious of the speed at which you were going. A better lesson than any of the ones I had been paying for.

Sacha, who had passed her driving test in France before the war and drove a Citroën when she and my father lived in Vence ('your father would seize the handbrake and pull it up in terror if I went at more than 30 kilometres an hour'), had to retake it in England. I said I would go out on the road with her and get her used to the new conditions, but when, at our first session, I made her do a three-point turn on a small country road, reducing both of us to near tears, she decided to take proper lessons and eventually passed her test on the hilly, traffic-laden roads of Brighton. After the oral, she told me, the examiner grudgingly said: 'You've passed, but only just.' 'That's all I want,' she said, whereupon he looked at her disapprovingly and she feared he would reverse his decision. But he didn't, which was fortunate as she loved driving. 'I can't believe it,' she once said to me, 'I live in a country where there is nothing to fear, you have a secure job so we know we will never go hungry, and *on top of that* we have a car.'

So much of our later life together seems, in retrospect, to have been spent in cars together. Sacha grew to hate the train, so we would drive to London together to go to concerts or plays or, occasionally, to visit friends, taking turns to drive. On one occasion, on the M23, sensing she was exceeding the speed limit, I warned her: 'Slow down, there's a police car behind us,' but she only put her foot on the pedal and went even faster until the inevitable happened and the police car overtook us and forced us to pull in. The driver got out and leaned down as she opened the window. 'Do you know what speed you were going at, madam?' he asked. 'I can't keep my eye on the road and on the speedometer at the same time,' my mother said, 'I'm sure it was under seventy'. He was not amused. 'I'd advise you to drive more slowly,' he said. 'I don't want to drive past one day and see your car all smashed up and you inside.' 'Yes, Officer,' my mother said. As we drove on she said: 'You turned away! You pretended not to know me!' 'Why did you speed up instead of slowing down?' I retorted. She did not deign to answer.

We would drive across the continent to go on holiday to the Dolomites, often going on to visit her cousins in Bologna or

Forte dei Marmi or her aunt in San Remo. Every year I would have forgotten how scary it was to be driven by Sacha, especially in an English car on continental roads where I felt the oncoming cars were heading straight for me as I sat in the passenger seat. I would ask her to slow down, then beg her, and finally scream at her. 'Control yourself,' she would say, tight-lipped. 'I can't,' I would reply, 'I'm frightened. Please! Slow down!' Eventually she would bring the car to a stop in a layby or on the hard shoulder and we would sit like that in furious silence. 'I'm never going to drive with you again,' she would say. 'And you know how I love driving.' I could never understand that. Cars for me are a useful and comfortable way to get from one place to another but driving has never been a source of pleasure in itself. Yet it clearly was to her. We would make up and she would promise to drive more slowly while I in turn would promise to try and control myself. And all would be well until the next time I felt she drove too fast and I could no longer control my fear and the whole scene would be played out again.

Yet it was also often as we took these long drives that we had our most fruitful conversations and that she would open up to me about her childhood and the war years. So my life, I now feel, would have been much the poorer had cars never been invented.

15.4.2020

Weather much colder but still amazingly sunny and dry. Set to change by Friday, apparently.

When the figures for deaths in care homes for the past week was finally released yesterday it turned out that it added huge numbers – I heard 5,000 being mentioned – to the official death toll from the virus. When the medical officers were challenged by the journalists in the briefing for comparing the death tolls in France with those in England without explaining that in France they included those not in hospitals while in England it was only those diagnosed with C-19 in hospitals, they deflected the questions and avoided giving an honest answer in the way of all politicians, thereby further undermining our faith in them.

Comedy

As an adolescent interested in art I was always trying to understand what 'art' was, what 'drama' was, what 'comedy' and 'tragedy' were. I soon came to see this led nowhere, and Oxford taught me a respect for the historical context of all art forms. Now I shudder at the thought of having to teach a course (as I once had to at Sussex) on Tragedy, and glow with pleasure on reading John Jones' wonderful book *On Aristotle and Greek Tragedy*, which not only shows how alien and strange Greek tragedy was, how far removed from Shakespeare and Racine and Ibsen, but, by showing how different Aeschylus and Sophocles are from Euripides, draws attention to the folly of even trying to speak of an entity called 'Greek Tragedy'.

And it is the same with comedy. I can appreciate the medieval idea that comedy deals with ordinary people whose fortunes go from bad to good while tragedy deals with highborn people whose fortunes go from good to bad, the reason why Dante entitled his poem *Commedia* (the 'Divine' was added in the Renaissance, and I resist the epithet, it 'skies' what is a wonderfully down-to-earth poem). I also feel I am getting somewhere in reading Auerbach's accounts of how Christianity transformed the rigid hierarchy of genres by stressing that Jesus was an ordinary man who came to save ordinary men, and that the evangelists used not an elevated or a low style to depict the great events of his life, but a 'humble' style, the *sermo humilis*. In the remarkable first two chapters of *Mimesis* he shows how in this the evangelists (or whoever wrote the Gospels) were merely following in the footsteps of the narratives of the Hebrew Bible. And I feel the same way reading C.L. Barber's *Shakespeare's Festive Comedy* (1959) and Robert Wiemann's *Shakespeare and the Popular Tradition in the Theatre* (1981), two remarkable books which have stood the test of time, and which seek to anchor Shakespeare, his clowns and fools, the songs and comic routines that fill his works, as well as his comic plots, in a vibrant popular tradition ,and to show how when a great artist happened to be born into such a tradition the combination led to the writing of works that transcend their time and place and can still speak to us today, much more powerfully of course if we take the trouble to acquaint ourselves with that tradition.

On the other hand I do think that a *comic spirit* pervades many of the books I hold most dear, from Rabelais and Cervantes through Sterne to Proust (Scott Moncrieff rarely manages to catch this, since in Proust the comedy is largely linguistic), Kundera's *Immortality*, all of Muriel Spark and most of Perec. And I would like to think my own novels (not all, not *Migrations* or *Everything Passes*, for example) catch something of this. It's at the forefront in *Infinity* (one reason why I like it more than almost any of my novels) and palpable, I think, in *The Inventory* and *Now*. Even books I have thought of as desperate and painful turn out, *après le coup*, to contain some comic scenes or phrases, such as the refrain 'She had other qualities' in *The Cemetery in Barnes*, which I never thought of as comic when writing but in T's mouth, as she uses it in other contexts, turns out to be so.

What I realise I yearn for as I write is that humour the other side of anguish which is the ground of Beckett's writing. Yet not like Beckett's, which is predicated on the laughability of the idea of a world created by God and in some way fulfilling his purpose, or one in which a mindless Victorian optimism pervades popular expressions of belief. This is the source of the bitterness of his titles, like *All That Fall*, which tells of a child killed in a fall from a moving train and makes a mockery of the verse 'The Lord upholdeth all that fall, and raiseth up all those that be bowed down', from Psalm 145; or *Happy Days*, which refers to the 1929 song by Jack Yellen, whose first verse runs:

> Happy days are here again
> The skies above are clear again
> So let's sing a song of cheer again
> Happy days are here again

and shows us a woman buried first up to her waist and then, in the second act, up to her neck in sand. Somehow my sense of the comic as a response to pain and despair is less culturally specific than Beckett's, perhaps for that reason less rooted. It is not an Eastern European Jewish combination either, though I love that in Bellow, Malamud and Shabtai. If there are any antecedents I suppose I'd have to say a mixture of Sterne and Kafka, though that sounds very odd as I write it down.

One of the plays I'm most proud to have written was called *Comedy*.

16.4.2020

More of the same – more people dying, including doctors, nurses and care staff; more Government faffing to cover their inefficiency and cluelessness; more cloudless skies.

Zeman responded to my email to him, with which I'd enclosed the diary entry above. He reiterated his 'scientific' analysis, claiming the small percentage with aphantasia were more abstract and likely to be scientists while those with hyperphantasia tended to be artists. Sounds like the kind of cliché scientists come up with, though he may well be right, whatever 'right' means. I suppose I don't care two hoots where scientists place Rembrandt or Kafka on a spectrum. But what of musicians?

Rosalind: I've always been amazed at how powerfully you respond to music, at how central it is in your creative work, and yet how little you know about it and you have often told me you can't really distinguish between performances or performers.

Ivy Compton-Burnett

She's the great enigma of twentieth-century British letters. Is she an eccentric lady novelist who writes indistinguishable novels about the Victorian world of her childhood? Or is she, as Pamela Hansford Johnson put it, the purveyor of 'a gentle tea-cosy madness, a coil of vipers in a sewing-basket'? Or, as Nathalie Sarraute wrote, a radical modernist who has been totally misunderstood in her own country?

Perhaps all three. It's quite possible, as Pamela Hansford Johnson remarks, that 'this piercingly wise, discreet, mannered Victoriana conceals abysses of the human personality'; and it is also possible that this is conveyed, that she feels it can only be conveyed, through a concatenation of dead-pan dialogues, with the reader being left to fill the gaps, imagine the drama for him or herself rather than having it done for them by a narrator. That would align her with Virginia Woolf rather than Elizabeth Bowen, with Sarraute herself rather than with Jean Rhys.

She is one of those writers – Jane Austen and Flaubert are others – who I like reading less than I feel I should, knowing what I do about them and seeing how they go about their work. With Austen I suspect it is that though I enjoy the wit and the craftsmanship I grow tired of the morality, however sophisticated, and of the relentless way the plot functions. With Flaubert I know it is the lack of warmth, a perpetual seeing of the worst in men and women, which, allied to the impeccable style, I find wearying and unrewarding. But with Ivy Compton Burnett?

I ought to adore her. After all, she does everything I would want to do in my writing: create, through the words people speak to each other, and only through those, a world, a universe, and allow events to be conjured up for us only by those words. I want to do that, I realise, because I sense that words are the only currency we writers have, so if we are to be honest we should deal solely in words, that is, in the words people speak to each other and to themselves; and because I sense that *in our lives* many things may happen to us but we only have words to talk about them, words that falsify, inadequate words. I think of what has happened when I have known that I am seeing people for the last time, whether it be Chickie when I left Egypt in January 2000 knowing that she wouldn't be alive whenever it would be that I would return, or Gāmini or Jonathan Harvey or Josef Herman as I knew they were dying and they knew it too, yet all we could exchange were words. I asked Josef as he lay on his day-bed, the only time in our long acquaintance I hadn't seen him standing or sitting: 'What has it been in your life that has made you most happy?' 'Gabriel,' he said in his marvellous Polish accent which he had not lost in sixty years in Britain, 'Gabriel, I alvays did vot I vonted.' Then he lay on the bed and I felt he was tiring and said: 'I'm going to go now, Josef.' 'Goodbye,' he said. 'Goodbye,' I said, and left.

Everything I know about Ivy Compton Burnett also makes me warm to her: living most of her adult life with her companion, one of those fine mid-twentieth century women – Marianne Moore was another – who were masters of their fates, kind to friends but not giving much away to strangers, journalists or critics, and thus wonderfully enigmatic to the last.

So why does she not sit in my pantheon with Kafka and Proust, or at least with Duras and Spark?

It may be because her work is *too* stylised. All those adults and children who speak in the same way and who are described in the same way: 'Fulbert Sullivan was a spare, muscular man of fifty .' His wife Eleanor is 'a tall, angular woman of forty-eight.' His son Graham 'A tall bony youth of twenty-one'. His daughter Lucia is 'two years older than her brother Daniel. She was in appearance a cross between her parents, but was shorter and rounder in build, with more colour in her eyes and skin and a more tightly chiselled face.' (All this from *Parents and Children*, 1941.) Such details seem to be pinned on to her characters, thrown out as though they were necessary labels. But if she is not interested in creating characters for us, as Dickens, for example is, why give these details? Clearly because the author sees them in her mind's eye and presents us with what she sees. But it only adds to the odd impersonality of the people who fill her books, their wooden, puppet-like quality. It is possible that if we persevere and do a great deal of work we will come to know them and live in and with them. But I'm not sure Ivy Compton-Burnett wants us to. In her best books there is a fascination in seeing individuality emerge almost despite the best efforts of the author, and in watching events unfolding which would not be out of place in a Greek tragedy, as critics have noted. But when I ask myself which are 'her best books' I am at a loss. Just as the people are relentlessly undifferentiated in the way they speak, so the titles – *Brothers and Sisters*, *Men and Women*, *Fathers and Children*, *Daughters and Sons* – are relentlessly similar. So, to find out which you liked and which you didn't there is no option but to read them all over again – not a bad way of passing the time, and yet…

Or is it just that I have not tried hard enough? I don't know.

And where Muriel Spark, who also relies on dialogue to a large extent, draws you in by her rhythms, her ballad-like repetitions and prolepses, Ivy Compton Burnett seems to spurn all this as beneath her. Take me as I am, she seems to say, or don't take me at all. Her books are there, real literature, anything but pap, but they make no concessions, feel as though they would not stoop even to think of the reader and his or her needs and desires, as though this would demean them in some way. And perhaps they would. Her austerity, the simple facticity of her books, have something both admirable and frightening about them. Will I be up to it? we ask ourselves as we take one of them off the shelves? Or will I be defeated? Will I enjoy it or will I need to just grin and bear it? There is nothing else like them that I know of, in English or any other language.

<hr>

17.4.2020

More bluster from the politicians and their scientific advisors in the face of questions of why Germany has had so many fewer deaths than the UK. More inadequacies highlighted all over the country in the provision of PPE and tests. The unnatural good weather has come to an end. Though the skies were blue when I woke up at 7 it is now grey, as it was for much of yesterday, and heavy rain is forecast.

Dreamed last night that Nigel Farage was giving an online interview from his house. At the end he said: 'But in these difficult times there is one book I would recommend.' He turned and reached into a bookshelf behind him and came out with two books. 'Montaigne's essays,' he said. 'I always go back to the large, two and a half inches thick edition [showing it] of the complete essays, but Penguin [showing it] have a nice little edition of three of them.' Then I woke up.

I'm amazed that my unconscious should be so witty.

Coronavirus

My grandmother died in the typhoid epidemic that swept Egypt in 1920 and in which Sacha herself, at ten, was struck down. And then, when I read Sacks' *Awakenings* in the 1970s I became acquainted with the great flu epidemic of 1918–26, which apparently killed more people than had died in WWI. In the past twenty-five years or so we have had foot-and-mouth disease in cattle, which kept us off the Downs for months, and then Sars, Mers and Ebola, which took place in far-away places like Eastern Asia and Africa. But the idea that a pandemic would occur which would kill thousands, if not hundreds of thousands, in the West and lead to the wealthy nations of Europe and America effectively shutting down for months, their economy simply ceasing to function, was the stuff of sci.fi. fantasy, or rather, if it was foreseen by scientists, was not a possibility ever contemplated by even the newspaper-reading public. And yet it's happened. In three months, since mid-January, the virus has dealt a blow to two centuries of the undiluted worship of Capital and Progress. Will such a worship simply step unscathed out of the pandemic when it is over and things just go on as before? Or will there be a massive change? This is what the pundits argue about non-stop on the airwaves and in the papers, and nobody knows. The best guess seems to be that even if the changes are profound they will be gradual, both changes leading to a return to the *status quo ante* and those leading to a profound re-orientation.

To my surprise I find that the pandemic, despite all the horrors it has brought with it, the suffering, the death, the despair at loss of loved ones and at the loss of jobs, the dreadful pathos of people having to die alone and families having to bear the deaths of parents and children without being able to be with them in their last hours or even to bury them with due ceremony – despite all this a part of me is glad that this has happened. I had felt for too long – for the past fifty years? maybe a little less, but a long time – that we had lost our way in a thick fog no one could get out of. That we, the well-off in the West, had become a consumer society, able to have more or less everything we wanted – food, travel, entertainment – while somewhere far away (even if it was only a mile or two, but safely out of sight) people worked in conditions we didn't want to think about in order to enable us to go on as we were, and everywhere the environment was suffering irreparable damage and animals were being slaughtered in appalling conditions to provide us with our food and whole species were disappearing. People wrote anguished books and essays talking about these things and 'sensitive' novels were devoted to highlighting them, but nothing changed. Politicians occasionally mouthed sympathetic words but Capital and Progress won out every time, for obvious reasons: who would want to lose immediate gains either out of compassion or to save a planet that showed no obvious signs of needing to be saved.

In the past few years even the nations of the West, and outliers such as Australia, have begun to experience the direct effects of global warming – floods, droughts, forest fires. As a result the trickle of voices urging that something needed to change if we were to save the planet for our grandchildren has turned into a stream. But as the Australian example shows, it is very hard for politicians in a country a large part of whose economy is based on coal extraction to ban this even when everyone can see the destruction to life, property and nature that the terrible fires there caused. And totalitarian countries like China, Russia and Turkey can simply ignore public opinion if in the view of the leaders the political cost of change would be too great.

One can be pleased with Covid-19 for alerting us to the fact that something seemingly invisible and purely hypothetical, like a global pandemic, can in no time at all be on our doorsteps, claiming the lives not of Bangladeshi garment manufacturers or Chinese car-parts manufacturers, but of our fathers, brothers and friends. But I don't quite mean, I think, that what pleases me about the pandemic is that it alerts us to the far worse prospects of global warming unless we take active steps to reverse it. I think what I mean is that it reacquaints us with reality. And the reality is that we human beings, after a brief life, have to die, and that our modern worship of Capital and Progress has written death out of the script, made it more and more difficult to accept. And when it comes, therefore, to our loved ones and friends, we don't know how to deal with it.

This of course is what thinkers from Kierkegaard to Heidegger and writers from Melville and Dostoevsky to Rilke and Eliot have tried to articulate. My love for the Middle Ages rests partly on my sense that they reflect this more realistic perspective. The art of the time conveys the feeling that for all the horrors, it was a time that had hope built into it, hope inseparable from the acceptance of limits. Those limits were codified in Christian teaching and described in the Christian story. That indeed is why, I suspect, both Eliot and Muriel Spark converted to a more rigorous form of religion than what they were raised in and saw around them. I have just read this in Rowan Williams' book on Dostoevsky: 'Even the controversial bowing down to the earth, commended to converted sinners, practiced by Raskolnikov and Alyosha, which has raised some orthodox eyebrows, becomes more intelligible when seen in the context that sin is in itself a defacement of the same material environment: that is, that the earth is another defaced icon, whose inner and non-negotiable dignity is secured only when its relation to the creator is acknowledged.'

But I don't think grasping what it means to have limits, what it means to die, has to be a matter of embracing a religion, Christian, Jewish or Moslem. I find it in Homer and Sophocles, for example. Nor does it have to be a matter of a 'basically religious culture'. That may help, but it is not necessary, as Rilke, whose whole life and art consisted in trying to understand what this meant, demonstrates. Raskolnikov kissing the earth is a very Russian and very Russian Orthodox expression of what we should all be able to acknowledge: that the earth is other than us, that it was there before we came and will be there after we have gone, and that we are part of it whether we like it or not.

Covid-19 has wrought terrible destruction, but it has also done something to bring home to all of us that life can never be reduced to the calculus of profit and loss.

18.4.2020

What this lock-down has done to the world is what Kierkegaard hoped his own writings would do to the Danes and maybe to all cultured Europeans of his day: it has forced people to stop and ask: What for? Why was I rushing around like that? A lot of people of course have no option, without rushing they and their families would starve. But this does not apply to everyone and some of those who worked the longest hours certainly did not need all the money that brought in. This has been the beef of the Germans and other Northern European (Protestant) countries against the improvident South, as they see it: 'They do nothing all day and then expect us to bail them out.' And there is a sliver of truth in that. But only a sliver. And one suspects that the anger is mixed with a certain repressed jealousy: 'Why are they able to enjoy life, poor as they are, and we aren't?'

But we are all Bartlebys now.

Of course, faced with the question: 'Why have I been rushing about all my life?' most people try to push it away. As Kierkegaard sensed, it's too painful to contemplate.

Crème Caramel

'I can't stand gefillte fish,' I said.

'But you should have tasted my grandmother's,' T said.

'Even your grandmother's I wouldn't have liked.'

'You would,' T said. 'The way she made it everyone loved it.'

'Well I'm sorry then I never had the pleasure.'

'And her cakes,' T said. 'You think my mother's cooking is good, you should have tasted hers.'

Why is it that the food cooked by one's grandmother should go on being remembered as so much better than anything tasted since?

In my case, since all my grandparents had died by the time I was born, it was my mother's cooking. And I was not the only one. 'I remember Sacha's cakes,' so many people said or wrote to me after her death. 'I remember her delicious meals.'

I don't think she was a superlative cook, but I think the combination of good food and a warm and inviting ambiance which she generated made tea or dinner prepared by her memorable for so many people. She had not learned from her mother, since her mother died when she was ten, nor from her grandmother, with whom she and her sister subsequently lived. 'When I got married,' she told me, 'I had no idea how to cook. Ahmed the cook, who you remember used to visit us in Maadi in his old age, ruled over the kitchen and no one was allowed near. So when your father and I set up house as students in Aix I had to do everything by the book. I remember if I put a little more salt into a dish than the recipe said I threw the whole thing away and started again.' But from such beginnings she had developed, by the time I was old enough to appreciate it, into someone who could make a tasty meal out of very little and with the minimum of fuss. Later, in England, while lamenting the paucity of the fruit and vegetables on offer (this was in the days before big supermarkets supplied us with food from everywhere in the world all the year round), she would still make mouth-watering dishes of all kinds with simple ingredients. I remember, when we were in a furnished flat in Oxford prior to finding the Woodstock house, I had invited Rachel Trickett, my undergraduate tutor, to dinner. She lived in college and claimed she did not know how to make a cup of coffee. Spaghetti with plain tomato sauce was first up and Rachel tucked into it happily, talking all the while and not refusing a second large helping. When the meat course arrived she said: 'Heavens! I thought the spaghetti was the main course. I wouldn't have eaten so much if I'd known!' And ever after she would recall that day: 'What a meal that was that Sacha served up the first time I came to dinner with you! The first course was so good and so abundant I thought it was the main course and ate far too much of it!'

In Lewes I recall Sacha shooing everyone out of the kitchen while she cooked, even if we only had a solitary guest. Francis Landy she found particularly difficult. 'Go and sit in the garden, Francis' she would say to him. 'I'll call you when it's ready.' But soon he would creep back in, stand close to her and go on talking. 'Francis!' she would say, turning on him. 'I told you: get out!'

For many years after her death I strove to make the simple cake she used to make called in French Quatre Quart, and which she would rustle up in an hour or less if she knew someone was coming to tea. She would make it with banana, caraway seed or chocolate flavouring, but what I preferred was plain. I couldn't remember the portions, though, and whenever I tried to make it it emerged too stodgy or too flaky or just plain tasteless. Eventually I gave up. It was only many years later, when I had been using a computer for a while, that it suddenly struck me that one can look up anything these days. Gingerly I typed in Quatre Quart cake and lo and behold! a dozen recipes popped up. Since then I have happily entertained friends to tea and given them something which, if never quite as good as what Sacha used to make, bears a fairly close resemblance to it. For me, though, it never tastes quite the same.

But what I loved above all and what I have seen nowhere else was Sacha's *crème caramel*. 'It has to be on the point of being burned,' she told me once. 'Leave it a moment longer and it's no good, take it off the fire before that point and it remains white and anaemic.' And indeed in most restaurants, in Britain at any rate, it is precisely that, white and anaemic – and much too sweet. Sacha's was firm, the substance a deep yellow and the surface a dark brown. But what really set it apart was the fact that she did not make it in separate little dishes but in one large one, which would serve six people. I have never seen anyone else serve it that way. I can still recall its appearance, the way it wobbled gently as she brought it to the table, its texture and its taste. I would not dream of trying to make it.

19.4.2020

Brief storm the night before last. Thunder and lightning, torrential rain. We'd almost forgotten what that meant. Then it passed. Yesterday was iffy, though we had a good walk, and today woke up to bright sunshine and blue skies again.

More chaos in Government. Because of shortage of PPE they have had to change their official instructions to NHS staff, ordering them to re-use some and to use ordinary aprons. Many doctors and nurses and of course their unions, outraged. Unions urging all who feel they don't want to risk their lives to stay at home. But what would happen to the patients? Terrible dilemma for the doctors and nurses. Reminiscent of First World War soldiers having to fight without adequate ammunition and equipment. A disgrace. So many have obviously died needlessly and will continue to do so. Germany, with a bigger population, has had under 4,000 deaths and falling, we have around 16,000 already and only flattening – and that's not counting the thousands as yet uncounted who have died in care homes and the community. The opposition and the media do their best but no real accountability for this shambles.

Crime

Most crime is messy, the householder hit on the head by the frightened thief, the irate driver who has got out to remonstrate with another surprised by a knife in the gut, the baby shaken to death by a drugged stepfather. Of course there are the brilliantly executed robberies or gruesome murders which touch the public imagination to such an extent that books and films are made about them for years after, but they are rare.

These days the mafia have moved from making their money through protection rackets to making it through world-wide drug operations which remain largely unhindered, though occasionally one border force or another seizes a large haul and for a moment the spotlight falls on it. Yet even here there is a secret fascination among the public with a system that yields such rich rewards and with the ruthlessness and lack of regard for human life which enforcing it requires.

Already in the Renaissance people were avid to learn about the underworld and the men and women who inhabited it, but it was in the nineteenth century that the crime novel and the detective story came into their own. Many attempts have been made to understand why this should have happened just then and why the detective story in particular remains so popular with the reading and viewing public (to judge by the number of police procedurals and television detectives filling our screens week after week). Some have suggested writers were simply being realistic and reflecting in their books the establishment of a national police force and the rise in real life of the private detective; some have linked it to the transition from a criminal justice system dependent primarily on confession to one dependent on the presentation of evidence; and Auden, in one of his quirkiest essays, 'The Guilty Vicarage', has put forward the idea that the pure English detective story in effect deals with the theme found in Greek tragedy of the expelling of pollution leading to the restoration of the health of society.

It's interesting to ask why Poe, often credited as the founder of the pure or 'closed-room' detective story, should also have written stories like 'The Adventures of Arthur Gordon Pym', with its uncanny closeness to Mallarmé's *Un Coup de dés*; like 'The Tell-Tale Heart', so close to Dostoevsky; and like 'The Fall of the House of Usher', so close in spirit to the darker tales of incest, murder and seduction that we find in the work of the Decadents and then of the Surrealists and their circle; and why Eliot and Perec were such *aficionados* of the pure detective story. Is there a link between the detective story and modernism?

One way into that might be to ask what it is about Agatha Christie that so captivated Georges Perec? I think it's her fascination with pure problem solving at the expense of character and, quite often, realism, which she shares with Poe, who was of course idolised by Baudelaire and Mallarmé. This culminates in her solution of what one would have thought was an impossible wager with herself, that of making the narrator himself the murderer in *The Murder of Roger Ackroyd*.

But that still does not answer the question of why it should be so captivating to a modernist writer. The answer must run along these lines I think. From Poe and Melville through Eliot to Beckett and Perec the central issue is: Why write in a world without meaning? The detective story is the apotheosis of genre in a world where genre as it was once known has long disappeared. It is, like all writing, arbitrary, but it revels in its arbitrariness instead of hiding it, as the 'serious' novel does. Like chess and Sudoku it is a beautiful way to pass the time. It is a crossword puzzle for those who have no gifts in that direction. The murder is committed for reasons dreamed up by the writer to get his (or, more usually, her) book going, and at the end the questions whodunnit? and how? are answered to everyone's satisfaction, the criminal is apprehended and we can breathe a sigh of relief. This if very similar to the way that in the classic novel the plot is tied up, just what Kierkegaard railed against when he said that the sign of a true writer is that they cannot write 'the last part'. By contrast Christie says: I can write the last part because it is precisely the part that will solve the problem I have set at the start. In life we know it does not work like that, and the trouble with the traditional novel, in the eyes of a Beckett or a Perec, is that it pretends that it does. The detective story reveals the (highly questionable) assumptions of the traditional novel and gives pleasure in so doing, in that sense not so very different from *Tristram Shandy*.

But that only explains one aspect of the fascination of crime, and especially of murder for the modern writer. Dostoevsky reveals another. Murder is the one irrevocable act: a stolen jewel can be recovered but a life taken cannot be given back. Hence Raskolnikov's fascination with murder. If he can commit a murder, he feels, he will finally prove to himself that he can act, for in his mind only what is irrevocable is a real action. What he discovers, though, is that though he cannot bring the two women he has murdered back to life again what he has done does not seem to constitute the decisive action he longed for after all. For such an action we have to wait till the final scene of the novel.

Dostoevsky shows us that it is only in crime stories, not in life, that the revelation of the identity of the culprit leads to the expelling of the pollution and the end of the story. *Crime and Punishment* is at once the greatest crime novel ever and the profoundest critique of the genre.

Meanwhile, as television viewers continue to gorge themselves on long-running crime series, young, mainly black men continue to be stabbed to death in the streets London and drugs continue to find their way into the cities of the world.

---

20. 4.2020

Most governments have made mistakes in the course of this pandemic and it's very easy to carp with hindsight; but it becomes clearer by the day that the British Government was fixated with Brexit, still planning absurd celebrations for the 31 January and the final exit, and was woefully slow in acting as and when it should have. It is also obvious that this particular leader and his cabinet have grown used to this manner of doing things – warm words, sloppy thinking, bland assurances that all will be better some time soon– and that they cannot now change their ways. They came to power with a single mad purpose, to get us out of the EU, and are singularly ill-equipped to run the country in normal times, let alone deal with a crisis of these proportions. Ugh.

Critic

Everyone remembers the exchange:

> *Vladimir*: Moron!
> *Estragon*: Vermin!
> *Vladimir*: Abortion!
> *Estragon*: Morpion!
> *Vladimir*: Sewer-rat!
> *Estragon*: Curate!
> *Vladimir*: Cretin!
> *Estragon*: (*with finality*) Crritic!

Not the finest passage in *Waiting for Godot*, but Beckett has built puerility into the fabric of the play and he is never averse to a cheap laugh. And we know, too, that theatre critics can make or break a play in a way literary critics rarely can with a book, so that playwrights are particularly averse to them.

But the word *critic*, even *literary critic*, covers almost as wide a spectrum as does the word *novelist*. It includes the reviewer, the writer of essays on books, the writer of books on books and the writer of essays and books on every aspect of literature from prosody to cultural history. And while I can understand Beckett's intense feeling that criticism and scholarship were not for him, as witness the reluctance with which he wrote his early Proust book as a jobbing *littérateur* attempting to make a living and his palpable frustration at his inability to say what he means in the conversations on painters he conducted with Georges Duthuit in mid-career, he was no mean critic himself, as these works and his sometimes hilarious comments on books and writers in his letters testify. I have never felt the same tension between criticism and so-called 'creative writing', have felt much more as I think Coleridge, Proust, Eliot and Auden have felt, that criticism is a form of conversation with oneself and the reader about the works and authors one likes or (though that is rarer) dislikes, and a chance to work out one's own aesthetics, or, if that is too grand, too philosophical a word, the nature of one's desires and ambitions.

There is nothing shameful about criticism, *pace* Beckett. It is more natural, actually, than 'creative writing', for every time one recommends a book or film to a friend with a little more than: 'You must read this, see that', one is doing criticism. Keats's letters and Kafka's journals and letters show them to be acute critics even though they never wrote a critical essay in their brief lives, and that is hardly surprising, for writers spend their lives thinking about writing, their own and that of others, and they know that there is no singing school but studying monuments of past magnificence.

Proust's essays in particular, those on cathedrals and painters as well as those on books and authors, I have found endlessly rewarding, but read the essays of any practitioner, Auden, Jarrell, Berryman, Snodgrass, Hill, and you come away enriched. But I have also found in the course of my life that even critics who are not practitioners have written works that have had as profound an impact upon me as have novels and poems. In my gap year between school and university, when I was devouring Dostoevsky and Mann and Proust, I also discovered Erich Heller's *The Ironic German*, which had recently been published. Though, as its title suggests, it is the study of one writer (Thomas Mann), it is much more. It brought out for me the profound interconnection between Romanticism and the great innovative writers of the early twentieth century and, in its scintillating prose, raised and examined the central issues with which modern artists have been concerned since 1800. But of course why the book was so important to me was that it spoke to my condition as well and, along with Mann himself and Proust and Kafka, gave me the courage to find my own way through the multiple impasses in my own writing.

Then as an undergraduate at Oxford I came across the essays of Maurice Blanchot in two books, *L'Éspace Littéraire* and *Le Livre à venir*. They bowled me over. Everything I had been struggling to articulate about Kafka, about Proust, about Rilke and Musil, Blanchot expressed in lucid, often beautiful prose, and in the extraordinary essays on Henry James's *The Turn of the Screw*, on Beckett, on Robbe-Grillet and on diaries, I found the answer to many of the questions I had been grappling with on those writers and on more general aspects of literature and of what it entails to be a writer today.

And it is not just the great explorers of modernism who have meant much to me. Other books on single authors or works have given me, over the years, almost as much pleasure as the essays of Heller and Blanchot: John Jones on Greek tragedy, on Wordsworth and on Dostoevsky; Del Kolve on the medieval Miracle Plays; Charles Singleton on Dante; C.L. Barber on Shakespearean comedy. They all do what Virginia Woolf said Proust did for her: make me feel more alive, more aware of the possibilities of the human spirit. I will never subscribe to Estragon's insulting 'Crritic!'

21.4.2020

Government incompetence more and more evident. The actions and inactions of those supposedly in charge are leading to the unnecessary loss of many lives, including those of doctors and nurses who should never have been put in the position of having to choose between their personal safety and their patients.

The glorious, unreal weather continues. I'm in danger of annotating this diary like Bonnard on the Cote d'Azur, filling in his daily diary throughout the turbulent thirties with a single word accompanying a sketch: 'soleil', 'ciel bleu', 'pluvieux', etc.

Death

I came face to face with death the day my mother knelt by my bed in the Road 9 flat and said: '*Lala est mort. Une voiture l'a écrasé.*' I knew then that I would never see him again, never take him for a walk, never watch him run by the canal or lie at my feet indoors. It was final. That was what death was.

Since then I have had to bear the death of many beloved animals. With Pilic, our wonderful epileptic giant collie in Lewes, I had to take him myself, alone (for once Sacha couldn't face it), to the vet, help him on to her operating table, and watch as she injected him and he slowly grew still. But even here, when I got back, there was the comfort of Sacha's company and we could mourn him as we had mourned all our other animals, together. Sacha's death left me alone, with no one to mourn with, although it was of course by far the worst death I had experienced.

To return alone to the house one has shared with a beloved person for many years, a person who had shared one's life for nearly all of its fifty-five years – that is not something I would wish on anybody. If I had not had my writing to fall back on I don't think I could have come through it as I did.

The received wisdom is that when your parents die you suddenly grasp the fact that you are next in line. That your parents in some way shielded you from death and now they are gone your shield is gone and you are face to face with it. I didn't feel this at first, though I did begin quite soon to feel the force of Proust's remark that when your parents die you become them. I looked at myself from the outside sometimes and was amazed to find myself doing and saying things my mother had said and done and of which, in her lifetime, I had disapproved of or found strange. And that feeling has only grown.

As has the thought of death, naturally enough as I have reached my seventieth year and now approach my eightieth.

I'm not sure 'thought' is the right word. The feel of it more, the growing acceptance that it is coming – though part of me, as I suspect is true of all human beings (except for Rilke?) imagines at the deepest level that they are immortal, that death, which comes to all living creatures, will not come to them.

I try to fight this. And at moments think I have succeeded. Who was it who said that we should not be frightened of death, that we should see it as a friend? Was it someone in Tolstoy? The trouble with wise words of this kind is that, written down, perhaps even spoken, they sound pious and, somehow, easy. They needn't be, but that is how they sound.

There is also the remark I heard from someone in the wake of Sacha's death: 'All deaths are messy.' And I still feel pain at the thought of her alone in hospital the last three weeks of her life. True, I came to see her every day. True, towards the end she was hardly 'there'; but if I could have one wish it is that those last days could be given back to us and I could have taken her home to die there, with me. Because it is obviously much easier to greet death as a friend, not to look at it with fear, if you are with your loved ones, if you know they are there and will be with you to the end. That Sacha, who watched over me from my birth, who saved me from death at the hands of the Germans, nurtured me, was always there for me, should be abandoned by me at the end is very hard to bear. I know that makes it sound worse than it is, that the doctors assured me she was getting better, and even at the end, when she and I realised it was all up, kept saying that perhaps she would pull through – and I had to believe them. Besides, I had no one to advise me and simply went along with it with a heavy heart. But nothing can gainsay the fact that she was alone those last days and nights, alone with her thoughts and nothing to support her. I can't bear even to write about it.

For the majority of the world's population death will always be messy – for those swept up in war, in epidemics, in the mindless brutality of city streets whether in London or Los Angeles or Bangkok, dying of hunger in Africa or overwhelmed by some natural disaster like an earthquake or a tsunami. But I hope that for myself it will not be. I think – I think – that I could face it with equanimity. I think of John Cruikshank, of Marianne, of Giglia, all diagnosed with cancer at a ripe old age (though John was much younger, but as a very religious man he felt that three score and ten was our allotted span and that should be respected), the two women having lost beloved husbands, who elected not to go into therapy, with all the suffering and degradation that entails. And of Giglia in particular, who really did slowly succumb surrounded by her children, grandchildren, and often by good friends. Hers was somehow, as she would have wanted it, a pre-modern death, and all the better for it.

The terror of death is bound up with the fact that we are leaving a life that was so precious to us, but also that as we die we are for the first time in our lives perhaps truly alone. Earlier cultures mitigated that by the belief in a deity and by rituals such as the administering of extreme unction, which made the dying feel they still, even as they died, belonged to a community. Most of us no longer have such comforting rituals. We must make do as best we can, the most fortunate among us waiting to see what their unique death is with fear and I suppose a certain curiosity.

22.4.2020
(A month since T arrived.)

Figures for non-hospital deaths from C-19 up from 200 plus a week ago to 1,000 plus yesterday. It's clear that care homes and the old and sick living there (and their carers) were ignored by the Government.

Deborah Levy on the one-o'clock news yesterday: 'My writer friends say they self-isolate anyway so life for them will go on as before. But there is a difference between solitude and isolation. I find that I need, when I go out, to make eye-contact with people, to stop for a coffee or a chat, even in the most intense moments of writing, so that I find our present mode of life stifling. I spend too much time on the news and then it's very hard to get back into the world of my fiction.' As always a lot of common sense. She's right of course, but I find I've always made do with what I have and not worried too much about ideal conditions – though it's true noisy intrusive neighbours such as I had a few years ago at number 62 made writing very difficult.

When she came to read an extract from *The Man Who Knew Too Much*, however, she lost me. She read well, and it's a novel much of which I admire, but the way she purrs over beautiful men and women (as she describes them) is almost pornographic – the woman combing 'her long silver hair' in the hospital was meant to convey a moment of warmth between her and the dying man in the bed – I only felt: why 'long silver'? I don't want this kind of thing intruding between me and the hospital scene.

Dialogue

'It feels more like a play than a novel.' How many times have I heard that from readers of my novels. I try to explain that the fact of dialogue is neither here nor there. A play has to be firmly grounded but a work of fiction floats into the reader's mind and body to do its work there. That is a massive difference. I love the freedom of fiction and though I have always enjoyed the challenge of play-writing it has never come as naturally as has fiction.

So why am I drawn to letting dialogue do the work of storytelling in my fiction? I have written about the enormous breakthrough that was, for me, the discovery, when writing my first novel, *The Inventory*, that I didn't want to describe either places or people, that as soon as I set about doing so I felt I was doing what I thought had to be done rather than what I wanted to do, felt drawn to doing. In the long interview with Victoria Best I elaborated on that and tried to tease out why this was what I wanted (and didn't want) to do. Why I felt I was taking part in a lie if I wrote down a description of the house to which the solicitor goes to take down the inventory of the dead man's possessions – a double lie in fact. First of all the lie that consists in spelling out in time (the time for me to write, the time for the reader to read) what, in life, it takes only a second to take in. If you are telling a story, as Dickens or Balzac felt they were telling stories, then you can do that and enjoy, as it were, the sound of your own voice describing; but if, like most modern novelists, and like me, you want to give the reader the sense that he or she 'is there', then that's a problem. I find I always tend to skip descriptions in novels, they never clarify anything and only hinder the forward momentum of the action. This I now discover may in part be due to my lack of a visual imagination, but I have always felt and still feel it is more probably due to my sense that I don't want to be part of the lie being perpetrated by the novelist. Certainly as a writer I feel strongly that I did not give my life to writing for this.

I am interested too in the way character emerges out of dialogue and event, not limited by a novelist's further exploration of motivation etc. – because I feel that motivation is usually so complex and in the end so unfathomable that it is better to allow the reader to respond as he or she wishes rather than directing them along one route or another. That is why I am drawn to the biblical narratives and to modern writers like Compton-Burnett, Duras and Spark. As well as to writers like

Faulkner, Claude Simon, and Thomas Bernhard, whose works consists in effect of monologues – quite different from first or third person narratives in traditional novels.

The latter is a form I employed, with my own variations, in *Moo Pak* and *Infinity*. And even with the dialogue novels, I have, I find, always been uneasy with absolute purity. And I like the staccato rhythm of 'He said/She said', as well as the message it sends that this is said by *a* person at *a* moment in time.

'Dialogue', has of course become a hugely popular literary and philosophical concept. Buber, Merleau-Ponty and Levinas have built their philosophies on the belief that our relation to the world is that of an 'I' *addressing* a 'Thou', not a passive viewer *looking* at the world; and Bakhtin has built a whole literary-theological edifice on the term and facilitated its dissemination throughout academia. I have problems with Bakhtin though. Dostoevsky, it is true, his prime example, builds his novels out of the laying side by side of different 'voices' and world views and letting the reader determine, to some extent, which is 'right'. That is why the novels are so great and his personal views as expressed in his essays, letters and speeches so often an embarrassment. But what neither Bakhtin nor his followers is prepared to acknowledge is how difficult real dialogue is for a writer to achieve, and how long and hard writers as different as Proust and Kafka had to struggle to achieve it.

Most of my critical work, I now see, has consisted in trying to bring out that difficulty and the nature of the subsequent achievement in a few exceptional cases. And it is a difficulty I have gone on encountering and gone on trying to overcome in my own fiction, novels and short stories. Indeed, I can say that unless I overcome it in the preliminary groping work on the way the novel or story will be written the subsequent work will be dead in the water.

23.4.2020

St George's Day, Shakespeare's birthday, etc. Not much celebration about though. Starmer in his first PMQs yesterday, almost empty chamber, online for many, no Boris Johnson, took Raab apart as he trotted out all the old excuses.

Weather supposed to reach 24 degrees.

Diary/Journal/Notebook

There are two sorts of diaries. Those, like Pepys's, which simply recount what he did during the day and which are of great interest to future historians, and those like Kafka's which, as well as sometimes recounting what happened on a specific day, are also the repositories for thoughts, self-questionings and the first gropings towards stories and novels. Of course Pepys has always been more than simply a source for historians because every sentence he writes seems to be imbued with his personality. Nevertheless, the contrast seems to hold between diaries that record events and those that give us a glimpse into an extraordinary creative struggle. Perhaps the second should be called Journals and only the former Diaries – yet though we have the Journals of Henry James, we have the Diaries of Kafka. But that may just be a question of nomenclature. After all, the French only have one word for it, which is also the word for a (daily) newspaper, *journal*, while the Germans use *Tagebuch*, day-book, for both as well.

Nevertheless, the diaries of Virginia Woolf are an instructive example. In 1953 Leonard Woolf published a single volume of extracts from the diaries his wife had kept from 1918 till her death in 1941 under the title *A Writer's Diary*. In other words he extracted from a large mass of writing those passages which showed Virginia Woolf groping towards her novels, in search of a new form for each new work, frequently depressed by her inability to find it and thus to get going, occasionally elated as she gets to the end of one of them and knows it is good and, more important, that she has nailed it. In the 1970s, as Woolf's stature changed from that of an interesting and difficult writer to almost a cult figure, her nephew Quentin Bell's wife, Anne Olivier Bell, began to edit the complete Diaries, eventually published in five volumes, to go with the six volumes of the Letters. Thrilling as I had found Leonard's single volume I found these boring and dispiriting; the riches of *A Writer's Diary* were submerged in a welter of trivia and I found myself in the presence of a person I had little desire to get to know.

Even if they did keep a diary or journal we have nothing in the public domain from Proust or Eliot. And their letters are most often stilted and 'public', a world away from those of Keats and van Gogh. The diaries or journals of James, Woolf (Leonard's version) and Kafka, on the other hand, belong with the letters of Keats and van Gogh . In them we can see, in the anguished present of the writing, the lineaments of modernism emerging. There is nothing more inspiring for the young writer, and, indeed, more reassuring. You read them and you know you are not alone.

I have never wanted to keep a diary and, reading Blanchot's essay on diaries I understood why. He distinguishes between diaries that are essentially an account of something done and those that are essentially an account of a doing. But that, to my mind, is exactly the difference between the kind of novels I am not interested in – the telling of a story 'about' this or that, x or y – and those I am – the making of something or at least the struggle to make something – for we are not talking here about an object or a machine.

I have kept a notebook ever since I came to England in 1956, at fifteen, the moment, I think, when I suddenly grew up. Or rather, since 1957 when, having secured a place at an

Oxford college and a State Scholarship to pay my way through my three years there, we moved to London and I had a year between school and university with nothing to do but read and think and try to write. I tend to date entries and to put on the cover of each notebook – there are more than a hundred by now – the date I started using it and the date I ran out of pages, so I know that for the years I was at Oxford, both as an undergraduate and as a postgraduate, I seem to have made no notes, though it's possible the notebooks just got lost. But for most other years there is something, sometimes much more than one notebook. I have also, at some times more than others, jotted down what happened during the day, what someone said, a dream I had, and so on. By and large, though, I have used these notebooks to feel my way towards a story or novel or to note something that might lead to a later story or novel. I'm not sure how useful all this is as I rarely re-read the notebooks, but I have the feeling that writing it down stores it away in my mind. And if in the course of scribbling I find what I am looking for I hold that page dear and frequently return to it in the course of writing the book.

Usually, though, these are preliminaries, what allows the book to get going. Once it is going it takes on a momentum of its own and I rarely have recourse to a notebook.

And there are times of emotional turmoil when much more personal struggles and anxieties are recorded, day after day.

Much as I love to read the diaries and notebooks of the writers I admire, and am fascinated to see works I know and love growing before my eyes as their authors feel their way forward, I have no desire for anyone to do the same for me. I want the books to speak for themselves and to make the scaffolding disappear. I want to move on to the next book, not think back to earlier ones. So when I said to Tim, some years ago, that I had left instructions for the notebooks to be burned after my death I was taken aback when he expostulated: But you can't do that, Gabriel. What does it matter to you when you're dead? You owe it to posterity to leave them behind.

I thought about that, but I was unpersuaded. Recently, though, I have had a change of heart. Is it that after Sacha's death and the writing of my book on her life, and later doing that long interview with Victoria Best, I have grown less attached to the idea of invisibility? And is that a failure on my part, a weakness? I don't know. But I suspect it has to do with the fact that while Sacha was alive I sort of knew I had a life, she had been the witness to it, as it were. But when she was no longer there I felt nebulous, unreal. And the writing of the book about her was a way of bringing not just her but me back to life. And perhaps that has been the deep impulse behind my new willingness to lay out my life, in all its strangeness, before others.

And Tim will be glad to hear that I have made provision for the notebooks and other bits and pieces to go the University of Sussex (and there join the papers of, among others, Virginia Woolf).

24.4.2020

Starmer two days ago in PMQs: 'There's a disconnect between what the government says it is doing and what we hear on the front line.' An example of that yesterday: A care home in Hove with sick inmates urgently requests the government for tests – which Hancock said would be available in every care home in the country. Gets a reply from some official saying: 'We have no plans to provide tests.' The Hove Labour MP Peter Kyle holds the letter up to the camera, then the BBC reporter talks to the manager of the care home: 'I'm distraught and angry,' she says. 'To get a letter like that! And my inmates are sick and dying. It's a scandal.'

Dreams

For many years I slept like a log and as far as I was aware never dreamed. Even when, as a child, I would stay awake out of anxiety at not getting enough sleep if I was taking part in a big sporting event the following day and Sacha had to take her mattress and put it down on the floor by my bed so that we could talk – even then I don't think I dreamed. Of course the experts tell us we only dream as we are waking up, so that the more often we wake up the more likely we are to remember our dreams. But even now, when I sleep badly and wake up at least twice in the night, often more, and have long confused often clearly anxiety-induced dreams, I rarely remember them in the kind of detail some people seem able to muster. I often wake up to the strong feeling that I have been talking in French in my dreams, and sometimes I can even remember snatches of the conversation, but usually it all fades before I can tell T or jot it down; and even when I manage to recall it quite vividly, as I 'tell' it I realise how boring and dull my account of it is. As boring and dull as other people's dreams usually are when they tell you them.

Clearly there is a disconnect between the feelings the dream has evoked – or has perhaps been constructed to account for – and how one seems to have to tell it. Dreams that are interesting when recounted also usually feel undreamlike and concocted. But it may be that I'm worse than other people at that and it is related to my inability to 'see' with an 'inner eye' – though I'm still sceptical about this new theory of aphantasia.

Butor wrote a whole book about one dream of Baudelaire's, and fascinating I found it when I first read it, though I've now forgotten both the dream and what Butor made of it. Certainly it was much more interesting than the dreams Freud recounts or the explanations of them he gives. But can Baudelaire really have dreamed so long and complicated a dream? Or rather, recalled it?

Perec kept a book of the dreams he dreamed when he was undergoing analysis. I tried to do the same at one point, when I was particularly anxious and woke up frequently, putting the dream, or what I could remember of it down as soon as I woke up. But I gave up after a while as I was sure what I was jotting down was of no interest whatever and that anyway I would never want to re-read the notebook in which I had jotted them. I feel with dreams a bit like Stravinsky with music 'given' to him. If I found one day as I sat down at my desk, he says somewhere, probably in the conversations with Robert Craft, that a new piece of music had somehow been given to me by the gods without my having to do anything, I would reject it. Working on a piece of music is what gives meaning and pleasure to my life, so what would be the point of finding it there ready-made? The same with me. Dreams are there, ready-made, as it were, and since I am only interested in the making of narratives and in the sense of satisfaction good making provides I find dreams of little interest – funny, sometimes, or terrifying or troubling when I can remember them – but no more. There's plenty of dreamwork, I have no doubt, Freud was right there, but it is, as it were, the work of someone else.

On the other hand Stockhausen seems to have dreamed many of his compositions. What he dreamed, it seems, was something visual and dramatic, but it was what would then drive the music he subsequently wrote. Thus for one of his finest compositions, *Trans* (1971), for orchestra and tape, he tells us that he had a dream in which he saw (ah!) a large number of violinists seated in a line on a stage, moving their arms like automata, producing a fascinating sound. And for a later composition, having been commissioned to write a quartet, not something he was in the habit of doing, he explained, he had a dream of a helicopter and heard its rotary blades very loud and clear, waking up with the sound in his head – and this became the notorious helicopter quartet, in which each member of the quartet plays from a separate helicopter and the sounds are somehow relayed back to the concert hall and blended. Not one of his most successful pieces, but once embedded in *Mittwoch*, the seventh of his operas based on the days of the week, and, performed (we saw the four helicopters by video-link) one afternoon and evening in a giant disused factory in Birmingham in 2012, it produced a memorable effect.

The shutdown, which, ever since it started on 23 March, has been carried out in the most extraordinary weather, blue skies and sunshine every day, which has meant a good walk, one and a half to two and a half hours every day, and a very regular life of sleeping, working at this, eating, walking, watching the news, reading, listening to music, and then sleeping again, seems to have been conducive to dreaming.

I've already mentioned the Farage dream, which rather pleased me with its wit. Today a rather more clearly wish-fulfilment dream. I had been called onto the pitch as a substitute in an important football match, it might even have been a World or European Cup final, and, playing really well, scored the final goal (it's true we were three-nil up at the time, partly owing to some earlier brilliant passing of mine), a long screaming shot à *la* Bobby Charlton, which squirmed past the goalkeeper, who half parried it, but it trickled into the net. The whole was being played in the rain yet indoors, though I could hear the crowds – but could not see them. I was saddened by the fact that this splendid performance of mine should have been played behind closed doors (literally, for we seemed to be playing in what was both a normal pitch and a very large room), but proud of my achievement. To be able to play like that at seventy-nine, I thought, wasn't bad. Afterwards there was some kind of drinks party, more literary event than post-match booze-up, and the coach grabbed me and drew me to a group that included a lady. 'She's your biggest fan,' he said to me. 'The best scout we have. It was at her insistence that I brought you on.'

T, who neither understands nor is the least interested in football, was not impressed when I recounted the dream to her.

'Another glorious day!' as Winnie says in *Happy Days*. And another day of Government bungling and inefficiency revealed last night. It's sad to belong to a country such as this has now become, run by a bunch of incompetent ideologues. Oh for some grown-ups.

Drink and Drugs

I have always been terrified of not being in control of myself – at least I have since we left Egypt when I was fifteen and I knew that I was on my own with Sacha and how my life turned out was very much up to me. But it may have been there even earlier. France? Leaving France? And how much is due to these circumstances and how much to natural pusillanimity? The fact is that both drink and drugs seemed to me to be things that had the potential to derail me, both momentarily, after ingestion, and permanently if I became addicted. And even if it they didn't, even if they produced in me states of euphoria such as other people seemed to experience when drinking or taking drugs, and had no after-effects, I was not interested in such states for their own sakes. I have always wanted my euphoric states to be produced by some kind of effort, some kind of sacrifice on my part, such as training for a big swimming championship day in day out, often hating it, but with the hope of being rewarded by triumph on the day of destiny; or getting to a particular spot in the mountains by a hard morning's climb and walk; or writing a book that was the best I felt I could have done after long months of struggle and hard work. Is that all too puritanical? Maybe. I've no idea, only that this is the way I've always felt – though often, when walking in the mountains, I wish it wasn't quite so tough, and, when writing a book, that it would suddenly come clear and I could reach the end without the pain and despair on the way. And I'm particularly happy with the rare books and stories I've written where it seemed as if I was merely copying what was already there as fast as I could and no difficulties seemed to stand in the way. That is what I felt when I was writing *Contre-Jour* and the later parts of *Infinity*. But of course if it had actually been there for me to copy I would have dismissed it as of no interest. What writing these gave me was the feeling of going very deep with surprising ease. Sportsmen describe the feeling as that of being 'in the groove', when all ones senses are that much sharper and for the duration of the match, the race, everything one tries comes off and everything seems effortless.

I did once get drunk, as a first-year undergraduate at Oxford, wanting to see what it was like. But, perhaps because my heart was not in it, all I felt was misery. Not afterwards but as it happened, when one is supposed to be so happy, to have the cares of the world lifted from one's shoulders if accounts of drinking are to be believed – though of course addiction to drink as to drugs seems to be anything but joyful. Whatever the reason, I remember cycling back to my digs on Hinksey Hill, south of Oxford, in the snow. I kept on falling, getting up, getting back on my bike, falling again a few yards further on, always with a headache and a bad taste in my mouth. After what seemed – and perhaps was – hours, I got to the house, only to find I had lost my keys. The house was dark and silent but there was nothing for it, I had to wake my landlady if I was to get out of the cold. I pressed the bell and stood there shivering. Eventually she opened the door. 'I'm sorry,' I said. 'I've lost my keys.' She looked at me stonily. 'Do you know what time it is?' 'No,' I said. 'I'm sorry.' 'Three a.m.,' she said, standing back to let me pass.

I did not repeat the experiment, and I have always been glad that I neither craved a drink nor needed to spend what little of my grant was left over for personal pleasure on drink. On the other hand I have of course, as with my seemingly visceral aversion to any form of pop music, felt that such an attitude cut me off from many if not most of my contemporaries. Even as an adult and with a little more money to spend I have not really ever enjoyed having wine with a meal as almost everyone else I know seems to, certainly not enjoyed it enough to counterbalance its inevitable ill-effects – headaches, the inability to get to sleep and all the rest of it.

I have been even more afraid of what drugs might do to me. None of my friends at university, so far as I know, took drugs of any kind, but that was probably more a question of the time when I was there. Later, at Sussex, it seemed that everyone smoked something or other, but I was not interested. Does that make me a dour puritan? I don't think so, because I have never minded what other people get up to, simply known, or thought I knew, what it was I needed.

And that, for a long time, included cigarettes. Trying to give up taught me the power of even a mild addiction, for though I smoked only five a day for many years moving from that to not smoking at all was very difficult. I tried to explain to my students that they had to think of the denizens of Dante's Hell as addicted: wanting to give up but not wanting at the same time. 'You all know about addiction, don't you?' I would ask, and they would look down at their books. I was never sure if my analogy worked for them though it certainly had for me.

I made many attempts to give up and finally succeeded in my early sixties, with the help of Nicorettes after I had been forced to stop for a fortnight by a bad bout of bronchitis. Apart from the chewing-gum what helped me was hating the idea of being addicted to anything and the strong sense that I did not want to spend the rest of my life keeping count of the number of cigarettes I had smoked so far during any one day and how many I still had left to get to my allotted five. There were better things to think about, I felt.

In the previous year or two the woman with whom I had been living, Burmese but raised in the States, could not bear smoke in the house and kept badgering me to give up. If we went to stay with friends of hers and I tried to steal a smoke in the bathroom before dousing the stub and flushing it down the loo she would immediately smell the smoke on my clothes and kick up a fuss. Though I knew she was right I felt I was damned if I would give up just because someone else wanted me to. I caught my bronchitis shortly after we had split up and I think her constant hammering on the closed door of my consciousness had really driven the need to give up deep into my being, so that now, without feeling that I was doing it under pressure from someone else, and of course with the help of those Nicorettes, I finally managed to stop. Such is the perversity of human beings.

26.4.2020

People talk of how things will be 'after the crisis', but more and more pundits are warning that that may be a long way away, many more months of lockdown and many more waves of it in the coming years, even if a vaccine is developed. A nightmare for those with businesses, very hard for most of the population, less so for me and my friends, most of whom are retired and/or have lived fairly solitary and isolated lives by choice and for a very long time. But we of course are the ones most likely to die of the virus – though it seems to spare no one except – thank God – for the very young.

Marguerite Duras

Well, *she* certainly drank. The depressing book written by her much younger lover, Yann Andréa about life with her in her declining years shows someone totally in thrall to drink and all the worse for it. Yet that wasn't surprising; rather like Berryman, she always lived – and wrote – on the edge. You felt there was no safety-net with her, either in her life or in her work. That was its strength and its weakness. She followed her instincts, more like a modern painter than a writer, feeling her way from a relatively conventional beginning, with books like *Un Barrage contre le Pacificque*, towards a totally new kind of writing, spare, driven by dialogue, each sentence heavy with unspoken resonances, and towards films which, from *Hiroshima mon amour*, with Alain Resnais to *Le Camion*, which she directed herself, also broke new ground. Yet amongst the mature novels and the films, along with the masterpieces, are works of excruciating dullness and/ or pretentiousness, as if she had gone so far out it had become impossible for her to distinguish the wonderful from the awful – in that too more like a modern painter than a writer.

It was in the sixties, in the early part of her mature period that I became aware of her. *Moderato Cantabile* was the book that did it for me. In barely a hundred pages it seemed that everything was said – and nothing. I loved the title. I loved the way an initial event leads inexorably forward to its reduplication – except that the novel stops short before anything that can be called an event happens. Alain Robbe-Grillet was exploring the same sort of territory at the same time but in a totally different way, through the slow accumulation of precise description which makes the reader feel more and more uneasy and grow more and more aware of that which is not said. Duras remains much closer to a traditional realist novelist, but works to bring out all that traditional novels don't and can't say. Take the opening scene of *Moderato Cantabile*, as Anne Desbaresdes sits suffering in silence as her son's piano lesson takes its course in the piano teacher's stuffy room in a more popular part of the seaside town than that in which she lives with her rich husband and child in a lovely villa surrounded by a large garden. In a few sparse words the drama taking place between teacher, child and mother unfolds.

> -Veux-tu lire ce qu'il y a d'écrit au-dessus de la partition? demanda
> la dame.
> -Moderato cantabile, dit l'enfant.
> La dame ponctua cette réponse d'un coup de crayon sur le clavier.
> L'enfant resta immobile, la tête tournée vers sa partition.
> -Et qu'est que ça veut dire, moderato cantabile?
> -Je ne sais pas.
> Une femme, assise à trois mètres de là, soupira.
> -Tu es sûr de ne pas savoir ce que ça veut dire, moderato cantabile?
> reprit la dame.
> L'enfant ne répondit pas. La dame poussa un cri d'impuissance
> étouffé, tout en frappant de nouveau le clavier de son crayon.
> Pas un cil de l'enfant bougea. La dame se retourna.
> -Madame Desbaresdes, quelle tête vous avez là, dit-elle.
> Anne Desbaresdes soupira une nouvelle fois.
> -A qui le dites-vous, dit-elle.
> L'enfant immobile, les yeux baissés, fut seul à se souvenir que le
> soir venait d'éclater. Il en frémit.

And so the piano lesson, or the hour of torture, if one prefers to put it that way, unfolds for all three, with the teacher eventually giving way before the child's stubborn silence: '*Ça veut dire, dit-elle à l'enfant – écrasée – pour la centieme fois, ça veut dire modéré et chantant.*'

Duras has hit on a fundamental truth, which made her the darling of the psychoanalysts but which had long been intuited by certain writers: What we say often does not bear any direct resemblance to what we want to say, but if presented with sufficient skill and a good enough ear it can lead us straight to what the character or the book wants to say. And for the writer who understands this it is a godsend, since words are the material of the writer. I will get people talking, such a writer thinks, and then I will get the reader to listen. Not to see, for appearances and settings are secondary, though the traditional novel has always relied heavily on them, but to listen.

As the unbearably painful piano lesson unfolds a cry is heard outside. All stop to listen, then the lesson proceeds, while down below there is the sound of a crowd gathering. Anne, always with the child, makes her way home, but not before discovering that a woman seems to have been killed by a man who is being ushered into a police van. 'Why?' she asks a bystander. '*On ne sait pas,*' is the answer. But as she becomes fascinated by what might have taken place and finds herself sucked deeper and deeper into this *crime passionel*, the novel takes its course, itself *modéré et chantant*, till its inevitable conclusion in which everything is understood and resolved and nothing is understood and resolved.

The characters and the setting are so clearly evoked one would have thought it was made to be filmed, and in fact no less a director than Peter Brooks had a go. But, interestingly, it was a failure. The reason I think is that the novel has perfectly judged what can be said and what can be seen for maximum effect, and the intrusion of a camera makes the visual primary and destroys the delicate balance. Only words, only Duras' words, can keep it in place.

Three years before she wrote *Moderato Cantabile*, in 1955, Duras had written an even sparser book that I now prefer to *Moderato*, *Le Square*. Two people meet on a bench in a square and talk. He is a commercial traveller and she a housemaid. They talk out their sad lives and their powerful desires and then they part. It's a beautiful book, bathed in melancholy, utterly true. The sort of book I wish I'd written. In the sixties she produced *l'Après-midi de Monseiur Andesmas*, *Le Ravissement de Lol V.Stein*, *Le Vice-Consul*, and perhaps my favourite, *L'Amante Anglaise*, as well as plays and films. What drives these novels is the powerful feeling of an overwhelming need for plenitude along with a sober awareness that to achieve that is to destroy yourself, and – this is what distinguishes her work from that of the Romantic artists to whom she is so close – a realistic awareness of the limits of the medium. She instinctively understands how much can be said through a combination of dialogue and event – an understanding that brings her best work close to the sparse and resonant narratives of the Hebrew Bible.

The danger is that the gesturing towards romantic fulfilment can itself start to become nothing but that – a gesture. And this leaves us with a kind of baroque dance of death in thrall to its own power. We see hints of this in two works that are central to her whole oeuvre, *Le Ravissement de Lol V. Stein*, and in *Le Vice-Consul*, both works that, to my mind, succeed, but come dangerously close to total failure. That happens with much of the later work, *Détruire, dit-elle, Abahn, Sabana, David*, and then lapses into the frankly and boringly pornographic with *L'Homme dans le couloir* and *Les Yeux verts* (both 1980). Here fantasy and the sense of her own total authority abruptly destroy the balance of realism and desire which was the glory of the earlier novels, and which goes all the way back to even a more conventional novel like *Les Petis chevaux de Tarquinia*.

Was it drink that did it? The surprising success of her version of her early life in *L'Amant*, which won her the Goncourt and propelled her to international stardom? Or a combination of the two? She still produced remarkable accounts of her tormented life: her childhood in French colonial Vietnam with a mother who played the cinema piano to keep them both alive; her being 'sold' in her teens to a rich Chinese suitor; her early struggles in France in the '30s as a communist intellectual; her marriage to Robert Anselme, later imprisoned in Mauthausen and who is no more than a living corpse when she and the man she has since fallen in love with, Dionys Mascolo (with the help of François Mitterand), bring him back to France after the war. And she still produced novels and films which had the power of her earlier work, such as *L'Amour* (not to be confused with the pot-boiler that won the Goncourt, *L'Amant*), and films like *Le Camion* (with Gérard Depardieu), but too often – to my mind at any rate – they are as boring as the dreams people insist on describing to you in great detail.

But those novels from 1952 to 1970 are among the greatest of the twentieth century. Though I sometimes despaired at her lack of humour I learned more from her perhaps about the power of sparseness and where I myself wanted to go than from any other writer.

27.4.2020

Finally, the extraordinary weather seems to be changing. Grey skies today and no sign of the sun breaking through later, as has occasionally happened in the past month.

A group of leading ecologists warn that the pandemic was made by no one other than man and more will occur unless we change our ways and abandon the self-destructive rampant capitalism that is the way most if not all nations function now. Fat chance.

The Echo-Chamber

It was so hard to write: a novel that moved forward into itself. Sounds simple but for months, if not years, I tried everything but just couldn't see how to do it. Every time I thought I'd got it, it turned out to be a false trail. In such cases I usually give up, turn to something else and hope that a few years down the road I will see the solution. But I couldn't shake it off. I felt I had to do it or I'd burst. Eventually, spurred by sheer desperation and by a diagram John showed me of, I think, shoe production in the Far East, from some Marxist book he was reading, I plunged in, crazily, not sure at all that I would come out the other side. I've never re-read it and have no idea if it's any good. But what I do know is that the title could apply to many of my works, so it clearly speaks to something very close to the centre of my being – or at any rate, of my being as a writer.

One example: when Martin Esslin, head of Radio Drama, invited me in 1972 to write a radio play for the BBC I immediately thought of something I had recently read in a book on Dostoevsky, that for Stavrogin in *The Devils* the world is nothing but an echo-chamber in which his own voice is echoed back to him, and that this drives him mad. And I conceived of a work in which the listener would experience the breakdown of a man with no privileged access to his thoughts or feelings but simply through fragments of innocent earlier conversations or remarks coming back at him, filling his head, in more and more mechanical and violent a fashion. Thus his wife's opening words as she draws the bedroom curtains: 'The laburnum's in flower', return to him, first as that precise phrase, dropping into a quite different exchange; then the first three words repeated three times: 'The laburnum's in – ' 'The laburnum's in – ' The laburnum's in – '; then cut up even more, and growing louder and louder, and so on. The effect, in Guy Vaesen's brilliant production with a wonderful cast exceeded my wildest dreams. Both Pinter and the normally critical *Times* radio critic were very complementary. I never wrote a better radio play in the twenty years I wrote for Radio 3.

I decided to call the piece *Playback*, but it could have been called *The Echo Chamber*. Proust says somewhere that every writer finds a title to one of their works which in retrospect becomes emblematic of them all: all Flaubert's books, for example, could have been called *L'Éducation sentimentale*, all Dostoevsky's books could have been called *Crime and Punishment*. By the same token all my books and plays could be called *The Echo Chamber*.

The first thing that tends to come into my head with a new idea or 'feel' as I prefer to call it, for a new work, is of it as a self-enclosed entity, a whole, a machine or an organism that starts with the opening sentence and comes to an end with the last word. And so naturally it tends to be 'about' madness or some equivalent and – in many cases – its eventual appeasement or relief. That I think is what led Pat Vincent, a mature student of mine who was also an artist, many years ago, when I had only written four or five novels, to describe my work with this wonderful phrase: 'Always the hope of the voice calling from out of the closed system.' I love the idea that hope can – and can only – reside in the voice calling, and the idea of a voice calling out of a 'closed system'. I would like to imagine this was the case, but I am not sure it is. Yet I comfort myself with the thought that she must have sensed something of that there to formulate it like that. It would explain why a naturally sunny person like me tends to write about madness and the collapse of inner worlds. I seem to be driven in my writing to seek what can be salvaged when there is seemingly no hope.

But there is another, less dramatic way of looking at it. This is that I feel the overwhelming need in everything I write to account for all the elements in the work. In other words, no background, nothing purely arbitrary. In life that means madness. In art it means – what?

28.4.2020

Woke up to the sound of rain. The first proper rain for 38 days, as if God, realising it was getting dangerously close to the biblical forty, had quickly put a stop to the unnatural bright blue skies and clear sunlight we have been having since 21 March. Johnson returns with an absurd speech from the steps of Downing Street still talking of fighting the enemy and 'wrestling him to the ground'. It may be that he thinks this will strike a chord in the general public, but I begin to think that is the way his mind works – one cannot call it 'thinking'.

England

13 September 1956. A bright sunny late summer's day in the South East of England. As the train took us from Folkestone to Victoria (or was it Waterloo?) my mother and I gazed out at the fields flying past and tried to understand the phrase that kept running through our minds: This is England.

My mother's main feeling, I imagine, was one of relief. She had cleared the last hurdle, albeit not exactly in the way she would have wished. While visitors to the UK were at the time automatically granted a three-month stay she had been unwise enough, when questioned by officials on board the boat that had carried us from Calais on the last leg of our journey out of Egypt, to reply in the affirmative when asked if she would like to stay in England for the duration of my year's schooling in the country. 'I see,' said the customs official, and promptly gave her a month's visa, telling her she could challenge that by writing to the Home Office. I don't know what I felt. I think that since we had decided to leave Egypt for good at the end of the previous year I had put my feelings on hold.

I wrote in *A Life* about our wait for the train to Gloucester in the café in Paddington Station, and how my mother and I turned to each other after a while with the same thought: How quiet it was, despite being full; everybody was whispering, and we found ourselves doing the same. This then was England. Very different nowadays, where the advent of mobile phones has led to people conducting business and even marital disputes out loud with no apparent awareness of anyone else. But even before that things had changed, for the worse, it seems to me, along with the loss of deference, which is of course to be applauded. Now even without mobile phones very few conversations are conducted in the hushed whispers of the past and all too many ignore the feelings of the other occupants of café, restaurant or railway carriage.

But England for me was not really about the people. It was about the miracle of snow that first winter in Cheltenham, followed by the miracle of spring, neither of which I had experienced in my eleven years in Egypt. It was about London in the year between school and university, and the museums and art galleries I discovered there. It was about Woodstock, six miles from Oxford, to which my mother and I moved when I started graduate work; about Blenheim Park, against which Woodstock clusters, where I would walk and try to work out how to move forward with whatever story I was writing at the time and where I always hoped, in vain of course, to meet the woman who would change my life; about the Cotswolds where my mother and I cycled at weekends and where, on one of our walks, we encountered one of the most charming cats we were ever to have, who decided we were the people for her and followed us home. It was about the various places we went to on holiday with our two dogs in the late sixties and early seventies, when we could finally afford a car, since the severe quarantine restrictions meant we could never travel abroad with them and we were reluctant to leave them in kennels: Lyme Regis, where we had difficulty finding a boarding house that would take two big dogs; Watendlath, the little lake off Borrowdale which we hit upon by chance on a trip to the Lake District, and where the landlady would bring us each a mug of hot chocolate before we went to bed; a flat in a large house by the sea at Welcombe in North Cornwall, owned by that irritable poet, Ronald Duncan, the librettist of Britten's *Rape of Lucrece* and author of, among other things, an epic poem modestly entitled: *Man: The Complete Cantos* (Pound had been a friend), and an autobiography, *How to Make Enemies*. He would sit in a large study surrounded by remaindered copies of his own works and a bust of himself on a pedestal, and receive the rent with barely a word, not, I now realise, because he was annoyed with us but because he wanted to get back to the hut he had built on the cliffs above Welcombe Bay and get on with his writing. And much else. We always said that holidaying in England would be a delight if it wasn't for two things: the weather and the food. Which is why, when both dogs had died, we took to travelling to France and Italy for our holidays.

But England was also Oxford, where I spent five years at a formative time in my life. None of them were what I would call happy but all were important. And as an undergraduate the walks in Christ Church meadows, Magdalen gardens and the parks were always a source of joy. When I went back many years later, first for a term at St Anne's and then at All Souls for two terms, little had changed, the place was as beautiful as ever. But always there hung over it, for me, the sense that I did not belong and did not really want to belong. It was too beautiful, too unchanging, too smug. None of that had bothered me as an undergraduate, I was used to settling into strange environments, but it did as a graduate and it did again when I was at All Souls. I recalled Eliot's remark in a letter: 'Oxford is very beautiful but I do not want to be dead', and realised that while I relished visits to Oxford, living there for any length of time was indeed, for me, a kind of death.

Despite feeling, when I got to the University of Sussex, to take up my first (and only) teaching post, that this was the place for me, in England itself I have never felt completely at home. Not that I had in Egypt or would have in France or Germany, both countries I at one time or another thought of settling in (Paris and Berlin would be more accurate). Until recently, when asked how I thought of myself I would say: As a Jew with roots in Egypt, and a European who lives in England. Brexit has changed all that. Suddenly that 'European' seems far more important than I would ever have imagined. I have felt, as the wretched Brexit saga has unfolded, as I imagine those Jewish denizens of the Austro-Hungarian Empire felt after the Treaty of Versailles, when, as a result of impersonal forces, they found themselves no longer citizens of a multi-national, multi-lingual entity, but of a tiny chauvinist land-locked Alpine state called Austria.

And yet, a few years ago, returning from a trip with Tim to Bavaria to look at the art in Munich, Nuremberg, Bamberg and Würzburg, as the plane circled before landing at Gatwick, I realised I was looking forward to getting home. Not England, not Lewes, but my own house in Lewes. That, it seems, was really home.

Interesting statistic: more people have so far died in Britain of C-19 than died in the Blitz. But of course they died hidden away from the rest of us and we have not seen here what we saw in Lombardy, corteges of army vans carrying away the dead for disposal elsewhere. In the Blitz the evidence of destruction was all round, in the buildings torn to pieces by the bombs, the rubble in the streets, the nightly rituals (in London) of seeking shelter in the underground. Now Johnson comes out onto the steps of Downing Street and announces that 'we have triumphed' because the NHS has not been overwhelmed. No acknowledgement that Britain looks set to have the highest death rate of any European country despite being last in line to have to face it and therefore the country with the longest time to prepare.

The English Language

When I was starting to write and finding that everything I put down was stale and bore no relation to what I wanted, yet had no idea what it was I wanted, one of the things I blamed was the language. I had come to English at the age of six and though I had then learned it rapidly, as one does at that age, it was in a country where the main language was not English and where the only English people I knew were my teachers. Yet here I was, saddled with the language, unable to write in any other. I looked with envy at painters and composers who worked with an international language and never needed to concern themselves with such things.

Even today I lament the fact that I am not inward with the language as, say, Muriel Spark was or Rosalind is, born and bred as they were in the British Isles. But as I forged a style for myself I began to see that if not being inward with the language was a handicap it was perhaps not a fatal one. I came across Stravinsky's remark that 'Had Beethoven had Mozart's lyric gifts he would never have developed his rhythmic capacities to the extent he did', and I kept that as a mantra to recite whenever I felt the disadvantages of not being a native speaker weighing me down. After all, coming at language as an outsider might have its advantages, as Beckett and Nabokov showed. I was no Beckett or Nabokov, but I was me, and I would have to find how I could work comfortably with what I had.

I was no Beckett or Nabokov, but they had a native language to bounce off, Irish English and Russian. And Beckett at least, after deliberately deciding to renounce his native language for his adopted one, remained happy to write in the two languages for the rest of his life. But what was my native language? Not French, which I spoke predominantly with my mother from the moment I learned to speak till we imperceptibly switched to English in my sixth or seventh year. I did not feel French and I did not and never have considered French 'my' language. Not Arabic, which was an alien language I had to learn at my English school in Egypt, quite rightly of course, but I knew I was not Egyptian and never learned it properly anyway. And obviously not English. But recently I have begun to question whether there really is such a thing as a native language. There is no doubt that the language spoken by mothers and grandmothers tends to have a special place in most people's sense of language. Kafka's famous diary entry on how the German word *Mütter* cannot, for him, represent his (Jewish) sense of mother is well known and a powerful testimony to the abiding presence of a native language. But long before Kafka Dante had also written passionately about this in his plea for Italian to be given as much respect as Latin was in his day. Without that native language, he writes wittily, my parents, meeting, would not have been able to speak and so to fall in love and marry and I would never have been born. And in the *Commedia* he makes a powerful case for the importance of the language of *mamma* and *babbo*, as he puts it. But there too he analyses how dangerous is the human tendency to look backwards and to assert some primal innocence. We must acknowledge where we came from, he says, but acknowledge too that this must be both integrated into our being and eventually transcended. If you are an artist working with language you must hone a new language, turning neither to Latin, the language of Authority, nor to childish babble, which does not know the full potential of language, but to that which you have yet to make. The *Commedia* is of course both an exploration of this issue in all its dimensions and an example of what he means.

The only writer I know who seems to have had precisely my problem of not being inward with any language is Derrida. In *The Monolingualism of the Other*, one of his most autobiographical pieces, he informs us that as an Algerian Jew he could not identify with French, the language of the colonialist, or Arabic, the language of the native majority, or even Hebrew, a language his family had lost touch with long before. But then, he points out, we none of us 'have' a language in the sense that we have a body, we *speak* a language. It is something we use, not something we possess. This makes sense to me and helps free me from mourning the absence of something which does not exist.

It doesn't quite answer the question of what Kafka, Nabokov and Dante felt as a gift and Beckett as a curse. But I discovered over the years that it was not so much the English language I was not inward with as English culture, whatever that vague word might mean. Just as I did not feel 'street-wise', so I did not feel 'English-wise' or Scottish or Irish-wise. I could feel it when I came across it but I did not have it.

And this is a big disadvantage. On the other hand the lack of something, as Stravinsky noted, only makes me more aware of how having such street wisdom too often stops English writers from writing much of interest. Of interest to me, at any rate. And explains to me why I warm to writers like Pinter and Spark, where inwardness with the language and culture is used rather than accepted by writers who do not feel themselves to be quite English. And this is true of Stoppard too, with Jewish parents and an immigrant background, and of younger writers like Deborah Levy, brought up in South Africa, and Kirsty Gunn, brought up in New Zealand, both of course growing up with English, but not with England.

In a recent *TLS* the Liverpudlian poet Nicholas Murray takes issue with Ian McMillan, himself a poet from Barnsley and a regular Radio 3 presenter of cultural programmes, who had lamented the absence from the BBC of newsreaders with local accents. 'Even if one concedes the richness and vitality of regional speech,' writes Murray, 'and the fact that it has no need to justify itself to anyone, I still hesitate a little over McMillan's call for more northern accents. First of all a radio voice needs to be just that: a *voice* that the stippled microphone takes a fancy to – rich, clearly audible, musical, resonant, pleasant on the ear. It doesn't matter that a Scottish Radio 3 presenter rhymes Brahms with 'rams' rather than 'arms' if the voice is doing its job with silky panache.'

Murray's point is the same as Derrida's: to fetishise the local origins of the voice is to substitute some mythical notion of identity (which can never be fully satisfied since all languages, including all dialects, have to sacrifice some modicum of uniqueness and individuality for comprehensibility) for the truth that it all depends on what is *done* with the voice.

In the end the writer has to do the best he or she can with what they have and leave it to others to decide if it is any good and if 'foreignness' had any part to play in it.

Johnson finally back but partner just had a baby, so now due paternity leave! Will absurdities never end with this man?

Ephemeral

From the Greek *epi+hemera* (day) – lasting but a day.

Ever since I started to think for myself I have been very conscious of the ephemerality of things – here today, gone tomorrow. And been conscious too of how difficult it is to hold on to that thought and how reluctant we all are to do so. And this consciousness has informed all my writing I think, from the first novel, *The Inventory*, to the latest, *The Cemetery in Barnes*.

I did not think about it at the time, but *The Inventory* is 'about' precisely that, the ephemerality of life. Yet what got me going was nothing so grandiose but simply the desire to write a novel, to be able to work day after day at a piece of fiction, which is what I felt I wanted/needed to do above all things. And then, as I struggled to find a subject and a form that would enable that, the word *inventory* came into my head and I knew by the quickening of my heartbeat that I had found what I was looking for. For here was a word that went in two directions at once: outwards into the world, since an inventory is a list of objects, and inward into the self, into the world of imagination and invention – though a glance at the dictionary showed me that we are dealing with two Latin words, *inventarium* and *invenire*. However, that was not important. What was important was that the one English word gave me both my subject-matter and my form – though it was some time before I hit upon the right form, a combination of dialogue and inventory lists. The subject, though, was given me by the word: the book would deal with a solicitor going through the inventory of the objects in the house of a man who had recently died with the grieving family. And I thought that in the course of handling these objects, once part of a life, now curiously empty and, so to speak, stranded, different members of the family would find themselves evoking the dead person, and that many of the details of these evocations would conflict, giving us the sense that the memories we have of the dead differ, depending on our relationship with them in life.

I have since been told that this kind of subject is 'very Jewish', but I certainly had no such thoughts when writing the book. When I wrote it, at twenty-six, there was nothing that I can think of in my experience to make me particularly concerned with death or with the objects that survive after death. But what do I know about it? Perhaps there was, but if so it was certainly not at the forefront of my mind. What was clearly there was an interest in how the objects people accumulate around themselves in the course of their lives seem so orphaned on the disappearance of their owners. It was exploring this tension between the permanence, the seemingly unchanging nature of these objects, and the brevity of human life that probably excited me in the writing of that book, as well of course as the challenge of making something out of nothing but fragments of dialogue and lists of objects.

The Inventory was written in 1966. *Everything Passes*, written in 2000–2002, was, as the title suggests, much more of a head-on confrontation with the ephemeral. Yet I'm amused at the failure of most commentators to note what seemed to me the central irony of the whole book, that what it deals with first and foremost is the inability of the protagonist to free himself from the compulsive return of something that has previously happened; for him, in effect, nothing passes, he lives the horror of discovering that everything returns. The book emerged out of the collision of the phrase, 'Everything passes, the good and the bad, the joy and the sorrow, everything passes', and the account I had read of a woman in an asylum who, over many decades, wrote every day to her husband, but never turned the page, leaving us with nothing but an illegible palimpsest. Though 'everything passes' does not have the bitter irony of 'happy days' in Beckett's play, and is not meant to, it is nevertheless challenged (I thought) by what emerges in the course of the book. But, again, who am I to judge? The book is written, it is out there, let it make its own way.

I could go on detailing the way all, or nearly all my books and stories try to force the reader (and, I suppose, as I wrote, to force me) to face the strange phenomenon that everything does indeed pass, and that one day, perhaps sooner than most people think, humanity will pass and, eventually, the universe, but that most of the time we live as though all was permanent, including ourselves. What rich soil for the artist!

1.5.2020

Mayday. And for the past three days, April weather. Went out first thing yesterday morning to avoid the showers forecast for later, breaking long routine of work first, walk later. Did get back in time to do an hour before lunch and an hour after, but it was hard.

Boris's first press conference for five weeks. Did not watch as I've grown disillusioned with the scientific advisors, who have turned out to be government stooges and are coming under increased pressure from their peers as they hunker down and spout the Tory mantra of things being tough but under control and, like their Tory masters, have learned never to say sorry.

In the *TLS*, which I read in bed this morning, a review by Judith Flanders of a book on the alphabet as an organisational device by a young scholar, James Waddell. She is lukewarm about the book but fascinating on its contents. Waddell quotes Coleridge's contempt for the *Encyclopaedia Britannica* (2nd ed. 1784), especially its organisational principle. He calls it a 'huge unconnected miscellany... in an arrangement determined by the accident of initial letters.' 'So convinced was Coleridge of the facile laziness of alphabetization,' writes Waddell, 'that he decided to embark on his own rival project, the *Encyclopaedia Metropolitana*. This work, he pronounced, would "present the circle of knowledge in its harmony," not like those shoddy alphabetical rag-tags "where the desired information is divided into innumerable fragments scattered over many volumes, like a mirror broken on the ground, presenting, instead of one a thousand images, but none entire."'

A perfect description of the reason why I love the form, as I love *Tristram Shandy,* and have difficulty with *Middlemarch.* 'Like a broken mirror' would make a nice title for this volume. (I recall how fascinated I was by discovering, when working on my Bible book, that the first codices or books as we know them, were Christian Bibles, while the Jews stuck to scrolls, the reason being that the Christians, like Coleridge, believed in unity and totality, and their Bible was to run from Creation to Last Judgement, an idea perfectly conveyed in the form of the book, while the Jews set the different scrolls in their Bible side by side, beginning with the most sacred, the Torah or Pentateuch, going on to the 'prophets' (books by named prophets and what the Christians called historical books) and ending with a miscellany, the 'ketubim' or books, such as Lamentations, the Psalms and the Song of Songs, that were considered holy enough for inclusion, but only just, and in no particular order.

Epiphany

Gk *epi* + *phanie* (to appear). English usage coloured by NT narrative of the 'showing' of the infant Jesus to the Magi. Hence: sudden and transformative revelation.

The power of such a concept for the modern artist. In a world no longer underpinned by belief in a Creator God all that is left for those with a sense that there is more to life than the daily grind, which includes all artists by definition, the idea of an epiphany, a moment of revelation which flashes forth and then is gone, is very tempting. It's what Wordsworth is left with, those spots of time, those moments when the heavens part and something appears, literally in the early 'Old Man Walking' when the moon, which has been covered, suddenly breaks free of the clouds, through to the moment he crosses the Alps and realises he is now on a downward journey, and on to the moment that ends *The Prelude* of the vision of emptiness in the fog above the sea in Snowdonia. But it also includes moments of terror, as when he feels something unnameable coming after him on the lake when he has taken a boat out to row or even when he emerges from his destructive fit in 'Nutting' and sees what he has done.

It punctuates *À la recherche* and *The Four Quartets*. It's so powerful when it occurs and yet I have never been drawn to it. Or rather, my writing has never felt able to express it – no that's not quite it either. I think my epiphanies are more negative, more ambiguous than the classic ones. Not as negative as Beckett's, whose Christian upbringing perhaps led him to feel very strongly that the real betrayal was the pretence (as he saw it) of epiphany. Better drag the notion in the dirt than subscribe to that lie. Hence those titles, like *All That Fall*, *Happy Days*, gesturing towards wonder only to show us how it really is, to paraphrase the title of the book that followed the trilogy. Or as negative as Bernhard's response to Molly

Bloom's *yes*, made so much of by sentimental commentators on *Ulysses*, in the title and last word of his novel, *Ja*:

> I recalled that I had said to the Persian woman, in the course of one of our walks in the larch-wood forest, that in our time so many young people commit suicide and that the society in which these young people are forced to live has absolutely no understanding of why they should do so, and it came to me that without any transition and with all the brutality of which I was capable, I had asked the Persian woman if she herself would kill herself one day. Whereupon she had contented herself with a laugh and she had said: 'Yes.'

So: not as negative as this, but negative just the same. Or rather, what I seem to favour is ending on an ambiguous note, leaving it open as to what will ensue. Closer perhaps to the half-true epiphanies of Virginia Woolf, the 'For there she was' of *Mrs Dalloway* or Lily Briscoe's feeling at the end of *To the Lighthouse* that she has finally nailed her vision and her painting, and which may, we are left feeling, be the product merely of wish-fulfilment. The most 'epiphanic' ending I ever came up with was that of *The Air We Breathe*:

> The light fell on the glass of water in front of her. Light is the lion. She heard the words, clear, quiet, inside her head. Light is the lion that comes down to drink. Yes, she thought. Light is the lion. Light is the lion that comes down to drink.

The line is Wallace Stevens', at the end of his poem, 'The Glass of Water', and I pondered long and hard on whether to put the quote in inverted commas, to have my heroine read the poem earlier, or to let it hang there, unmotivated, unattributed. Finally I decided the last was the right thing to do. I sort of half-wanted to take responsibility for it, but only half, since it is such a well-known line, though not in the category of 'to be or not to be' or 'season of mists and mellow fruitfulness'.

But that's an early novel. I have usually preferred to let the reader decide how to take a book, putting the elements of it together and allowing the juxtapositions to do the work. In the case of a book like *Infinity* I suppose I hoped the absurdity of Pavone the man would be subsumed into a larger whole which would include the beauty of his music and the pathos of his end; in that of a book like *Now* that the heroine's inability and refusal to speak would reveal more than was visible to those destined to be with her day by day; in that of a book like *Contre-Jour* that the lack of contact between the painter and his model wife, which leads to her intolerance of other people and compulsive washing, would be tempered by the sense that in the end, though they might not have been able to say it to each other, they each literally meant the world to the other. In all those cases if epiphany occurs it occurs beyond the comprehension of the characters, as a result of the multiple interactions which make up the book. That, after all, is what Bonnard's paintings, which were the inspiration for *Contre-Jour*, repeatedly enact for us.

But, looked at closely, does it not seem as if the epiphanies described in the writings of Wordsworth, Proust and Eliot are themselves ambiguous? It may be that 'ridiculous the waste sad time before and after,' but what we get in *The Prelude, À la recherche* and *The Four Quartets* is not a string of epiphanies but a great deal of before and after, and the gradual recognition that 'only in time is time conquered'. Eliot may give this a Christian interpretation and see in Christ, both man and God, the ground for such a belief, but in both Wordsworth and Proust it is free of doctrinal trappings. As Blanchot points out in a wonderful early essay on Proust, though the epiphanic moments are the keystones of the whole vast edifice, the lesson of *À la recherche* is that without the waste sad time before and after there would be no epiphany and no book, just as without the epiphany there would be no book and Proust the man would have wasted his life as he felt the Goncourts had wasted theirs, for all the realistic accuracy of their many observations.

2.05.2020

Weather set fair again after the early April weather of the past week. Blue skies. Sunshine. Hardly a breeze.

The government and their scientists keep insisting that we are now 'on the downward curve' and that soon we can begin to think about re-opening shops and sending children back to school. But I see no sign of that in the figures, which continue to be grim: over 700 deaths a day.

Failure

The great lesson Proust taught me was that failure is unimportant, what is important is what you make of it. Marcel fails in every sphere: in love, in his desire to write, in his attempts to understand why he remains unmoved by his first experience of seeing La Berma. But compare his response to failure and that of others. Swann, who stands guard over the entrance to *À la recherche*, falls passionately in love with a woman far beneath him in social standing and who at first he does not even find attractive, but when the affair is over all he can say is: 'She was not my type'. Marcel, in the various setbacks he encounters to his need for love and security, from his mother to Gilberte to Albertine, works away at trying to understand why it is that his love affairs always follow the same pattern, and if this doesn't help him in his life it gives him the subject of his book. Indeed, what he learns is that to shield yourself from the pain of rejection is to shield yourself from life. The lesson is thus at once moral and artistic, and in Proust the two cannot in fact be separated.

I don't think I understood any of this when I first read Proust at the age of seventeen, but I felt it, somehow, and I found it enormously exhilarating. It told me that my attempts at writing, which I could see were pitiful, were not a reason to give up but a necessary road to some future where things might get better. In other words it both gave me hope and made that hope concrete. Writing, I knew, was not like the sport I had been so good at in Egypt, where hard work always paid off; its progress was unpredictable and there was no such thing as method. But there was also no such thing either as an insurmountable wall. Or rather, what Proust taught me was that if the wall was insurmountable what you had to do was find a way round it. Later, in the fount of wisdom that is contained in the volumes of Stravinsky's conversations with Robert Craft, I found the old maestro remarking: 'If you cannot find an answer perhaps the question is wrong.' And for the rest of my writing life, when I am embarked on a book and cannot find a way forward and yet the book goes on crying out to get written I am buoyed by my memories of Proust and by Stravinsky's remark.

The grimmer aspect of Proust's lesson is that however much one understands one never learns from one's mistakes, in life or in art, but is destined to repeat them ad infinitum. But then that is also its joyous aspect: not to repeat them is to choose death to life, the death of the heart for the sake of a peaceful life. Failure is what living is about, as much as joy. A hard lesson to learn, and in fact not one we can bear to learn, so we go on failing and we go on being tormented by our failures.

The depressing news shows no sign of easing. We wait and watch, strangely insulated from the horrors going on elsewhere yet knowing that at any moment we could be part of them.

Flow

We are caught up in the flow of life. It has no beginning and no end. And our own lives are the same. There is no beginning. We come into consciousness and we learn about the circumstances of our birth (in most cases) and certain incidents in our earliest childhood, and no doubt those early years are important, perhaps vitally important, in our development. But we never have a sense ourselves that 'this is when it started', 'it' being our life. That is why I prefer the opening of *Tristram Shandy* to that of *David Copperfield*. The latter deals brilliantly with the conventions of autobiography (and of fictional autobiography) in Dickens' time, but the former tells it how it is.

I was once commissioned to write a play and I called the play that ensued *Flow*. It was the best commission I ever had because it was so precise and as a result I dared do something I would never otherwise have dared to do and produced something I didn't know I had it in me to write. Caroline Blakiston, who had been in one of my radio pays, had joined The Actors' Company, a group of actors including Ian McKellen, Robert Eddison and Edward Petherbridge, who in the early 1970s formed a company which would choose its own directors and appear alphabetically on the billboards and not by degree of celebrity. They had been invited to the Edinburgh festival and planned to put on a Shakespeare play, a Chekhov play (*The Bear* I think), and, at lunchtime, a double bill consisting of Petherbridge's adaptation of R.D.Laing's

Knots for the stage, and a new half-hour play. Was I interested? asked Caroline. Was I hell. They wanted a half-hour play for five virtuoso performers and very few props. Precisely the kind of commission I had always dreamed of. (Stravinsky again, to, I think, Lincoln Kirstein and the New York City Ballet, who asked him to write a work for them – we give you *carte blanche*, they said. I don't want *carte blanche*, retorted the composer, I want a precise length and the precise number and make-up of instruments, and then I can write something for you.)

For the first days or perhaps weeks after accepting I was petrified. Could I do it? Had I not been rash in accepting? It soon became clear that with that brief there would be little scope for the actors to exit and enter. I needed to have them all there for the whole half hour. But doing what? Saying what?

That is the advantage of a commission. Even when there seems to be no way through you keep pressing and a way opens up. I don't know when the idea dropped into my mind, but there it was: Five people, facing forward, each engaged in a monologue (whether internal or external never seemed to be an issue, they were both). These monologues would run simultaneously, or rather, overlap, so that we (the audience) would have to block out the four others if we were to fully take in any one strand and, if we switched 'strands', block out what we had just been listening to.

Ridiculous? Pointlessly difficult? I didn't think so. I had always been fascinated by the fact that most of the time, in life, if I listen to someone in a crowded spot, a café or a bus, for example, I am also overhearing other strands of conversation. In fact most of our interactions with others are of this kind, passing by them rather than stopping time and looking them full in the face. Yet all art, as far as I was aware, asks us to look at it 'full face' and give it our whole attention. The experience of half-overhearing was just what I was interested in. (I subsequently wrote a novel called *Conversations in Another*

Room and then a novel about Bonnard, an artist, I discovered, who specialised in playing with angles and perspectives precisely so as to make us aware of how different lives go on at different speeds in the same space.) My five characters, then, would each be living their own lives as though the others didn't exist, but we, the audience, would know that they all occupied the same world, our world.

I wrote the piece in one go, 'hearing' the overlaps and intercuttings as a continuous whole. Afterwards I went back and checked that I had not inadvertently given one character a much larger or much smaller 'role' than the others, and found that this had not in fact happened. Naturally I had to tweak a bit here and there, and rewrite this bit or that, but really, once I had the conception and dared go with it, it came by itself. And I would never have dared go with such an idea had I not had that commission.

The rehearsals, to which I was invited, were unbearably exciting. The very effort the actors were making to keep going, to concentrate on their own monologue while cuing in to the others was part of what made it so. Of course there was no way, if you got lost, that you could find your way back in again, as you can in most plays. Here you were by yourself – and yet had to pay the utmost attention to the rhythm and pace of the others. It felt at times like that children's game of passing an object unseen from one to the other and the person caught with the object having to pay a forfeit. Except that here if someone lost their way or dried up everyone payed the forfeit. And this is where we hit a problem. One of the actors kept drying up under the pressure. Not every time, but often enough for Petherbridge, who was directing, to have to make a difficult decision. With three weeks to go before the opening should he persevere and hope for the best or cut his losses and decide to equip each actor with a script and a lectern? In the end prudence prevailed and he settled for lecterns.

Naturally, this at once removed the element of danger and turned the play into a performance. The audience might perhaps at times be able to forget the lecterns, but probably only by closing their eyes. And in that case why not a radio play? One reason why not was of course that a radio play, being pre-recorded, removes precisely that theatrical element of something happening NOW, in front of you. And yet having the actors reading from lecterns, even though they were still physically present (and, being fine actors they naturally made their presences felt), robbed the whole thing of a crucial dimension.

That, however, is how it was done at the Lyceum in Edinburgh and subsequently at the Shaw in London. It still carried a certain punch, but so much less than I had hoped.

I still long to see it done as I envisaged it.

4.5.2020

Andrew McNeillie sends me a couple of poems he's written. He tells me he's still working on the third stanza of the second one, and I too am not sure about the bracket at the start. But even as it stands it feels to me like the authentic voice of poetry itself, and a call to arms to all of us who feel the need to think about what is happening but have difficulty doing so, distracted by the fact that there are always so many things to do, fresh books to think about, food to order, walks to be undertaken, news to be watched and listened to.

> As (...)
> you struggle to make sense of what's happening,
> with one eye on the weather
> And an ear to what they're saying about
> The latest turn of events,

As one thing leads to another
But nothing changes or even relents –
Consider the lilies of the field for once.

Think what it means to have time on your hands,
Time if not space to dwell, to see
What it means, simply to be
At the beck of no one's commands,
To be stuck ashore, yet all at sea.
Didn't you always want to break free?
Haven't we all heard you cry 'If only…'
Well, now's the time to give only a try,
Because only is here and lonely.

We are all 'stuck ashore' yet most of us are unable to think through what that means, do not know how 'simply to be', and so, after a vague thought that it would be good to do that, move on. 'Teach us to sit still', wrote Eliot, and this was not some vaguely Buddhist mantra but, again, a call to stop rushing. We who deal in prose and in fiction rather than in poetry, can perhaps catch something of that by bringing out the utter craziness of constant movement – there is a story in Beckett's first book, *More Pricks than Kicks,* that is specifically about just that (actually all the stories in that volume are about just that), and we know that Beckett, as a young man, would lie in bed all day and when friends called to take him out to a picnic, ask: 'What for?' But at that point he seemed to be in what I would call the Bartleby bind – he would 'rather not' take part in the meaningless activities the world around him was apparently engaged in yet could put nothing in its place except total passivity, the foetal position. Andrew's poem swerves into Larkin territory as it moves towards its conclusion, 'Haven't we all heard you cry "If only"?' it asks, as Larkin reminded us of the joys of saying: 'I'm going!' and slamming the door behind us. But his is a more hopeful tone than Larkin's, beautifully bringing to the fore the word which we have just so thoughtlessly used: 'Well, now's the time to give only a try, / because only is here and lonely.' Perhaps if we are sharp enough mentally and spiritually to do so the word will cease to resonate as a solitary specimen and will find other words, other thoughts, or perhaps a deeper word, deeper thoughts, to rhyme with it, relieve its solitude – ah, but there it is, the poem, the work on the poem, has found it.

And what is my writing this every day, day after day, but an attempt to do just that? Of course too often, when I have had similar feelings and have tried to write them out of me or write myself into them, I have found that the act of writing and the substance of what I write has simply taken me away from them. And I have often had the same feelings since I have settled down to this project. But I have learned over the years that to be too dismissive too soon is a mistake, that sometimes simply keeping going brings about a surprising swerve back to what set the writing going in the first place. Not always though.

What Andrew says in this poem is very close to what Proust keeps returning to: Marcel is on the point of 'understanding', of 'opening the door' as he puts it in *Contre Sainte-Beuve*, but then laziness or external events draw him away and he loses it. Or perhaps that is how it was meant to be and in a strange way it is his persistence, his readiness to bounce back from failure, that eventually leads to success.

Always the question though: How do you give only a try?

Foreign

I have always felt foreign. First in France, then in Egypt and finally in England. It hasn't bothered me overmuch, except, as I wrote above, in the case of having to write in a language with which I do not feel 'inward', where I look in on the language instead of simply employing it. Actually that is a good way of putting it. I have, for as long as I remember, always 'looked in' on the natives of the countries I have lived in. I suppose I feel a little more 'at home' in England than I did in Egypt, because the natives speak my language. But I think I felt more at home in Paris, during my brief sojourn there twenty or so years ago than I do in London – or Lewes?

Last night listening to a programme about A.J. Ayer on the radio. Educated at Eton and Oxford, Professor of Logic at Oxford, knight of the realm, darling of the media, at the end of his life he confessed to his successor in the Oxford chair that he could never shake off the feeling that someone would one day tap him on the shoulder and ask what a dirty Jew was doing there. That – rather as with Steiner – would account for his constant insistence that he was the greatest philosopher in the world and, when asked who he was, always giving his full name and honours: Professor Sir Alfred Ayer. Were such feelings specifically linked to the descendants of Ashkenazi Jews whose families had made good? Was it because they were at once part of a history of prejudice and discrimination in Eastern Europe and yet now so deeply embedded in the English Establishment that they feared being 'found out'? Certainly I have never felt that way, have simply accepted that I would always be 'foreign', but that this was not a big deal. I have never felt 'at home' in any setting, except perhaps, to some extent, at Sussex in the early days. And I went on feeling that way with George, and even with Larry who hardly agreed with me about anything and yet I felt did accept me as I was and respect me. But though that was a very good feeling, even at Sussex I sensed that I did not quite 'belong' in the way Larry and George, Tony Nuttall and Stephen did. And in 1966, after three years there, blissfully happy, I knew that if I was unable to write the novel I felt I needed to write in the term's paid leave

I had been given I would – however reluctantly – have to leave. And even after I had published *The Inventory* and felt that the University recognised that my heart would never be totally in my teaching, that part of my time and energy would always go into my writing, I was always reluctant to take part in school and subject-group meetings or become chair of the group and all the rest of it – though I found I could organise lecture courses and put on poetry readings as well as or better than the next person. But then Sussex in those days was a place where the odd and the unusual were not just tolerated but respected and even admired. Where, nowadays, would either Stephen or George ever get a job, neither of them ever publishing a book in his lifetime? Yet everyone recognised that *they* were the heart of Sussex arts. Sadly, Sussex itself has now changed and become much like all other universities, starved of cash, its teachers overworked and ignored in all the big decisions, tutorials a thing of the past, more a degree-awarding factory than anything else. The admirable faculty have long ago learned to ride with the punches, try to do something individually for their students and get on with their own writing and reading lives.

Foreign. Sacha and I used to say we never felt like tourists in France or Italy or Egypt, but that tourists always had a country of their own to return to and we didn't. This struck me afresh when planning the book on Sacha after her death and reading the accounts of growing up in Egypt by Priscilla Napier and Penelope Lively. Both are brilliant and both seemed to capture much of the world Sacha herself grew up in – yet of course they were both expats, both had a *patria* to return to, whereas the Jews of Egypt, like all other Jews, had nowhere else to go. Even when the State of Israel was established the Jews I knew and the Jews of my family would no sooner have thought of Israel as a 'home' than Jakarta or Timbuktoo, and when they left they settled in Italy, France, England, Canada,

Australia or the States, never Israel. André Aciman's *Out of Egypt*, which came out the year Sacha died, 1996, and which I re-read recently seems, on the other hand, though it deals with a Jewish Sephardi family, to be equally alien to me in many respects. Partly because though Aciman brilliantly exposes its growing alienation from its religious traditions, his family was still much more deeply embedded in a Jewish culture than I or my mother ever were; partly because the milieu he describes was a business milieu whereas our family had lost its fortune and was made up more of professionals, doctors, lawyers, etc.; and partly because he himself only left with his immediate family in 1964, enduring eight years of an Egypt, which had been denuded of its British, French and Jewish elements and which was growing more nationalist and anti-foreign by the day. As he describes it, those last eight years, coinciding with his secondary school years, reminded me very much of accounts of Jews in Germany who clung on after 1933 because, they felt, this was where their businesses were, and because 'we have nowhere else to go,' and anyway, 'it's just a matter of lying low for a while and all this will blow over'. Very different from my own experience, since Egypt never felt like home in the first place.

Why, when I have watched European football competitions at national and cup level, has a part of me always rooted for the European opposition? Does that make a traitor out of me? An enemy of the people? Or is it not rather that I have been enraged by the chauvinism of the commentators and felt they always underrate European teams? It may be that if I were listening to French or German or Spanish commentators I would feel the same thing. I don't know, though Brexit has revealed the horrible strain of arrogance and sense of entitlement which lies deep in the English (probably not Scottish or Welsh) psyche, not just in the Tory elite but in the furthest recesses of the country. The longer I live in England the less I understand it, I realise, and I certainly find it hard to take seriously the sense of exceptionalism and the myth of how England won the war on its own – I thought this was the stuff of *Beyond the Fringe* satire and suitable as the frozen settings of P.G. Wodehouse novels. But no, it's still there and it's real. So now, after Brexit, I feel more foreign than ever.

Of course there is no such thing as England, let alone Britain, except in the fevered imaginings of fervent Brexiteers. I feel at home in London but not in England, T says. And she means the metropolis in all its messy variety, having lived in Kensington, Wimbledon and Kentish Town and taught at schools and colleges in Wembley, Tottenham and Islington. Liverpool is not England, Bernard assures me. Brighton is not England, my colleagues used to tell me. Nevertheless, England, and for the moment, Britain, is ruled by people who no longer seem to believe in democracy or democratic institutions, and who would want to live in such a country? But when T and I talk of emigrating rather than live in a Tory-dominated Little England we have trouble deciding where to settle. Not because of the vast choice on offer, but on the contrary, from the feeling that there is nowhere we would feel at ease in. Edinburgh and Dublin are possibilities, but the former, where we have good friends, is too cold and grey for our Mediterranean senses, while in the latter we have too few friends. France is the obvious choice, but might it not soon be in the hands of Marine le Pen? Italy? Is it too not infected by the Fascist poison? Canada and Australia? Too dull. Fine I'm sure if you grew up there, but to *choose* to live there? In the Thirties, we joke, Jews in the German-speaking lands could emigrate, if they fulfilled the necessary requirements, admittedly a big if, to countries where democracy and the rule of law were the bedrock, Britain and the States. No more. Such countries no longer exist.

5.5.2020

It's official – the UK has the highest number of deaths of any country in Europe, over 32,000 and rising. Probably end up around 50,000. As the Westernmost country in Europe, and the last to get the virus it should have been the best prepared and have among the lowest death rates. A shame on our country and its leaders.

France

Before England there was France. On our way from Egypt to England we stopped first in Venice, where the boat landed and where my mother wanted to show me the city she loved. Yet I have no good memories of those few days spent traipsing over bridges and through churches as I mourned the sudden severance from my friends and my dogs and waited anxiously for the next stage of my life to start, a year of school in England. From Venice we took the train to Geneva, where Sacha had to go to whatever bank held the meagre sums she had managed to smuggle out, and then to Paris to see one of her surviving uncles. More traipsing, more stifled anxiety. It was only when I finally started school in Cheltenham and felt I was engaged in something I could at last do and do well, that I began to relax.

But once at Oxford, and with my friend Theo living in Paris, I began to frequent that city, nearly always its Left Bank. I still remember the stink of the fish from the fishmonger's stall at the front of the block in which Theo had his first flat, a dingy affair on the rue du Bac. Then as a graduate student, now with a scooter, I remember driving down to Paris with Gordon on the back to stay, in his absence, in Theo's latest flat in St Cloud. Later, teaching at Sussex, I discovered it was possible to board the ferry at Newhaven and get the train from Dieppe to Paris for £12.50 return, staying this time with Lydia Farahat in her crazy higgledy piggledy flat in the smart rue du Dragon, five minutes from the Place Saint Germain des Près. The strange rule of the flat was that no one had their own bedroom, one simply slept in any bedroom that happened to be unoccupied. The residents were Lydia, a close friend of my mother's from Egypt, her husband Raoul, and their daughter Ingy, about my age, with her brother Jean sometimes staying over. Later I was put up by another friend from Egypt, this time of about my age, Marcianne, whose father, I learned, had once been a suitor of my mother's. She taught philosophy at the Sorbonne in a junior capacity and then switched to law. She had a wonderful top floor flat, itself on three floors, in the rue d'Ulm close to the École Normale where first Beckett and then my colleague and friend George Craig had taught English. And later still, when Dan had settled in Paris and was teaching at the American University, I remember staying in his flat in the 18me, above a street market, where sleep was impossible after 5 a.m. when the vendors began setting up their stalls.

My abiding memory of all those visits, from the age of eighteen to my fifties, is of excitement at the city's variety and beauty and of melancholy solitude. More recently, with T, staying either in Peter and Sian's tiny flat by the Jardin des Plantes or in Nina's just below the Panthéon, these visits have been happy occasions, the joy of being with T, the joy of seeing Nina. The pleasure, too, of seeing my books published in French, for our trips have often been dictated by my French publisher's desire to have me read and talk about the latest translated book, until recently– a further source of pleasure – with my brilliant and fascinating translator, Bernard Hoepffner. My last memory of him, before his terrible death, whether by accident or design, off St David's Head in Wales, a spot he had spent time in as a young man and returned to regularly, is of a stroll round St Germain, ending in Delacroix's studio, after the award of a prize to both of us for his translation of *Infinity*.

Once Tamar and I stayed in Sophia's flat on the other side of the Butte Montmartre, and once in a strange hotel on the Paris side of the Butte, close to the famous Bateau Lavoire where Picasso, Chagall and co. lived as struggling young artists at the turn of the twentieth century. The reason for the change of venue from the Left Bank was the six month period in 2003 when I taught at the American University in Paris, invited by Dan, and rented Jean-Michel Rabaté's flat in Abbesses, at the foot of Montmartre. I taught one course a week, on my own work and any works I associated with that, to about twelve enthusiastic and mainly articulate students, nearly all American, so had plenty of time to write and to wander. That was when I got to know Paris away from the Left Bank, walking on Sundays over the hill to the flea market at the Porte de Clignancourt, often treating myself to a very French set Sunday lunch in one of the many bistros around the Porte.

But Paris is not France, and for many years, before we started going to Bressanone, Sacha and I used to drive through France to holiday in the South, stopping at the great cathedral cities of Rouen, Chartres, Tours, Bourges and Orleans, and the wondrous Romanesque churches and cathedrals further south. At one time we would go and stay with another friend of Sacha's from Egypt, Gougou, a painter and potter who lived in a farm not far from Nice. It always made me happy to see Sacha with some of her old friends, a sense of her (and therefore me) belonging somewhere.

What does France then 'mean' to me? A place where I feel at home, perhaps more so than in England. Paris in the first place, but the regions as well. I probably know it better than I know England, though I don't feel I really know either very well. But it is certainly a part of me in a way no other country is. Even Egypt, which, because I spent such formative years there, is a repository of more powerful memories than France, feels strange, alien, in a way France never has. Even after Brexit, I keep trying to remind myself, France will be there for me, in reality and in the imagination.

6.5.2020

The Government scientists and even some ministers have admitted there were mistakes made early on. It seems the decision to move from test and track to 'herd immunity', which cost the country a precious week and led to far more deaths than necessary was the result of the discovery that there were not enough tests available at the time. In other words, the Government lack of preparedness, the result of ignoring previous reports on the likelihood of pandemics at some point in the near future, the running down by the Tories since 2010 of the NHS, the starving of councils of funds and the shutting down of various committees which would have overseen preparedness. Exacerbated by total concentration on Brexit in the past three years and by Johnson's entrenched belief in British exceptionalism and his aversion to thinking ahead in the mistaken belief that he would always be able to talk his way out of anything, which had stood him so well throughout his life. Not this time.

The fine weather has returned. I'm happy just to keep going as I am, day after day, though there is the nagging feeling that I am not taking advantage of these out-of-the-normal-time conditions to think things through. Yet I know that I cannot do that, that breakthroughs only come by writing, and I'm glad to be writing this.

Freedom

I've never felt the lack of freedom and in that I suppose I've been lucky. I can understand the Israelites under Pharaoh, the slaves in the American South, the natives in Apartheid South Africa wanting to be free – free of something specific: the tyranny of Pharaoh or of the white minority in the American South and in South Africa. And the slightly more nuanced cases of countries where their own rulers were oppressing them, France in 1789, Russia in 1917, Romania under Ceaucescu, the Arab countries of the Middle East in the Arab Spring. In many of these cases, though, sadly, the cure turned out to be no better than the disease.

But the so-called student revolutions of 1968 left me cold, especially in England. My personal freedom had come with getting a job I loved in an institution I believed in – though before that too I had never felt that I 'needed to break free' and I would certainly have accepted a job in a run-of-the mill university and got on with it.

The idea of artistic freedom, like that of the avant-garde, is, I feel, usually the province of those without much talent, more of a slogan than anything that corresponds to reality. I love free spirits though, like the Muriel Spark who emerges from her autobiographical novels, especially *Loitering with Intent*, with its triumphant final sentence, quoting Benvenuto Cellini: 'And so, having entered the fullness of my years, from there by the grace of God I go on my way rejoicing.' Or like the Beckett who emerges from the four volumes of his letters. I'm not so sure about Evelyn Waugh and Kingsley Amis: what emerges from their letters and biographies, though not from the novels and the poems, is of an admirable independence of spirit turning into a rigid orthodoxy of right-wing prejudices. But certainly that is what I look for in art and what quickens my pulse when I encounter it: independence of spirit, whether in a Sterne, a Wordsworth, an Emily Dickinson, a Yeats, a Proust, a Kafka or a Wallace Stevens. And in people: Rosalind, Stephen, Nuttall, George, Kirsty, my composer and painter friends. That is what I warm to.

The principle, as I see it, remains the same: Don't give me *carte blanche*, tell me how long you want the piece to be, how many instruments, and which ones. The difficulty with making art today is that no one, except in very rare cases such as that of Stravinsky and the New York City Ballet, gets that kind of commission. Writers on the other hand, more usually get reminded by their publishers that the last book hasn't sold as much as they were hoping and that unless they change tack they are unlikely to be able to go on publishing them. At least this is what I hear. I have been fortunate in that no publisher has ever said that to me; they simply dropped me after one or two novels (until I had the good fortune to meet Michael, who has published me at Carcanet since 1986). I suppose they knew talking to me would do no good. Nor have I felt, what is perhaps even more insidious, that there were unspoken pressures, that unless I wrote in a certain way… This happens of course in the world of art as well. Andrzej told me that for the whole of the time he was at the Marlborough he felt he was being tolerated rather than loved or at least respected, until they finally announced that they would no longer go on representing him. Fortunately he found Purdy Hicks, a smaller gallery but one that cherished him, gave him the feeling that they were proud to represent him. Sadly, that did not happen to Rosalind with her writing. Rightly unwilling to bow to 'market pressures', yet also feeling that she had not given up so much in her life only to write for the drawer, she was always – and still is, despite the late success of *Our Horses in Egypt* and its winning the James Tait Black Memorial Prize – too uncompromising for the many commercial publishers who seem to have forgotten the old adage that successful authors help finance less immediately successful ones. Or perhaps have forgotten what good writing looks like.

But this is not really what I wanted to get into here. Rather I wanted to touch on what led Warhol to quip, in answer to the question of what it was he most desired: 'A boss on retainer.' That is a compressed and witty expression of what every modern artist desires: someone who will tell him what to do but who he can fire at will. An impossible condition, as Mann's *Dr. Faustus* brings out in excruciating detail. The delightful OULIPO, whose adherents are encouraged to create their own constraints, brings out clearly that constraints as such are no solution. With Queneau and Perec they were a spur to creativity, but the majority of OULIPO products have been spasmodically amusing, sometimes delightful (Roubaud's book-length *Ode à la ligne 29 des autobus Parisien* in perfect French Alexandrines), but too often tedious. Nor can one argue that Queneau and Perec had 'something to say' and the others did not. It's deeper and more complicated than that. I remember Max in a pre-concert talk, when asked about his use of magic squares in the works he wrote on first settling in Orkney, saying: 'In themselves such constraints are nothing. I've written good works using them and bad works using them.' Unfortunately he did not go on to suggest why he thought this should have been the case.

In my own experience subject and form must come together. I have had what I thought were brilliant ideas for novels but was never able to find the right form and the whole thing never got off the ground; and I have had brilliant formal ideas for which I was never able to find the right subject matter. One sees Virginia Woolf in *A Writer's Diary*, struggling with this, especially with *The Waves*, which is the book whose genesis she writes about most fully there. From the moment she experiences the overwhelming sensation brought about by what she describes as 'a fin breaking out of the water', she searches – for what? Not exactly a subject but a mixture of form and the interaction of characters that will *realise* that experience. And she cannot rest till it is found and *The Waves* emerges. Even there, though, her own sense that she had found it, pinned it down – whatever 'it' might be – does not guarantee that novel's success in either artistic or commercial terms. It was the first VW novel I 'got' – I was twenty-two and had tried *Orlando* and *Mrs Dalloway* but without ever really getting into them, and then I read *The Waves* twice in four days, unbearably moved. Recently, though, trying to re-read it, I found it mannered beyond belief. Who was right, my twenty-two-year-old self or my seventy-five-year-old self? And what does right mean anyway?

7.5.2020

Another spell of perfect Spring weather. Yesterday up to Mt. Harry via the big sloping field and then down and round the big racecourse, West side, through the wood and down between the fields. At that point the hawthorn blossom all round us overwhelming. Never seen it so full, so white, especially the triangle between the fields opposite, on the Eastern side of the slope. But everywhere it hit us. And every time we pass them the two oaks that guard the slope up to Mt Harry have subtly changed. The beauty of great single trees, marking out their space in so many different ways, but always satisfyingly. For most of my life just the big racecourse was a long enough walk but now we double it and think nothing of it. It shows how with practice one establishes new norms.

Boris J. at Prime Minister's Questions facing Starmer for the first time. Feel they are both sparring, Starmer holding back so much, Boris acting the shamed and contrite, most unusual for him, but clearly a strategy now he can no longer bluster in the face of the overwhelming evidence that the UK has on the whole done worse than most other countries in terms of preparing and planning for this pandemic. He admitted all failings, unlike his terrified lieutenants, who just revert to the old Tory tactics of answering damaging questions – about schools, care homes, lack of PPE, whatever – by showering the questioner with statistics and talking of money spent. But as we're seeing with this crisis, they may spend money, they may, for all we know, have the best of intentions, but the rhetoric and the reality simply don't match up. Even the BBC keep calling it out by interviewing, in this instance, care home managers and headmasters who say PPE has still not arrived and the lunch voucher scheme is unworkable, leading – in the latter case – to schools and sometimes even individual headmasters paying out to get the food and then using their staff to deliver it.

Friendship

'You have a gift for friendship,' Marianne said to me once, and I was very struck by the remark. I had not really thought about it. Why should it be? What does it mean, to have a gift for friendship?

She may have been right, yet that gift goes hand in hand with a natural tendency to isolate myself. Both, I think now, grew out of the peculiarities of my life, thrown together with my mother from my birth in France at the start of the war to our later life in England, knowing that I had her absolute love (an instinctive knowledge only grasped after her death), but also finding in her not just a protective mother but, as I grew to manhood, a friend with so many of the same interests as me. Her love gave me the confidence to believe that whoever I felt could become a good friend would be only too pleased to have me as a friend; her friendship gave me the sense that I didn't need other friends.

Yet I did need them, and the confidence given by my mother's love (it may have been absolute but that did not stop it often being critical – she was never a *doting* mother) was I'm sure a big factor in my ability to make friends. I can see now that often a new friendship was akin to sexual passion, though never with a sexual or should I say a physical dimension to it – just the same need to see the other person as often as possible and to endear myself to them. And with some friendships, as with what I took to be love, I would gradually realise that my need was greater than the other person's and as a consequence I would find my ardour cooling.

That is why I so disagree with Proust's dismissal of friendship, his insistence that while sexual desire (usually unrequited in the case of Marcel) feeds our search for fulfilment by enriching our understanding of ourselves and of the world, friendship is merely a way of avoiding facing ourselves, like attending dinner parties and musical soirées. On the contrary, I find, it is often friends who help us find ourselves, fulfil our destinies – though of course I recognise that friendship is no substitute for the actual (solitary) work of writing and thinking.

I had no friends in my first five years, which is understandable enough. Other people (I look at Tamar's daughters, nieces and nephews) grow up with siblings or cousins of roughly their own age and even if they drift apart in later life there is always that bond of shared memories and experiences. I had none of that, yet it was in first childhood that my friendship with my mother started, in La Bourboule, as I watched her carve the tops of walking sticks into faces or played with the wooden letters she carved in order to teach me the alphabet.

I have no friends I am still in touch with from my years in Egypt, from the age of five to fifteen, though I was a gregarious child and, unlike most of my contemporaries, could count my friends among both the European boys I mixed with at the club and the Egyptian boys with whom I took part in swimming training and competitions and in games of football and tennis. Being good at sports was clearly part of what made friendship easier, as became clear when I spent a year as a day boy in an English public school and learned how to play rugby, hockey and even that most weird of games, fives.

Always boys, in Egypt. There were plenty of girls, but they never seemed to become friends, only objects of desire and adolescent lust.

Any friends I had from Egypt were dispersed round the globe in the autumn of 1956, when the Suez war broke out, in the aftermath of which the English, the French and the Jews (less promptly) were expelled. They ended up in Italy, France and the States (and no doubt elsewhere), from where news of them dribbled through to me in the ensuing years. But when, some time in the early years of this century (it may have been 2006, the fiftieth anniversary of Suez), I received an email from someone I had been at school with, now living in America, informing me that there would be a grand reunion in Cairo of the 'last sixth form of Victoria College', and that I was cordially invited, though I toyed with the idea in the end I turned down the invitation. What, at sixty-six, did I have in common with those people? A reunion would only be an embarrassment as we all scanned unfamiliar faces on unfamiliar bodies and tried to give them names. For a few intense childhood years our lives had intertwined, but that was then and now I at any rate did not – I realised – have any desire to see those 'friends' again.

That all changed when I went up to Oxford. The few friends I made there were of paramount importance to my life. Four in particular. David Phillips, the quiet modest butcher's son from Cardiff who loved Haydn and only wanted to teach music when he graduated, and with whom I went on a number of walking holidays – to Scotland, to Wales – and who vanished after graduating. John Mepham, the biochemist turned philosopher, the most intelligent man I have ever had the good fortune to get to know, who followed me to Sussex. I have said more about him in the tribute to him I wrote after his sad early death. Gordon Crosse, the composer who first introduced me to new music and with whom I shared a flat in our last year as undergraduates. And Robert Henderson, the graduate student from Durham at work on a thesis on a sixteenth century Scottish musical manuscript, who looked like James Mason and who got me reading books as different as Augustine's *Confessions* and James Hogg's *Diary of a Justified Sinner*. In the end I found his willed withdrawal from the world too much to bear and, sadly, we drifted apart.

I wish, like Kurtag, I could write a series of musical (or, in my case, fictional) tributes to the friends I have made since then, both at Sussex and in the wider world, celebrating them and bringing out all they have given me and how much poorer my life would have been without them. But I can't and this will have to do.

8.5.2020

When, in 1962, we finally acquired British passports, my mother said: 'Now wherever you go you will be treated with respect.' Fast forward to 2020 and here is a sample of the world's view of Britain's handling of the pandemic. Italy's *Corriere della Sera* (partly no doubt because Italy is no longer seen as the country worst affected): 'a nightmare from which you cannot wake up but in which you landed because of your own fault and stupidity.' Britain 'lost the advantage fate and Italy gave it and is served badly by 'a very weak cabinet' and Johnson's own character: 'He's not Trump, though there is something similar in their approaches. In this kind of challenge you need to work hard on details. He's not a details person.' Germany's DPA: 'Only a few weeks ago Britain had the reputation of a country in which the coronavirus was only spreading cautiously. Politicians were already slapping each other on the back and praising the health system which was better prepared for the pandemic than any other country in the world. But that has quickly revealed itself to be a fallacy... There are now many signs that the government massively underestimated the pandemic.' Greece's daily, *Ethnos* opines that Johnson is 'more dangerous than coronavirus', and adds that one of the greatest tragedies of the pandemic is that incompetent leaders such as Johnson and Trump 'were at the helm in a time of emergency.'

Northrop Frye

No one outside academia knows the name of Northrop Frye these days, and even within the profession he is hardly ever mentioned, while interesting minor critics such as Bloom and Empson go on being written about and praised as if they were Coleridge or Eliot.

I am not surprised, though saddened. Even in his heyday, in the fifties and sixties, Frye was treated as something of a crank except by a few devoted readers and students. I read his finest book, the book he was born to write, *Anatomy of Criticism*, as an undergraduate, probably in my second year, in 1959 or 60. It was like a breath of fresh air. The study of literature at the time was dominated either by the harsh morality and narrow interests of Leavis and his disciples, or by New Critics, unconcerned with history or the writer's background but wishing to look at each work (mainly poetry) entirely in and for itself, an approach which went back to I.A. Richards and Cambridge in the 20s. And there was still of course the cohort of old-fashioned scholars wedded to a historical and positivist view of the arts. *Anatomy of Criticism* (1957) came out of none of these traditions. Frye claimed that it grew out of his study of Blake, which had resulted in a massive book on the poet published in the previous decade, but I suspect his response to Blake was itself the result of a peculiar temperament and a peculiar, indeed unique background.

He was born in Canada, studied there and taught there all his life. But I think that rather than trying to see his work as somehow peculiarly 'Canadian', whatever that might mean, it's more helpful to consider it in the light of a remark he makes somewhere that when he was young he could not decide whether to become a pianist or a Baptist preacher. I think we need to see his criticism as an amalgam of the two. And since 'pianist' is a very vague term it is worth remembering that a later volume of his, devoted to the art of criticism, is called *The Well-Tempered Critic*, which suggests that he was drawn not to the Romantic repertoire but to Bach's keyboard works, those quasi-exhaustive studies of all the possibilities of the well-tempered clavier and the tonal system that had developed over the course of the previous century. (The harpsichordist and music historian Malcolm Proud describes the word Übung, Practice, used by Bach for his Partitas, *Klavier-Übung*, as having 'broader implications than just practising an instrument, more of somebody exercising their talents or practising their profession.') It also, in the quietest and most modest way possible, sets its face against the polemical tone of both the Leavisites and the New Critics, as well as asserting that it had nothing in common with the often informative but usually dull productions of the scholars. Rather, it will look at literature as Bach looked at the keyboard: as a world of partially realised possibilities which call out for anatomisation.

But before I understood any of this what won me over to *Anatomy of Criticism* was the sheer range of his reach and the extraordinary sensitivity and astuteness of his judgements. I remember, when in my third year at Oxford I was sharing digs with the composer Gordon Crosse, running down the index of *Anatomy* out loud for Gordon to hear: accent and stress; Achilles; Adam and Eve; Addison, Joseph; Adler, Alfred; Adonis; Aeschylus; aesthetics; *agon*; *alazon*; alchemy; Aldhelm; Alger, Horatio; allegory; ambiguity and association; American Indians; Thomas Amory; Amos; anagogic meaning; *anagnorisi*s (cognition, recognition, discovery) – *see also* epiphany; *ananke*; anatomy; Andreyev, Leonid; Andromeda; Angelo; Angst; antimasque; Apemantus; apocalypse and apocalyptic symbolism; Apollo and the Apollonian; Apuleius; *Arabian Nights*; archetypes and archetypal criticism – and we have not even finished with the 'a's.

But, I said, after Gordon had shown himself suitably impressed, this is not just a widely read person showing off. Here he is on Aristophanes: 'In Aristophanes there is usually a central figure who constructs his (or her) own society in the teeth of strong opposition, driving off one after another all the people who come to prevent or exploit him, and eventually achieving a heroic triumph, complete with mistresses, in which he is sometimes assigned the honors of a reborn god.' And on *Hamlet*: 'In Hamlet, as Mr. Eliot has shown, the amount of emotion generated by the hero is too great for its objects; but surely the correct conclusion to draw from this fine insight is that *Hamlet* is best apprehended as a tragedy of *Angst* or of melancholy as a state in itself, rather than purely as an Aristotelian imitation of an action.' On *Ivanhoe*: 'one very common convention of the nineteenth-century novel is the use of two heroines, one dark and one light. The dark one is as a rule passionate, haughty, plain, foreign or Jewish, and in some way associated with the undesirable or with some kind of forbidden fruit like incest. When the two are involved with the same hero, the plot usually has to get rid of the dark one or to make her into a sister if the story is to end happily. Examples include *Ivanhoe, The Last of the Mohicans*,

The Woman in White, Ligeia, Pierre (a tragedy because the hero chooses the dark girl, who is also his sister), *The Marble Faun*, and countless incidental treatments. A male version forms the symbolic basis of *Wuthering Heights*. This device is as much a convention as Milton's calling Edward King by a name out of Virgil's *Eclogues*, but it shows a confused or, as we say, "unconscious" approach to conventions.'

What we sense in all these passages, is not just a naturally compartmentalising mind but a passionate reader, alert to differences as well as similarities, wishing all the time to illuminate the literature he is talking about, not to fit things into a pre-ordained scheme or score points. Eliot is not rebuked for his remarks on *Hamlet* but we are asked to reconsider his criticism of the play by setting it in a new context. One can imagine Barthes alerting us to the unconscious symbolism of the nineteenth century novel to make a political point about the bourgeoisie or in some way to 'free' his readers from the false magic of a Scott or a Melville; Frye too seeks to free his readers, but only so as to enable them to enjoy literature the more. And enjoy literature he certainly does. Taking the term in its very widest sense, his book finds a place for Rousseau, Macaulay, Kant, Newman, Oswald Spengler, the *Mahabharata* and the Bible, as well as the cartoonists of the *New Yorker*.

Too often Frye has been reduced, even by those who admire him, to a kind of structuralist *avant la lettre*. Of course he had an ordering, classifying bent of mind. But that is deployed for quite other purposes than Levi-Strauss or Genette. At the heart of his work is an apocalyptic, mystical vision of the possibilities of the imagination, no doubt linked to his youthful wish to become a Baptist preacher, but, as with Dante's mysticism and Bach's Lutheranism, it is so rooted in a human and humane vision of life that one does not need to share his beliefs to be affected by his work. This quote from his Blake book brings it out beautifully:

And in Rabelais, where huge creatures rear up and tear themselves out of Paris and Touraine, bellowing for drink and women, combing cannon balls out of their hair, eating six pilgrims in a salad, excreting like dinosaurs and copulating like the ancient sons of God who made free with the daughters of men, we come perhaps closest of all to what Blake meant by the resurrection of the body. Rabelais' characters are what Blake called his 'Giant Forms', and they are the horsemen who ride over the earth in the day of the trumpet and alarm, where we, in our sublunary world, see nothing but anguish and death.

Rabelais, like Blake, gives us an image of what the unfettered imagination can make of desire (male desire at any rate!). For Frye (as, I suspect, for a Blakean like Tim) this is a Utopian vision we must strive for and may one day acquire; for me, while it is wonderful to imagine, it is highly dangerous to believe that we can bring it about on earth, and those who have tried, like Thomas Müntzer, who led the short-lived Peasants' Revolt in Germany in the sixteenth century, and Stalin and Hitler in our own time, have brought nothing but suffering, death and destruction. I think Rabelais is of my mind, and again and again shows up in his books the folly of believing such an illusion. I also think that there is a melancholy side to Rabelais that links him to Mallarmé and Beckett rather than to Blake, a feeling that once literature meant something but now it floats free of the world and if writers wish to be true to their calling they must somehow come to terms with this. But I grant that there are aspects of his books, moments in his fictions, where the image Frye has of Rabelais is more apt than mine. And the quality of the imagination on display, both in his work and in Frye's, makes me happy to contemplate their Utopian vision.

Frye has probably been less of an influence on my own thinking about literature and culture than have Erich Heller and Maurice Blanchot, explorers of the disinherited mind, the unanchored vision, but he has shed a sort of benign light on all my subsequent reading and indeed on my whole life. It is difficult to describe except perhaps, returning to the title of *The Well-Tempered Critic*, as the feeling one has on listening to a master of the keyboard performing Bach, summed up in an author and a play that were close to Frye's heart: 'How beauteous mankind is! O brave new world/ That has such people in't.'

---

9. 5.2020

Yesterday was the seventy-fifth anniversary of VE Day. One can imagine what Boris was hoping to make of it: We stood alone when Europe was overrun; plucky Britain defeated the evil German foe; etc. Fortunately the pandemic scuppered his plans. It might have been thought that the rules about staying indoors and keeping two metres apart and so on would have made a damp squib of it, but it seems on the contrary to have enhanced it. The Queen even came on at 9 p.m., the precise hour at which her father George VI had addressed the nation on 8 May 1945. Of course she made the connection between then and now and delivered an uplifting message about how 'we, the British people', had stood together and never wavered in 'our' belief that 'we' would come through – but she managed also to stress Churchill's plea that 'all the nations must work together to rebuild', etc. And left the country to reflect on the obvious fact that the virus was not an enemy who would surrender on a certain date but an unseen killer which might never be stamped out.

Meanwhile chaos reigns in government as Sunak fights for a quick re-opening before the entire economy lies (as he and those like him see it) in ruins, while Hancock and Johnson, terrified at their inability to substantially lower the rate of infection and death, struggle to articulate a coherent strategy, and the scientific advisors on SAGE make their feelings known about their reports to the government being so heavily redacted before being allowed into the public domain.

Fugue

Fugue, at its simplest as well as its most sophisticated, is a figure of movement, not movement towards, but round and round. It is always a flight and a chase, that is, it always involves two elements, and it is often difficult to tell who is fleeing and who is chasing, and there is no end to it.

It must have been in the late seventies or early eighties that I wrote a short story called 'Fuga'. I had become fascinated by the paintings of Vuillard, those strange rooms in which it takes a while to distinguish the occupants – mainly women – from the wallpaper, leaving one with an uncomfortable feeling of oppression. I discovered that Vuillard's mother and sister were seamstresses and that both he and his sister were very much tied to their mother and their world with her and unable or unwilling to escape from it. I was about to write or had just written a novel 'about' Bonnard, *Contre-Jour*, and I found – as I still find – it natural to try to find equivalents in language for what has moved me in a work of art. (I think the first time I did anything like that was the little story I wrote about one of the Vermeers in the National Gallery, 'Woman at the Clavichord', with its multiple mirroring effects, and then I tried it again with that extraordinary Otto Dix painting of the brothel in Hamburg (or was it Brussels?) with the naked prostitute on the uniformed officer's knee mirrored ad infinitum on the walls, ceiling and floor.) I began to develop a little story about a woman desperate to escape a stifling family, but also desperate not to leave a nurturing family, and the story seemed naturally to take the form of a fugue.

Thomas Mann writes so beautifully about music in *Dr Faustus* (helped, one gathers, by Adorno), and one of the musical highlights of that book is Wendell Kretschmar's lecture on Beethoven and the Fugue, and why Beethoven turned to fugue late in life, most notably, of course in the 'Grosse Fugue' that was to end the B Flat Major uartet but which was found at first to be incomprehensible and unplayable and for which he was persuaded to substitute a shorter, lighter, 'easier' finale. But though I had read and savoured Kretschmar's lecture when an undergraduate, it was not till many years later that I found myself writing the Vuillard story – such is the way with 'influences'. And it was not till many years after that that I found myself returning to thoughts about fugues and flight, when writing *Goldberg: Variations*, my 'take' on Bach's keyboard masterpiece.

I'd never thought of writing such a work. I had wanted to celebrate the 250th anniversary of Bach's death in 2000 with a little story based on the anecdote told by his first biographer, Johann Nikolaus Forkel, about the origins of the *Goldberg Variations*. I didn't want to write a piece of historical fiction – as I didn't with the Bonnard book – and so decided to transplant Forkel's anecdote from Germany to England and from music to literature, so that instead of a harpsichordist being invited to the court of a German princeling to play in order to relieve him of his insomnia, I dreamed up an English country gentleman inviting a writer to come and read to him. Unfortunately – as I thought at the time, perhaps fortunately I now think – I had happened to hear Judith Weir talking on the radio about how much Bach still meant to modern composers and sent her the little story. She wrote back to say she had read it in one go on a train journey, liked it very much, and when could we expect the other 29? (Beethoven wrote 30 variations, with, as prologue and epilogue, what he called an aria, out of which the rest emerges and to which it returns.) I wrote back to tell her that was not something I was planning to do, that I had neither the skill nor really the wish to do so. But the idea, once lodged in my mind, would not leave me, and eventually I felt I had to see where it would lead. As I say, I had no desire to write a work of historical fiction, but while one can evade the issue in a short story it could not be evaded, I felt, in a whole book. So how and where and above all when to set it?

I struggled with the problem and with writing it for years, giving it up for a while but finding it kept on asking to be resolved and going back to it in the late '90s. In the course of that I found a way to talk about the form Bach had made his own, the fugue, but I did so in a variety of ways, including a meditation on Kierkegaard's *Either/Or*, a work made up out of the argument of two antithetical types, each arguing for the truth and validity of his position, his way of life.

Whether any of this has added to either the enjoyment or the benefit of mankind is of course a moot point. But I think one can see in a number of modern writers that the unease with the linear direction in which the traditional novel seems constrained to run has led to a proliferation of alternative forms, many of them, such as the ballad and the fugue, resurrected from more ancient poetic and musical practices. And of course not only in the realm of fiction but also in that of art and music. But that is for another time.

10.5.2020

A hundred days since the coronavirus first surfaced in the papers in Britain at the end of January, when the Johnson government was still wrapped up in the 31 January celebrations as their

Brexit project came to fruition and Britain officially left the EU; and roughly fifty days since T arrived and I started this diary (21 and 22 March). It is now widely recognised throughout the world and partially so in Britain that this country is the sick man of Europe, having managed the outbreak worse than any other country except for Trump's America and still clearly struggling to plug the gaps in equipment, testing and tracking essential to stamp it out and to send out clear signals to the public about what lies ahead.

Hot again yesterday and again up to Mt Harry and then back along the perimeter of the old racecourse on the Eastern side. Wish I could distinguish all the beautiful birdsongs we hear and all the wild flowers we see – or even some of them. As always I find myself signally ill-equipped, as someone naturally drawn to nature, to give names to what I see and hear. This is less of an issue for T, who, while moved by landscape and light, especially by bright blue skies and sunshine, is more interested in people than in flora and fauna. But it is sheer joy to walk out onto the Downs in fine weather at this time of year as we have done every day since T arrived. And as we walked along the Eastern perimeter of the great valley sloping southwards, with the sea visible at Newhaven in the distance and the sound of the ewes in the field above us calling to their young ones in deep tones and the lambs responding in their shriller voices, I felt my heart moving to a different and deeper rhythm, as when walking by the sea and hearing the pulse of the waves breaking onto the shore, retreating and returning.

What this lockdown has done is make me focus more intently on what I can recognise as what is good for me, as happens so often in S. Pietro or Bressanone, when there are none of the distractions of normal daily life. Except that this is even better as I have my mornings to work and then the rest of the day to walk, talk, read, eat and listen to music.

Gabriel

I don't really know how other people feel about their names, though I did know two young women who felt so dissatisfied with the ones their parents had given them that they chose a new one in their late teens (T is one of them). Personally I'm perfectly happy with my name, it's common enough in England for people not to look baffled when I give it (though the barely literate will add an l and an e at the end, giving me what I consider a very ugly girl's name), while unusual enough not to feel every Tom Dick and Harry has it. It is also a Jewish and biblical name without being aggressively so, like Isaiah or Joshua.

In Hebrew the name means 'strong man of God' or 'champion of God', *gibor el*, which is also pleasing. In Egypt the little boys would run after me holding out their hand and shouting *'gib riyal'*, *'gib riyal'*, meaning 'give me a *riyal*', a piece of money. I would shoo them away while admiring their punning. People who have tried Gaby on me have been quickly squashed, for much as I like the full name the shortened form has always struck me as unpleasant and even demeaning.

My mother told me she chose my name not because it was Jewish or biblical but because she had been reading a book by Chesterton called *The Poet and the Lunatics*, in which an eccentric poet called Gabriel Gale employs his extraordinary gifts of empathy to solve or prevent crimes perpetrated by madmen. It is often difficult, in these stories, very Chestertonian in their deployment of paradox and with their concern with the imagination, sin and salvation, and clearly precursors to the Father Brown stories, to tell which is the poet and which the lunatic. Why my mother was reading the book at that time I never found out. She talked to me about reading Queneau in those years in France before and during the war, and Char and Éluard as the war was raging ('They were very important to us at the time,' she said, 'though when the war was over they seemed rather thin to me.') But she never talked about reading any English literature. I wonder where the Chesterton came from.

She and my father had another child, a girl, two years younger than me, but she died after ten days, as a result, my mother said, of malnutrition (my mother's). 'I felt guilty,' she said on one of the rare occasions she talked about the whole sad episode, 'because I starved myself to give you a little more than the rations allowed, and then this happened.' I mention it here because after my mother's death, when I was trying to write about her, I realised that I did not know the name of my little sister. I wrote to my aunt asking if she knew and she wrote back saying that she thought it was Elizabeth. I find that hard to believe. Even in 1943 my mother would not have chosen such a Christian name for her child when something as neutral as Eva or Nelly, her mother's name, would have done. I thought at the time I could probably find out by writing to the authorities in La Bourboule, who would have a birth certificate, but something held me back. As it still does.

When my mother died and I organised a memorial event for her in the Meeting House at the University, hosted by my dear friend Andrew Robinson, the priest in charge of the University Chapel, who had been visiting her at the time of her death in the Brighton hospital, and by Jeff Newman, the friend and rabbi who had officiated at her funeral, and when the large gathering grew silent as the official starting time for the event approached, Jeff leant over to me and said: 'I'm going to introduce it. But I need to know Sacha's Jewish name.' 'Jewish name?' I said. 'I don't know that she ever had one. That was her name, Sacha Elena.' I learned afterwards that it is a custom among English and American Jews, who seem often to have terribly 'English' names like Arnold and John, to have a Hebrew name as well. I had never heard of such a thing in Egypt, and it makes me wonder: Do I have a Jewish name that is hidden even from me? An intriguing thought. Or is my name quite Jewish enough not to need it? Not, I have to say, a question that has ever kept me awake at night.

11.5.2020

Monday. Start of the eighth week since lockdown. Boris on television last night to announce that while everything must stay as it is, everything can also change! He alters the slogan from 'Stay at home' to 'Be vigilant', a meaningless term, first used in the aftermath of terrorist strikes, and which has always reminded me of those signs one sees on roads in the Italian Alps: 'Pericolo! Caduti Sassi!' – 'Danger! Stones falling!' The cautious motorist will creep along, looking out anxiously. The paranoid motorist will avoid the road entirely. Most of us keep driving, treating it as part of the landscape, since we have never actually seen stones falling off the mountains. And so it is with the new slogan: the anxious will wash their hands even more often, look under their beds, never venture out; the reckless will do what they wish, feeling the government has at last released them from unwelcome shackles; and most of us will go on doing what we were doing before. Especially nonsensical given that while the curve may have started to flatten, in the new jargon, it has certainly not started to decline and there are still huge numbers infected every day and large numbers of deaths.

Gardens

I don't and never have gardened – have always felt that if it's a fine day I'd rather go out for a walk than break my back weeding or planting. Yet I love the idea of gardens and gardening, especially if that includes a vegetable patch. It's only that I've never learned how to grow anything and wouldn't trust myself to set about it correctly even if I had the time and patience. And while I like the idea of books by people who have made and lovingly tended gardens, just as I like the idea of books about nature, I can only rarely bring myself to read them because somehow the gap between what the author feels and what his or her words convey remains – for me – unbridgeable. As it does with travel books.

Yet I myself have written a book with a garden, or at least a park which includes a garden, at its centre: *Moo Pak*. I can't remember when the idea of Moor Park came to me. What there was at the start was the sense of two people walking and talking – or rather, one person talking and the other listening as they walked through the parks and heaths of London. But then it became clear to me that what the talker would be talking about (among other things, I wanted a free-wheeling form which would allow him to ramble both figuratively and literally) was a book he was trying to write, and that this book would have Jonathan Swift and especially his time as secretary to Sir William Temple, the seventeenth century diplomat and writer, and his country house at Moor Park in Surrey, at its centre. As a graduate student at Oxford I had begun, rather desultorily, a B.Litt on Swift's *Tale of a Tub* and how it fitted in to the narrative traditions developed almost two centuries earlier by Rabelais and Erasmus in response to the crisis of authority that then engulfed Europe. Swift wrote *A Tale of a Tub*, his early masterpiece and, to my mind, the best thing he ever did, apart perhaps from the much slighter late *Directions to Servants*, in the years he had been Temple's secretary, the 1690s, and I had been fascinated by the relation of his writing to the slightly smug and confidently orthodox writings of his patron. Swift was also there as tutor to the young charge of Temple's sister, Lady Gifford, a bright girl called Esther

Johnson. It was a position fraught with ambiguity – was the secretary and tutor a servant or a member of the family, was his place at table above or below the salt (which by tradition was placed in medieval times in the centre of the table)? – and one that would remain so throughout the next century and a half. Intelligent and educated youths of the Romantic period often resolved it by falling in love with the mistress of the house – Hölderlin is the most famous example, and Charlotte Brontë gives us a female variant. Swift fell in love with his tutee.

Be that as it may I soon saw that while the young Jonathan Swift might be the obsession of my walker and talker, an even more central theme to my book would be the opposition between human and animal and between human languages and animal languages, topics that fascinated Swift, and, even more generally of the raw and the cooked, that is, the cultivated and the wild. Country houses in both England and the continent at the time had gardens divided into a cultivated area round the house and a much larger area of moorland and woodland beyond. I decided the spine of the book would be the metamorphosis of Moor Park over the years into a variety of institutions: among others, a lunatic asylum, a centre for the study of primates, and eventually a local school in which non-native English speakers, asked to write a history of Moor Park itself, would misspell it as Moo Pak. All of this, I felt, would allow me to explore the Swiftian themes of madness, and animal languages and Swift's own tormented life. The notions of *moor* and of *park*, garbled in the title, would control the whole.

None of the many metamorphoses of the house were true, they were all invented by me, but I hoped they were plausible. And a letter I received when the book was published gave me the satisfaction of feeling that in this at least I had succeeded. It was from a descendent of Charles Darwin, informing me that during 1857–59 the young botanist had taken the water cure treatment at Dr Edward Wickstead Lane's Hydropathic Establishment at Moor Park, near Farnham in Surrey, and asking me why I had not included this in my book. Of course while I was delighted at the thought that my fantasies had managed to impose themselves on readers with the force of historical reality, I was furious with myself at the thought that my refusal to do any research into the actual history of the house – a refusal driven by my dislike of the whole notion of 'doing research' for a novel – had robbed me of a heaven-sent opportunity. For would not Darwin have fitted perfectly into all the topics I was exploring?

Driven by the idea of the tension between *moor* and *park* I did do a little arbitrary exploration of the history of the English and European notion of a country estate, and learned much about eighteenth-century landscape gardeners like Capability Brown and about the landed gentry's desire to incorporate into their estates both the wild and the tamed. I also came across a book, Claudia Lazzaro's *The Italian Renaissance Garden*, which included, as well as splendid photographs of actual gardens, some magical frescoes, especially the ones at Villa Lanta at Bagnaia, near Viterbo, much more resonant, to my mind, than even the garden itself, painted in the 1570s by a young Emilian, Raffaelino di Reggio, who died at twenty-eight. One of the reasons these bowled me over is obviously that photographs of gardens can never be a substitute for actually walking through them, feeling the air, smelling the smells, but that paintings can evoke such feelings; Rafaellino's frescoes, all pale washes of bluey greens and pinks, corresponded in some strange way to my dreams of what my book would be like. That fresco garden is the one I would really love to walk in.

I still find it very difficult to grasp what this enforced lock-down is giving me. Something important, of that I have no doubt, but what?

Perhaps the only way to find out is to keep working.

The strange novel stirred up by Magritte's *L'Assassin Menacé* has been given impetus by repeated hearings of Bach's fifth partita in G Major, played on the harpsichord by Malcolm Proud, the Irish harpsichordist and Bach scholar. Impetus and form.

Part of me still thinks it's mad. But I am beginning to be intrigued.

Cloudless blue sky, but forecast is that this will change after 12. A shame as I love going out on the Downs when it's like that, but I seem only able to work in the mornings. If you can call it work.

Genealogy

Suddenly everyone is at it. Grandparents mainly, but not only them. Partly this is driven by the internet and the ability nowadays of everyone to find out a great deal about their families without leaving the comfort of their homes. And even people who have never thought about it are bombarded by online researchers offering their services for 'a modest fee'.

But Nicolette, my distant cousin in Ringmer, was already at it twenty years ago, when I really got to know her. Dashing with Jimmy her husband to Alexandria, to look at the inscriptions on the tombs in the Jewish cemetery (where she broke her leg falling into an unseen hole), attending events in Ferrara in honour of the city's Jews and Jewish past (Bassani is of course Ferrarese, and our family, like so many Italian

Jewish families, is convinced *Il Giardino dei Finzi-Contini* is about them), becoming bosom friends with a strange couple from Manchester, he an Egyptologist at the BM and she a genealogist with whom Nicolette could discuss her findings. And she certainly does know the history of our family, from the time our ancestor (my mother's great grandfather), Dottore Elia Rossi, left Ferrara for Egypt in 1843 down to the present, every scandal, every elopement, every premature death, she knows them all. And now her knowledge is displayed for all to hear in Bea's two hour and forty-minute interview with her for *Sephardi Voices UK*.

I had suggested both Jimmy and Nicolette as ideal subjects for Bea's project and she arranged to come down and interview both of them on video. She arrived in Ringmer with her cameraman at 10 a.m., and as Bea had said she thought she would be done by late afternoon I went round at about 5. She was taking a short break in the interview she was doing with Jimmy (in the end she did not leave till 10 p.m.). 'How was Nicolette?' I asked. 'She's a star,' she said. 'An absolute star.' This surprised me. I love Nicolette but would never describe her as a star. But the interview, which I subsequently saw, bore her out. Nicolette spoke slowly, looking at the camera, choosing her words, talking without any hesitation, and revealing not only a fascinating family history but also a difficult life of her own, plagued by personal tragedy, all without a trace of self-pity or sentimentality. One of the best interviews of this kind I have ever seen, and since getting to know Bea I have seen a fair number of them.

I suppose in the old days family lore tended to be passed down from mother to daughter, or, sometimes, from grandmother to grandchildren. And births and deaths were often inscribed in the family Bible. As with everything, we know so much more today but perhaps know it less well, less viscerally. When I wrote *A Life* I had got nearly all my information from my mother and then from my aunt, who was reliable, or at least informative about their childhood together, but much less so about their ancestry. Nicolette had lent me a book she possessed which proved very helpful, a published biography of our ancestor Elia Rossi written shortly after he died by a member of the Ferrarese Jewish community, full of the grandiloquent language common to tributes of the time, and of that distinctive Italian Enlightenment language, eliding the God of the Jews with the God of Kant, which was no doubt Elia's too.

Where does it get us, all this passion for genealogy? I suppose it may help future historians, but from a Nietzschean perspective does it not smack of a fear of death? But then could one not say the same about diaries? About writing in general, art in general? Is it not more about curiosity, the child's natural curiosity about his or her parents and ancestors? Is it not a wonderful gift that the internet has given us, that we can now find out in a day what it might have taken a lifetime and huge cost in time and travel to find out before?

A few years ago, probably in 2015, I got a message on my email from a certain Mark Baker. I am an Australian journalist, he said, writing a biography of the famous Australian war correspondent Philip Schuler. While researching his book, he explained, he had to face the fact that Schuler seemed to have been engaged to a lady from an Egyptian Jewish family, Nelly Rabinovitch, and was indeed still engaged to her when he was killed on the Western Front in 1917, aged twenty-seven. But try as he might Baker had not been able to find out anything more about this enigmatic lady – until, via the internet, he came upon my book, *A Life*, in which I recount the episode from the perspective of Nelly and of her daughters, my mother and my aunt. At that point the whole of his book came together and he knew he would be able to finish it. He was writing to thank me and to say that, married as he was to a Turkish Australian lady and in the habit of visiting her family in Istanbul regularly he wondered if he could come over to England when he next did so and meet me. He also wondered if I would give him permission to use one or two of the photographs of my grandmother which I had included in my book.

This was extraordinary. I had known of Philip Schuler merely as an Australian journalist who met my newly widowed grandmother when he was in Cairo with the Australian troops prior to their deployment in Gallipoli, and that is how I had described him in my book. I had no idea that he was 'the great Australian war correspondent', or, indeed, anything about him.

My grandmother had lost her Russian doctor husband in 1915, but they had been estranged for a few years before that, after he had developed the symptoms of the dementia that would eventually kill him. She was in Cairo with her two little girls, aged five and six, when she met Philip Schuler. I had thought that this had led to a rapid engagement, since Schuler was due to sail for Gallipoli; that, having survived that campaign he had been sent to the Western front where he had been killed. In my mother's memory what was mainly lodged was the day they received news of his death. The girls were in bed when they heard a peremptory knock at the door and two male English voices in urgent conversation with their mother, whereupon she came up to their bedroom and, kneeling by their beds, told them the men were friends of Philip's who had come to say that he had been badly wounded. But they knew from the tone of her voice, said my mother, what she told them the following day, that he was in fact dead. He had been killed by a stray shrapnel and the men had brought her the silver cigarette-case she had given him and which she showed them, bent out of shape by the missile.

What Mark Baker explained, when he came to see us in London with his beautiful wife, was that Philip Schuler was already a star of Australian journalism, himself the son of the then editor of the Melbourne *Age*, for which he wrote, and that, having covered the Gallipoli campaign for the paper, he had returned to Australia and written a book about that defining episode in the forging of the Australian national consciousness, a book that had been published to great acclaim and the royalties for which he left in a strange will he wrote before returning to Europe, no longer as a journalist but as a soldier, to a mysterious 'Nelly Rabinovitch of Cairo, Egypt.' Mark Baker's biography, he told us, would be published to coincide with Anzac Day, 25 April 2016, the Gallipoli centenary, and he promised to send a copy, which I duly received and read in one go.

In lucid prose Baker told the story of the brilliant young journalist, his run-ins with the devious journalist father of Rupert Murdoch, then a young reporter, his remarkable dispatches from the font line, his wish to return to the theatre of war not as a journalist but as one of the men he had grown to admire so much at Gallipoli – and of course of his doomed engagement to my grandmother, herself only twenty-six. The book, published by Allen and Unwin in Australia, has been a great success and has of course been bitterly attacked by the Murdoch press. But the damning portrait it paints of Keith Murdoch will strike anyone who has followed the career of his son as entirely plausible.

What is extraordinary, to me, is how two worlds which merely touched for a moment in the love affair of a beautiful young widow with two little girls and a dashing young journalist in Cairo in 1915–16, the world of my Italian Jewish grandmother and that of an idealistic Australian, and which had remained distinct for so long, were brought together by the internet. Mark Baker's fine book has thrown a new light on my family history, just as my family history has thrown a new light on a very Australian story. The genealogy doesn't change, since Nelly and Philip did not have a chance to marry and have children, but history, for me and my cousin Anna, as for Philip's family, has grown that little bit larger.

13.5.2020

As the government's confused instructions for easing the lockdown start to be implemented Scotland, Wales and N. Ireland are firmly distancing themselves from it, all feeling the infection and death rates have not fallen significantly enough to warrant any changes. David Hunter at Oxford predicts a certain rise in both as a result of the suggested changes and a second spike. In all this one feels incompetent ideologues are playing with people's lives – with my life, it seems, since at seventy-nine I appear to be in a very high-risk category. Not a pleasant thought.

Unsettled weather still, though we are promised some warm sunny days ahead. Lovely though cold walk yesterday.

God

Like so many adolescents in the Western, Protestantised world, at seventeen I was obsessed with the question of whether God existed or not. After all, many of the books I was reading were full of it, and those that weren't seemed thin, somehow, disappointing. That and the related question of an afterlife. I remember I liked the response of one of Dostoevsky's characters to the question: 'Do you believe in the afterlife?' 'Yes, I believe in an afterlife here and now.' I had no idea what it meant but felt I understood it. We must, I knew, put out of our minds the notion of an afterlife as a sort of perpetual continuation of this one; on the other hand the idea that there is no God and nothing apart from *this*, also flew in the face of my experience. Life was not just random and everything was not permitted – but if so, then what?

At Oxford I began to read the mystics, encouraged by my aunt, a great fan of Blake and Jacob Boehme. In the Bodleian I called up Gershom Scholem's *Major Trends in Jewish Mysticism* and plunged into that. I saw myself very much as someone passionately interested in mysticism, so it was hard to have to accept, as I gradually had to, that I was not. Suddenly the whole God thing lost its hold on me. Girls and my writing filled my thoughts, not God or even seeing God in a grain of sand. Thus as a graduate student I found myself thinking about God in a completely different way. Attending John Burrows' wonderful lectures on *Sir Gawain and the Green Knight* and talking to Del Kolve about the book he was writing on the medieval miracle plays made me think again about the wisdom of completely orthodox medieval thought and I realised how much more interesting it was to me than the individual ecstasies of a Meister Eckhard or Julian of Norwich. And I began to understand, as I went deeper into Erasmus, Rabelais, Cervantes and Swift and their powerful critiques of religious bigotry, both Protestant and Catholic, how profoundly the modern world was still influenced by ideas that had been formulated in the course of the Reformation, on both sides of the religious divide, and what a narrowing of human possibility both Puritanism and the Counter-Reformation had led to. I was particularly struck by John Burrows' reading of the end of *Gawain and the Green Knight*, when Gawain returns to Arthur's court from his encounter with the Green Knight and abases himself in public, showing to everyone the green belt he is wearing as a sign of his unique sinfulness, and Arthur counters this not with words but by instructing the entire court to wear a similar girdle – in a sign, Burrows point out, that Gawain is not more sinful than anyone else but neither is he unique. No, says Arthur by his instruction to the court, you are no worse but also no different from the rest of us mortals. Gawain's attitude is not very different from that of Stavrogin in *The Devils*, confessing before Tikhon that he is the most depraved and evil of men, and the holy man quietly rebukes him for his arrogance and fear. And I was also very struck by an essay I read at the time on the medieval English play of the sacrifice of Isaac, which argued that Isaac is at once terrified *and* accepting of his fate, whereas in post-Reformation depictions of this episode he has to be one or the other. The medieval vision, the author argued, was much closer to traditional Christianity in having no difficulty in recognising that our feelings are often in conflict, whereas in the wake of Luther's reforms the notion arises that there is no room for complexity and contradiction: if you are afraid you must root out the fear, if you are weak you must banish the weakness. This is when debates become fierce about whether Christ felt anguish or not as he endured his fate, with the emphasis falling either on his human pain and anguish or on his godlike lack of anguish and fear. Of course these debates had been raging since the beginnings of Christianity, and writers like Swift lose no time in linking Puritan zeal to the Gnostic rejection of Christ's human nature.

In those years, both at Oxford and at Sussex where I began to teach at twenty-three and had the chance to develop ideas that had started to emerge in my last year as an undergraduate, those pressing questions about God fell into abeyance. In my thirties, though, as so often happens, I began, for one reason or another, to think about my Jewish roots. With my wonderful high Anglican friend and colleague Stephen Medcalf I started a course on the Bible and English literature, driven by the belief that it is impossible to understand most English literature up till the twentieth century without some knowledge of the Bible, and that this was becoming more and more rare among our students. At the same time, in the seventies, a new colleague arrived, Michael Wadsworth, an Anglican priest and a semiticist who had been at Oxford writing a thesis under Geza Vermes, and who immediately started recruiting for a class he wished to give, teaching biblical Hebrew to whoever wanted to learn. This led in time to a reading group Stephen and I set up, which in much mutated form is still running, but now in London, in which we read the biblical narratives of the Hebrew Bible in our own time, trying to respond both to the language and the implications of the narrative. I became more and more convinced that reading the Bible in a modern language, while better than nothing, was a poor substitute for reading the Hebrew. And in time both these informal sessions and the teaching, as well as my growing admiration for the way these narratives were written led to *The Book of God: a Response to the Bible*.

As I worked on that book I became more and more aware of how the sparseness of the Bible's narrative style, its reliance on simple statement of fact and dialogue without any attempt to probe the psychology of the characters, was something I was striving for in my own writing and admired in a few modern authors, such as Marguerite Duras and Muriel Spark. Far from this lack of 'psychologising' leading to a paucity of psychological understanding it brought out how complex the underlying motives of the characters were and how often they did not themselves understand why they engaged in certain actions or said certain things. Indeed, it suggested that act always comes before thought – something Dostoevsky alone among the major nineteenth-century authors seems instinctively to have understood.

In all that time, owing to the friendship of many remarkable Jewish friends, including Francis Landy, who became a distinguished scholar of the Jewish prophetic tradition, and

Jeff Newman and Jonathan Magonet, alumni of Leo Baeck college for Reform rabbis, and, in Jonathan's case, subsequently its Director, I had grown to understand Jewish tradition a little better. In writing *The Book of God* I had found the writings of Martin Buber and his friend Franz Rosenzweig of immense help, as well as the brilliant commentaries on Genesis and Exodus by the Italian biblical scholar Umberto Cassuto, and I had begun to grow disenchanted with most Christian writing on the Hebrew scriptures. It had become clear to me that Jews don't ask the question: Does God exist? Or: Do I believe? Rather, they are content to get on with things, to keep the practices enjoined upon them with more or less rigour depending on the nature of the tradition they adhere to, and to let the 'big' questions rest. And I can see why that is not a way Christians, and especially Protestants, can easily follow, for Christianity has from the first been a religion that rested on belief, specifically on the belief that the crucified Jesus is the Messiah and the Son of God. Judaism has its own store of miracles but it does not depend on them for its very essence, what it depends on is a community and a tradition. At this stage in my life, and while not really being part of either, that seems good enough for me.

14.5.2020

The full extent of the Care Home disaster is beginning to emerge. It turns out that up to 40 percent of all the deaths from Covid-19 have been in care homes, a figure the government gives as 'in excess of 10,000' but which experts estimate at being more like 'in excess of 20,000'. More, probably, since it is estimated that Britain now has experienced over 40,000 deaths from the pandemic, far more than any other European country.

Weather still uncertain. T woke up yesterday hardly able

to move, her back was so bad. It improved a bit in the course of the day but she had difficulty lying in any comfortable position last night and is bad again this morning. To cap it all, her computer has seized up. In ordinary times she would go and see an osteopath who would set her on the right path and look at her manuals for the computer, but no osteopath is working and her documents are all in London!

Grandparents

Just as I never missed my father so I never missed my grandparents. My paternal grandfather, Albert Josipovici, author with his brother-in-law Albert Adès of the highly successful novel *Goha le Simple*, short-listed for the Goncourt the year Proust won it for *À l'Ombre des jeunes filles en fleur* (1919), died in 1932, at only forty (Adès died even younger, in 1921, at twenty-nine). I don't know when my paternal grandmother died, but I think it was before I was born. My maternal grandfather died in 1915, of dementia, in his brother's clinic in Neuilly, where he had been incarcerated for a year. My mother was five at the time. My maternal grandmother died five years later, a victim of the typhoid epidemic that swept Egypt in 1920.

Recently, and especially since being with T, who has a vivid recollection of both her grandmothers, I have begun to understand the importance of grandparents in a child's life. Both T's grandmothers lived on as widows for many years after the deaths of their husbands and it was not till T was in her forties that she lost both of them. Her father's mother was a real Cockney, born just off Commercial Road 'within sound of Bow Bells', and she ended her life in a mansion flat in Maida Vale, on the floor above her two sisters. In between she had lived in Israel in the thirties, running a hotel in Tel Aviv, where

T's uncle, who still lives in Israel, was born. So she had a fund of stories not just about growing up in the crowded poverty of London's East End at the start of the century but also about pre-war Tel Aviv. Her maternal grandmother was born in Poland, grew up in Hungary and Austria, married the highly successful publisher Béla Horovitz, the founder of the Phaidon Press in Vienna, whose foresight enabled his family to move to London in the immediate aftermath of the Anschluss with most of their wealth. After Béla's untimely death, when her daughter and her husband, T's parents, for a while took over the running of the Phaidon Press, and then, having sold it, set up their own publishing firm, Harvey Miller, she lived in a large house on one corner of Thurloe Place opposite the Victoria and Albert Museum. She is the person most elderly people who meet T claim to remember: 'Oh, Lotte! What a *grande dame*!'

The two old ladies, in T's memory, coming from such different worlds and with such different lives, nevertheless got along wonderfully well. Her father's mother in love with all things plastic, forever trying to foist on her friend this gadget or that for making life easier; her mother's mother, who curled her own butter and peeled her grapes, only too happy to hear about pre-First World War life off the Commercial Road.

I remember Judith Weir telling me that when she was travelling round Scotland talking about her opera based on Scottish folk tales, *The Vanishing Bridegroom*, prior to its first production in Glasgow, people who came up to talk to her afterwards would nearly always begin with: 'I remember my grandmother telling me'. She said it was very rarely 'my mother telling me'. And we know from accounts of the great nineteenth century collectors of national folklore material that it was nearly always an old nurse or a grandmother the stories were said to emanate from. And that is understandable. The mother is busy with the other children – and, in T's case, as with other modern mothers, with her job – and so it is left to the grandmother to tell the family stories.

Sacha made up for my lack of grandparents by herself telling me stories, first in France during the war and then in Egypt, and finally when we lived together in Lewes. I think it must be terrible to have no parents or grandparents, but if one has a parent who will share her past and the stories she herself has been told, then surely that is enough. Grandmothers are a nice bonus for children (and for the memoirs they will go on to write, as ably demonstrated by André Aciman in his memoir of his extended family in Egypt and after, where a central role is played throughout not only by the grandmothers but also by the paternal great-grandmother). But they are not indispensable.

And has becoming a grandfather myself made any difference to the way I think about the subject? Not really. But then I'm not a very good grandfather, whatever that means, and certainly don't feel any wiser, nor, really, any older as a result. So, not very wise and rather old.

15.5.2020

Weather set to improve. Cold nights (minus 3 or 4 degrees in some parts of the country) and bright blue skies, sunshine. Experts predict a new spike of infections as the English lockdown is eased. (And again I think of Bonnard writing only 'soleil', 'beau', 'pluie' in his diary as the war raged in Europe and North Africa.)

The nonsense of saying you can pay golf and go to garden centres but those who have to work and have to use public transport must do so. Shows the world these people live in and want to go on living in.

The Grass

I remember reading a review by Philip Toynbee in *The Observer* (it must have been 1960 or '61, I was home from Oxford for one of the holidays) of the translation of a book by a French writer unknown to him, he said, but one he would not soon forget. And he went on to give an impassioned account of its content and its form. Lead reviewers in Sunday papers these days rarely review a translation, unless it is of an Italian or French bestseller (Ferrante or Houillebecq, say). But Toynbee was adamant: he wanted his readers to go out and buy the book. He invoked Proust and Faulkner. I went out and bought it, though obviously in French, *L'Herbe*, not in English. But I keep it here under G because what is important about it is the notion of grass along with a haunting epigraph from Pasternak, an author I on the whole dislike: 'No one makes history, we do not see it, any more than we see the grass grow.'

But that one sentence and the book, it is not too much to say, transformed my life and my understanding of what is possible in fiction. For of course it was true. We do not see history, though we may see – on TV at least – memorable events such as the shooting of Kennedy, the fall of the Berlin Wall or the attacks on the Twin Towers. But history, like our lives, moves on invisibly and no one can see it moving, any more than we can see the grass grow. Writers have of course commented on this before (I love George Oppen's one-line poem entitled 'Old Age', which goes: 'What a strange thing to happen to a little boy'), and some, like Proust and Faulkner, have explored ways of conveying this, but no one I had come across before Simon had ever dealt with it so simply and so directly, though Beckett in *Endgame* comes pretty close ('Something is taking its course,' Hamm keeps saying). And the amazing thing is that by the end of the novel you do feel as though you have actually come close to seeing the grass grow.

I naturally bought Simon's next book, *La Route des Flandres* (but all his books could be called *The Grass* and have the Pasternak quote as their epigraph), and that I remember much better. More abrupt in its cutting from one voice to the other, more violent in its content, and more desperate in its articulation of the impossibility of speaking that which concerns us most directly, it is, to my mind, his masterpiece, though he had written many books before that, starting in 1939, and would write many more after it till his death in 1995. Simon, amazingly, was in a cavalry regiment (yes, in 1940) which was overrun by the German troop and tank advance across Belgium in 1940, and the book is an account of that event, spoken by a survivor in bed with his lover as he tries both to relive and to forget the experience. And just as it recounts, among many other things, the vision of a dead horse slowly disintegrating and being absorbed by the mud of the Flanders fields, so it struggles to keep going as darkness and silence overwhelm it.

The German invasion of Belgium, Holland, and France started on 10 May and took barely a month. By 10 June the Germans had entered Paris and on 22 June the French and Germans signed an Armistice. As news of the invasion reached the capital Parisians began to flee southwards, in cars, in carts and on foot. Many a film has shown the line of fleeing civilians repeatedly strafed by German planes and many a novel has tried to give an account of those tumultuous days and to give us the feel of what those days were like. But by 'telling a story' they smooth things out, drain it of its confusion, because the narrative voice itself remains clear and unconfused. Simon's account of the overwhelming of the French cavalry by the German *panzer* divisions is completely different. This is not because it tries to capture the confusion and horror by itself being confused but because it manages to convey in words the terrible lack of words we have to describe such events and the feelings they arouse. The traumatised soldier lying in bed with his lover, who cannot separate in his mind past from present as events reappear in different guises and he needs desperately to *speak* them, who returns compulsively to that horse gradually becoming one with the mud as he does to pre-war sexual betrayals and moments of sexual bliss, emerges through his repetitions, confusions and moments of lyrical beauty in a way none of the characters of a writer like Irène Némirovsky, dealing with the same subject, ever does. By the time we have finished the novel we have not been told a story, we have experienced something shattering, life-changing. David Jones manages to do this in his version of the confusions of a Flanders field in an earlier war, *In Parenthesis*, but the mythical elements of that book, beautiful though they are, to my mind do not enhance the central theme but rather detract from it.

After *L'Herbe* and *La Route des Flandres* I bought all Simon's earlier books and read them avidly. He had started out as a painter and it is fascinating to see him growing in confidence in his increasingly radical approach to narrative, until, in the three novels, *Le Vent* (1957), *L'Herbe* (1958) and *La Route des Flandres* (1961), he finally finds his voice. And though he went on to write many more books and to win the Nobel Prize, I find it interesting that, like so many painters, it was the works he wrote when he was still not absolutely sure of himself that are his best. The later works feel a little more formulaic, the wonderful tension has gone out of them, and, by the end of his career I had ceased to read him, somehow ceased to care, the decline perhaps not quite as visible as in a Hockney or a Kitaj, but not dissimilar. As though the struggle to understand and articulate, the feeling that at any moment he might lose it, were itself a part of the experience the great central books convey to the reader. No one sees the grass grow yet grow it does, and to convey that is never going to be easy. But in a sense it's the only thing I've ever wanted to do in my own writing.

Johnson's rambling statement on the Sunday, trying to look presidential at his desk in Downing Street, succeeded only in confusing everyone, including his own most fervent supporters. It's clear that with their eyes firmly fixed on keeping hospitals going the government sent patients with the virus out of hospitals and back into the care homes. Hardly believable, but it happened. And yesterday we learned from Michel Barnier that in the EU negotiations the UK has still not understood the EUs position, is still trying to have its cake and eat it, however they dress it up. So on top of everything else Johnson is going to pitch us out of the EU without a deal on 1 Jan. Happy new year.

Gravity and Grace

I have always loved the title Simone Weil gave to her most famous book, *La Pesanteur et la grace*. It came out in 1947 and when it was rendered into English (in 1952) the translator, Emma Crawford, came up with this inspired title. It is better than the French, since it binds the two parts of the title by alliteration where in the French one has difficulty holding them together. My aunt Chickie was mad about Weil and kept on at me to read her. I was of course impressed by her while finding, as many have done, that her powerful intransigence became wearying after a while.

Emma Crawford's brilliant title alerts one to the fact that the word *gravity* has multiple meanings. We probably first come across it in our first physics lesson, when we are told about Isaac Newton and the apple. Later we perhaps read about people being *grave*, not a word that is all that common in modern English, unlike French, when *un air grave* is commonplace. In fact we have to use the French terms when, dealing with French words, we talk about an *accent aigu* and an *accent grave*.

The noun *grave*, a place of burial, has nothing to do with the Latin *gravis*, heavy, important, from which the meanings I have been looking at are derived. It comes from the Old English *græf*, the root of *grafan*, to dig, the word which also lies behind the verb *to engrave*. The Old Teutonic root of this, **grað*, **groð* (hence modern German *Grabe*, grave), somewhat surprisingly appears not to be connected to the Greek *graphein*, to write).

Gravity then, in modern English, means both the force Newton discovered, which makes an apple fall to earth, and the first meaning the Shorter OED gives for *grave*: '*adj.* of persons: Having weight or importance; influential; authoritative – 1749.' Yet the first quotation it gives is from Menenius's address to the patricians in *Coriolanus* (1609 or thereabouts): 'Most reverend and grave elders'. The trouble is our more irreverent, or perhaps more democratic age, would find it hard to attribute this as praise to anyone, old or young. For at least since Dickens, and perhaps since Ben Jonson, 'having weight or importance; influential; authoritative' all too often means: '*thinking of yourself* as having weight or importance, etc.' In other words, *pompous*, which once meant 'characterised by pomp; magnificent; splendid' (Shorter OED again) and now means only: 'characterised by an exaggerated display of self-importance or dignity', and is commonly linked to the word *windbag*. Geoffrey Cox, the preening Attorney General in the last Conservative Government, is the archetype of this, pompous in manner and pompous in style; but though there are many such in English literature, from Lady Catherine de Bourgh and Mr Collins in *Pride and Prejudice* to Podsnap and Twemlow in *Our Mutual Friend*, to gage how far we have come from taking a man of gravity at his face value we have to turn to Virginia Woolf's depiction of Sir William Bradshaw in *Mrs Dalloway*, a man so full of himself that he cannot see that it is simple human affection the shell-shocked Septimus Warren Smith needs if he is ever to recover.

Woolf of course knew all about those who see themselves as having weight and importance for her father Leslie Stephens was the editor of the *Dictionary of National Biography*, a repository of the great and the good, the very men – generals, colonial administrators, members of parliament and so on – who had sent young men like Septimus to fight in a war not of their own making with inadequate arms and bungling superiors. *Jacob's Room* and *Mrs Dalloway* are Woolf's plea for men like Smith to be given their due and for men like Sir William Bradshaw and the political leaders and generals whose incompetence led to their deaths in such numbers to be seen for what they too often were: all pomp and no substance.

But the suspicion of gravity goes back much further than Jane Austen. We can already see it in Aristophanes and in the comedians, both Greek and Roman, who followed him. It comes to full flower in Rabelais, Cervantes and Shakespeare. In the eighteenth century we find it in Fielding and in Sterne it becomes something of a credo. Sterne even goes so far as to adopt the name of the court jester Shakespeare conjures up for us out of a few words of the Gravedigger and Hamlet, and entitles his collected sermons *The Sermons of Mr Yorick*. In *Tristram Shandy* he explains why:

> For, to speak the truth, *Yorick* had an invincible dislike and opposition in his nature to gravity; – not to gravity as such; – for where gravity was wanted, he would be the most grave or serious of mortal men for days and weeks together; – but he was an enemy to affectation of it, and declared open war against it, only as it appeared a cloak for ignorance, or for folly; and then, whenever it fell in his way, however sheltered and protected, he seldom gave it much quarter.

This is perfectly judged. The truth is that humour and irony in serious matters went out of the window when Luther nailed his theses to the door of the castle church in Wittenburg. And in his arguments over free will with Erasmus one can see why. For Erasmus Luther is in danger of throwing out the baby with the bathwater; for Luther Erasmus is merely sitting on the fence. 'Here I stand. I can no other.' Luther's cry rings out again and again in the course of the next centuries, and one has to take it seriously. Mann's *Doktor Faustus*, with its depiction of the tense friendship between the Erasmian Serenus Zeitblom ('serene flower of the time'!) and the Lutheran Adrian Leverkühn gives us the reason why. The trouble is zeal can too often turn into taking one's own vision for the truth and attempting to impose it on the world, and a world which has witnessed Hitler and Stalin is even less likely to treat it kindly than the one that witnessed Cromwell's reforms and the Anabaptist takeover of Münster.

The trouble with the ironic deflation of gravity is that it can too often turn into the sneering dismissal of anything serious. We see that in the way first Evelyn Waugh and then Kingsley Amis mutated from being great (in Waugh's case at least) comic writers, brilliantly deflating gravity and pompousness, to being reactionary bores attacking as pretentious and hollow anything they could not understand. Both extremes, sadly, are on daily display in contemporary Britain, both in public life and in the art that is produced, which is either full of itself and empty of substance or snidely jeering and while it sees itself as honestly deflationary is in effect as thin as what it is attacking.

My heroes in such a climate are, of course Yorick, both in Shakespeare and in Sterne, and such writers as Thomas Bernhard and the later Milan Kundera, such composers as Stravinsky, who found a way to marry wit with plangency, and Bonnard, both in his life and in his art. Gravity and grace – never the one without the other.

Kafka's parable of Ulysses and the sirens casts light on the topic, though as always with Kafka, it still remains for us to decipher what exactly is to be seen in that light. He prefaces it with the remark that what follows provides 'proof that inadequate, even childish measures, may serve to rescue one from peril.'

To protect himself from the Sirens, Ulysses stopped his ears with wax and had himself bound to the mast of his ship. Naturally any and every traveller before him could have done the same...; but it was known to all the world that such things were of no help whatever. The song of the Sirens could pierce through everything, and the longing of those they seduced would have broken far stronger bonds than chains and masts. But Ulysses did not think of that, although he had probably heard of it. He trusted absolutely to his handful of wax and his fathom of chain, and in innocent elation over his little stratagem sailed out to meet the Sirens.

Now the Sirens have a still more fatal weapon than their song, namely their silence. And though admittedly such a thing has never happened, still it is conceivable that someone might possibly have escaped from their singing; but from their silence certainly never. Against the feeling of having triumphed over them by one's own strength, and the consequent exaltation that bears down everything before it, no earthly powers could have remained intact.

And when Ulysses approached them the potent songstresses actually did not sing, whether because they thought that this enemy could be vanquished only by their silence, or because the look of bliss on the face of Ulysses, who was thinking of nothing but his wax and his chains, made them forget their singing.

But Ulysses, if one may so express it, did not hear their silence; he thought they were singing and that he alone did not hear them. For a fleeting moment he saw their throats rising and falling, their breasts lifting, their eyes filled with tears, their lips half-parted, but believed that these were accompaniments to the airs which died unheard around him. Soon, however, all this faded from his sight as he fixed his gaze on the distance, the Sirens literally vanished before his resolution, and at the very moment when they were nearest to him he knew of them no longer.

This is not a manifesto of how great art has gone on being made in what Erich Heller has called the era of the disinherited mind; it is, rather, a demonstration of it.

And it shows me that in taking the theme of Trust and Suspicion as the subject of the lectures I gave at Oxford in 1996, and that subsequently became the book *On Trust*, I was talking about issues that had troubled me ever since I began to think and which have gone on troubling me to the present moment. And I did at one time think of calling those lectures *Gravity and Grace*.

17.5.2020

Last night at Paul Griffiths' request tuned in to a Zoom session run by the indefatigable David Collard and handed over by him to the Manchester Nick Royle, who publishes new short stories in attractive format. Listened to two of his authors talking and reading, but then felt it physically impossible to continue and went off to read some Dostoevsky and Roussel. Never again.

German football has restarted – and I find myself filled with sadness at the thought. Never imagined I would feel like that about sport – but I realise this lockdown has been a wonderful relief from the daily and weekly intrusion of the world – I know that if there is sport on TV I won't be able to stop myself watching, yet want to keep this strange bubble going – very selfish I'm afraid.

Happiness

What an extraordinary thing to put into an official document: the American Declaration of Independence gives three examples of what it says has been given to all men and women: 'Life, Liberty and the pursuit of Happiness.' Life is indeed an inalienable right, and liberty, if that means the right not to be a slave, owned by someone. But the pursuit of happiness? It may help explain why I so loathe what America stands for: the resistance to gun control in the name of the freedom of the individual, all those health manuals and videos that are in effect a vain attempt to keep death at bay, etc. The pursuit of happiness is surely a recipe for unhappiness. Happiness, in my experience, comes to you unexpectedly or not at all. Though, come to think of it, can I recall any such moments? Enormous satisfaction and often relief, of course, as when I won that 100 metres freestyle under-fourteens event in the Egyptian National Swimming Championships; or when I learned I had got a First and so would be able to get a grant for my graduate work and one day a University job if I was lucky; or when I got the Sussex job; or got that letter from Raleigh Trevelyan saying Michael Joseph were going to publish my first novel, *The Inventory*. But happiness? Perhaps I simply don't have anything to compare it with and so don't know what it means.

I think I understand the word *joy* a bit better, at least when Dante or Proust talk about it. Indeed, the fact that joy is so central to both their works is part of what makes me love them so much. People find *Paradiso* the most indigestible part of Dante's *Commedia*, but it is anything but dry theology. Rather, it is an amazing exploration in words of how joy can fill the human soul – joy and light. At the start of Canto 21:

> Already my eyes were fixed again on the face of my Lady, and with them my mind, which was withdrawn from every other thought...

what joy it was to me to be obedient to my heavenly guide...

Where sorrow in hell comes from feeling that you are the centre of the universe and you alone matter, joy in paradise comes with recognising that there are other lives than your own, and it always comes with the sense of purposeful as opposed to purposeless motion. Paulo and Francesca are tossed this way and that on the winds of desire, never appeased, while at the very end of the poem we the readers, like the poet himself, are transformed by joyous motion:

Here power failed the high phantasy, and now my desire and will, like a wheel that spins with even motion, were revolved by the Love that moves the sun and the other stars.

All'alta fantasia qui mancò possa;
   Ma già volgeva il mio disio e'l velle,
   Si come rota ch'igualmente è mossa,
L'amor che move il sole e l'altre stelle.

But even at the start of the poem, when, in his terror and confusion the poet encounters a figure who reveals himself as Virgil and who says he was sent to guide him (to move him!) through the circles of both Hell and Purgatory, the note of joy creeps in – significantly, a joy generated by the recognition and acknowledgement of another:

'Or se' tu quell' Virgilio e quella fonte
   che spandi di parlar si largo fiume?'
   rispuos' io con vergognosa fronte.
'O delli altri poeti onore e lume,
   vagliami 'l lungo studio e 'l grande amore
   che m'ha fatto cercar lo tuo volume.

Tu se' lo mio maestro e'l mio autore;
  tu se' solo colui da cu' io tolsi
  lo bello stilo che m' ha fatto onore...'

'Are you then that Virgil, that fountain which pours forth so rich a stream of speech?' I answered him, my brow covered with shame. 'O glory and light of other poets, let the long study and the great love that has made me search your volume avail me. You are my master and my author. You are he from whom alone I took the style that brought me honour.'

Dante's words are not simply reverential; they are suffused with joy at the unexpected encounter, and it is this that stays with one long after the complex theology of the poem has evaporated.

The joy that flares up in Proust's novel is quite different from the feelings generated by Joyce's epiphanies, which remain always tinged with that Christian sense of revelation Joyce could never escape. In Dante and in Proust joy is a spontaneous, bodily feeling, and the memory of it remains with them through all the dark times.

Beckett, perhaps like Joyce too imbued by Christianity ever to wholly shake it off, can only drag any feelings he or his characters might have of joy down to ridicule: happy days indeed! Not so Stevens, whether walking by the sea in Key West or experiencing an ordinary evening in New Haven. 'The Emperor of Ice-Cream' manages, amazingly, to balance without either irony or disgust the pleasures associated with that very modern and demotic food with the dead body lying in its room awaiting the pall-bearers. As does Bonnard with those late paintings of Marthe in the bath, where our sense of her as a corpse is balanced by our sense of her as a triumphal offering on the altar of light and colour.

But in my life I have never expected happiness and so I

suppose only rarely been truly unhappy – unhappy as Sacha was, she told me, when, with both her parents dead, she went to live with her grandparents at the age of ten; or as T tells me she was for large periods of her own childhood. Sacha shielded me from that and when she was no longer there I did indeed have a number of years when I would go to sleep in pain and wake up in pain. Yet even then the energy of writing saved me. I recognised Bacon's wonderful remark, 'I'm a pessimist by nature but I have an optimistic nervous system' as applying very well to myself. If I can walk and if I can write I cannot be truly unhappy. But happy? That is something else.

18.5.2020

What has been so wonderful about the last two months alone with T is that my natural desire for isolation, for time and space to work things out for myself, has not had to fight against the push of society, the multiple things that usually have to be done (though I'm good at avoiding most of them). The last two months have been special and it's sad to see this start to disappear.

Home

The first time I became conscious of the place we lived in as a home and a refuge was the flat in Road 18, round the corner from Chickie. Before that, in the flats in Road 9 and Road 6, I was probably too young, simply took things as they came – even the horrors of the Road 6 flat, the constant worry that the dogs would tear the *galabiyahs* of the owners in the top two flats, leading to screaming and the threats of police action and the extortion of money for new *galabiyahs* – which my mother would gladly have paid, but the climate of fear generated by the screaming led her to think that as often as not she was being made a fool of and being asked to reimburse them for non-existent tears and wounds. I remember an incident when two of the men from upstairs not only shouted and raved, threatening to kill the dogs, but actually kicked out at her head as she stood on our basement stairs and they stood above her shouting.

It was a relief then when we learned that a flat was free in a house owned by a friend in a much quieter part of town, very close to my aunt and cousins. It was on the ground floor this time and I don't remember much about it except that it had a guava tree in the small front garden, and a bathroom with a bidet in which my mother would put the clothes to be washed and in which we would find our cat, Batly, lying fast asleep on his back with his four feet in the air when we returned from a walk or the club. Is it my imagination or was there no bath but only a round metal tub into which the hot water had to be poured? I certainly remember washing in such a tub, like the one Bonnard paints his wife Marthe washing in before he starts to paint her in the tiled bath, but that may have been in the Road 9 flat.

I also remember coming back from school and polishing the door-handles or something of the sort, to make the house look good for when Sacha came home. Was she already working at Victoria College, looking after the boarders after school hours and before their meals? That paid my school fees, she told me, and she explained how she would go in once a month to see the bursar, who would count the cash out into her hand, and then she would hand him back the money he had just given her. Could it have been exactly the same sum? Certainly that is how I remember her telling it.

It does seem funny to me now, looking back, to think of a little boy trying to get the house clean for his mother to return to. But it had to do, I think, with the sense, clearly already strong in me, that it was us on one side and the world on the other – not in a violent sense (the previous landlords were an exception), but as a fact of life. And this led, for me, to a valuing of where we lived, to the home Sacha made for us. That feeling grew when we were finally able to move into the bungalow by the canal that Sacha had bought with the money from the sale of the Bulac house which she had inherited from her grandparents. It was the most beautiful home we ever had, along with the Woodstock house outside Oxford in the early sixties. But even the cottage we lived in during my year at school in Cheltenham, on top of Battledown Hill, and the Putney flat we lived in when we moved to London from Cheltenham, both of which left much to be desired, became, while we were there, home and not just lodgings, a place to feel proud of – perhaps because we were in England at last, with the traumas of leaving Egypt and being allowed to enter the country finally behind us – though it was not till 1962 or '63 that we both finally acquired British nationality and the need to report regularly to some police station or other was thankfully behind us.

Perhaps the only place we lived in which did not feel at all like home was the newly built house I bought from the University in Kingston outside Lewes. I had got it because the University persuaded me it was a good investment unless one left within three years, but in fact we decided to cut our losses and leave after two. Partly it was the fact that not just the house but the whole estate it was in that was new, with as yet no trees and gardens that were bare plots needing to have turf laid on them. Partly it was the identical newly built houses with big windows, giving one the feeling that one could never really be *inside*. And partly it was that so many young university families were living there, that one saw the same faces when one got home as one saw at work, so that, again, there seemed to be no escape from scrutiny. After two years of this we looked at each other and said: We've got to get out, haven't we? I had thought we could make a home anywhere, in any slum, but this middle-class open-plan enclave with no place to hide was just too much.

Of course in retrospect there were advantages. Certainly for all the young families there were quiet carfree streets for the children to play in and a chance for both children and parents to get to know each other. Sacha made many friends there who remained close to her till her death thirty years later. But it was literally intolerable for both of us and we only began to breathe again properly when we got to Lewes, to an ordinary house built around 1900, but that had rooms one could make comfortable, a grate in the living room for an open fire, and, above all, a sense of having been there for a long time in a street that had been there for a long time, in a town that had been there for much longer. I have been in that house ever since, with no desire to move again, though there are many things wrong with it, and I have the strong sense that it is indeed home.

After Sacha's death well-meaning friends urged me to move, saying I needed to 'start afresh'. I stayed put, partly out of inertia, but also because I sensed that once I had got over the pain of her immediate absence I would find that she actually would still be there, a benign presence giving her blessing to the place. And so it has proved.

After writing this I went up to my room to go on sorting my postcards – trying to get them into some sort of chronological order – as I have set myself to do during lockdown. Among them I came across an image from the Luttrell Psalter sent me by someone who has not written a message or even signed, merely quoted a fourteenth century Japanese writer: 'There is a charm about a neat and proper dwelling-house, although this world, 'tis true, is but a temporary abode. Even the moonshine seems to gain in friendly brilliance, striking into the house where a good man lives in peaceful ease.' Kenko, *Essays in Idleness*. And by the word 'house' the anonymous sender has put an asterisk and another by the address on the right. Very strange.

19.5.2020

As more becomes known about what has been going on behind the scenes it becomes clearer and clearer that the government won't listen to WHO advice, won't learn lessons from how other countries have coped with the pandemic, and is consequently all at sea and always playing catch-up. But also that ministers who were picked to bamboozle the public with soundbites about Brexit and its amazing benefits cannot change their mindsets. And, most damning of all, that this most right-wing of governments has compounded its errors by awarding contracts for vital PPE equipment and the rest to large private companies as it has been used to doing in the days before Covid-19, and have ignored local councils and smaller local firms who would have known how to go about contacting and tracing. I suppose we should have expected no more, but somehow one thought they would shed their ideology for a moment and concentrate on saving lives. Liberals like me never learn.

Great walk yesterday via the wood, where T recorded amazing birdsong, to Mt Harry and then back on the east side of the valley. Weather warming up.

Homer

In the heyday of *The Independent*, when it was a serious broadsheet and Robert Winder was the splendid literary editor, he had the idea of asking one of his regular contributors to write a review each month not of the latest book but of some classic. I chose the *Iliad*, and I still have the cutting, dated Saturday 20 Feb 1993. I stand by what I said then:

'Old books are there to remind us of ways of looking and thinking that we have forgotten or that modern culture has kept hidden from us. And of no book is this truer than the *Iliad*.

'Where Virgil is the poet of subjectivity, of pathos, of the unspeakable sorrow at the heart of things, Homer is the poet who more than any other tells us how things in fact are. There is a kind of ruthlessness in describing a warrior falling off a chariot, a spear through his neck, as like a diver plunging into still seas; or of a warrior, his face a bleeding mass, his neck broken, as like a poppy in a field beaten down by a spring shower. Shocking, yes, but that is not the intention, nor, I think, is it quite the effect.

'We are merely being asked to see things from a non-human perspective, one which stands outside human concerns, and from which the eruption onto the Trojan plain of a horde of armed men is simply an aspect of life on earth, like the flight of migrating birds or the sudden emergence of a swarm of bees. From this perspective human beings are like leaves on a tree, "one generation of men will grow while another dies", and it is well to know this and have no illusions about our place in the universe.

'But that is only half the story. Homer's objectivity is not the disillusioned, even cynical objectivity of Ecclesiastes, which, I suspect, he would see as being as one-sided as Virgilian pathos. Unlike leaves and bees human beings long to make something of their brief lives in the sun and, unlike them, they find it difficult to cope with the knowledge of their own death and of those closest to them. Indeed, the *Iliad*, far from being the great poem of war, is in fact the great poem of mourning. Its central question is: how can we cope with the death of those we love and find ways of making our acute sense of what they have meant to us something enriching rather than destructive?

'Achilles, who has not been able to bear the shame of having his concubine, Briseis, taken away from him, discovers that even the funeral games in Patroclus' honour have not made the death of his beloved friend any more bearable. Yet in the final book he finds rest at last when he is able to return the body of Hector, the slayer of Patroclus, to his grieving father. And he can only make that gesture of generosity when he has made the imaginative leap of understanding what the old man is feeling. 'You must be brave indeed,' he says to Priam, 'to come here to face the man who has killed your son.' So the two of them weep together, Priam for his dead son and Achilles for his dead friend and also for his old father, brought to mind by seeing Priam. And we, who know he will soon die himself (though the poem, with typical restraint, includes neither that event nor the fall of Troy in its pages), and who have ourselves suffered loss and tried to mourn in a world where the public structures which used to facilitate such things no longer exist – we are helped by Homer's poetry and his wise realism to come to terms with the most important thing in our lives: death.'

I now realise that I wrote this just a couple of years before Sacha's death and I must have been internally preparing for it even then. But that does not mean I don't stand by what I said. Our classical Greek reading group still flourishes, and even during the lockdown we are meeting on Zoom. We have, however, taken a break from the Odyssey, since not all of us want to continue in this virtual form, and are having a look at the Homeric hymn to Hermes, that delightful, tongue in cheek celebration of the trickster god, a poem worthy of Thomas Mann. But I go on reading the *Odyssey* on my own and have recently come to the end of the Circe episode and the start of Odysseus' visit to Hades. And a couple of passages there, dealing with the death of Odysseus' companion Elpenor particularly caught my attention. I now see why and how it forms a fitting companion to what I wrote so long ago about the *Iliad*. Here is the first passage, in the Loeb translation:

> There was one, Elpenor, the youngest of all and not over valiant in war nor of sound understanding, who had laid him down apart from his comrades in the sacred house of Circe, seeking the cool air, for he was heavy with wine. He heard the noise and bustle of his comrades as they moved about [making ready to depart], and suddenly sprang up, and forgot to go to the long ladder that he might come down again, but fell headlong from the roof, and his neck was broken away from the spine, and his spirit went down to the house of Hades.

It is all so direct and simple. Homer tells it as it is: Elpenor climbs up on to the roof to get some fresh air, as is still common in the summer months in the Middle East today, but in his case it is not just the heat that drives him there but an excess of wine. When he wakes up, hung over and in his hurry to join his comrades, he forgets where he is and tumbles from the roof, killing himself. Homer is very precise: 'his neck was broken away from his spine', but then adds what was just as clear and down to earth for him but which we have to make an imaginative leap to understand: 'and his spirit went down to the house of Hades'.

At the start of the next book, Odysseus has reached the place Circe told him he had to go to in order to summon the spirits from Hades, and the first to appear, when he has carried out the appropriate rites, is none other than Elpenor. For, as Odysseus explains, 'not yet had he been buried beneath the broad-wayed earth, for we had left his corpse behind in the hall of Circe, unwept and unburied, since another task was urging us on.' Seeing him, Odysseus goes on, 'I wept and my heart had compassion on him.' How did you get here so quickly? he naively asks him: 'Thou coming on foot hast outstripped me in my black ship.' Elpenor explains: 'Son of Laertes, sprung from Zeus, Odysseus of many devices, an evil doom of some god was my undoing, and measureless wine.' Again, the calm realism. Elpenor acknowledges that 'measureless wine' was the cause of his death, but also 'an evil doom of some god'. Today we might ask why just he should have decided to climb onto the roof when presumably his comrades, also full of wine and in need of fresh air, lay down to sleep in the hall, and we would have no answer. Earlier, it is true, Odysseus has told us that Elpenor was the youngest of his surviving comrades and not the bravest, but, we might again ask, what made him like that? We have no answer, only an infinity of possibilities. The Greeks closed this off with the simple phrase: It was 'an evil doom of some god'. That evil doom might have been with him from the start, leading to a weakness for alcohol perhaps or an inability to hold his drink. The Greeks do not speculate. The important thing is that Elpenor is dead and unburied, and thus begging Odysseus to rectify this in some way: 'Burn me with my armour, all that is mine, and heap up a mound for me on the shore of the grey sea, in memory of an unhappy man, that men yet to be may learn of me. Fulfil this my prayer and fix upon the mound my oar wherewith I rowed in life when I was among my comrades.' Odysseus promises to do as he asks and the two then talk until the spirit of Odysseus' mother appears and attention shifts to her.

It is instructive to see how Virgil treats this episode in his rewriting of Homer. At the end of Book V of the *Aeneid* as Aeneas's fleet sail towards Italy and their destination (I am quoting the Loeb translation here too):

First before all, leading the close column, was Palinurus; by him the rest are bidden shape their course. And now dewy Night had just reached its midgoal in heaven; the sailors, stretched on their hard benches under the oars, relaxed their limbs in quiet rest; when Sleep, sliding softly down from the stars of heaven, parted the dusky air and cleft the gloom, seeking thee, O Palinurus, and bringing thee baleful dreams, guiltless one!

The god of Sleep, in the semblance of one of his comrades, speaks soothingly to him: 'The hour is given to rest. Lay down thy head and steal thy weary eyes from toil. I myself for a space will take thy duty in thy stead.' The helmsman protests: Never! he says, I must do my duty. And he clings to the tiller ever more firmly.

But lo! The god, shaking over his temples a bough dripping with Lethe's dew and steeped in the drowsy night of Styx, despite his efforts relaxes his swimming eyes. Hardly had a sudden slumber begun to unbend his limbs when, leaning above, Sleep flung him headlong into the clear waters, tearing away, as he fell, the helm and part of the stern and calling oft-times vainly on his comrades.

A wonderful evocation, with the use of mythology, of the power of sleep over us, and of the way there is nothing we can do to control it even when our lives are at stake. But see how we are made to pity Palinurus and how his sense of duty is brought to the fore. How human-centred the episode is, in contrast to Homer. We may pity Elpinor, but there it is: wine and the god did for him and what is important is not that we should identify with him but that he should be buried. Virgil wants us to feel pity for Palinurus and so, in a sense, for ourselves, guiltless but born into a cruel world. Virgil, I feel, lies behind most of the great art of the post-Renaissance period I so much dislike, Homer behind all I love.

Now that it is openly acknowledged that the UK made a total mess of dealing with the pandemic (and shows no sign of improving its performance) the government and the scientists advising them are starting to try to shift the blame onto each other. The scientists are making it clear whenever they can, at the daily press briefings and in the media, that they merely put forward various scenarios and the politicians make the decisions as to which one to choose; the politicians for their part are either attacking the scientists directly for giving flawed advice, or, in more nuanced mode and recognising that an attack on the very people they appoint to advise them would not look good, are blaming not the scientists but the science ('They didn't know the full facts' etc.).

And to add to the pathos we also learn that of the 21,000 'fully trained' and newly recruited contact tracers many are complaining that they were ready and eager to learn their new roles but training has been hopelessly inefficient, the private company recruited to do the job clearly not up to it. When they have raised a question they have been told to go online or to YouTube, and many report standing by all day and no one ever contacting them.

Meanwhile, in Europe, the countries with the most stringent lockdown measures, such as Italy, are returning to some semblance of life. In the UK yesterday the death toll of the previous twenty-four hours was still over 500.

This and Brexit have finally put paid to the notion in the world at large that the UK is a country to be looked up to. Now the US and the UK, Trump and Johnson, are laughing stocks and examples of how not to do things.

Honesty

I have found myself, in the past few years, using this term to myself to describe art of various kinds. Recently, listening to the harpsichordist Malcolm Proud playing the Bach Partitas on an instrument that is a copy of a 1624 harpsichord by Johannes Ruckers of Antwerp from the Interlinden Museum in Colmar, I jotted down 'honest' in my notebook. What I meant I think was that since on the harpsichord, unlike the piano, each note is plucked, there is no possibility of 'cheating'. What do I mean by cheating? Am I accusing the piano, somehow, of cheating? Or just certain pianists? No one, surely, would accuse Andras Schiff of cheating. And indeed his Bach playing is wonderfully crisp, as near as it is possible to get, one might say, to playing the piano as if it were a harpsichord. Or do I mean I prefer Bach to Beethoven and Beethoven to Chopin? On the whole that's true, and also that the Beethoven I prefer is the most Bach-like, the late-piano sonatas and quartets. And that I love Bartok's *Second Piano Concerto* precisely because he uses the piano not for nuanced effects but for its rhythmic power, uses it as a kind of percussion instrument.

But why honesty? As if I feel that Romantic music (Chopin, Schumann, Wagner in particular) is in some sense *dishonest*? Is it that I feel it is trying to persuade me to succumb to something by a sort of sleight of hand? Away with profundity! I feel like saying. Away with sublimity! Up with the humble, the modest, with all that promises little and delivers much rather than promising much and delivering the false, the meretricious.

Why, when I read this, the opening paragraph of *Don Quixote*, do I feel not just amused, but elated, as if something murky had been scrubbed clean? 'Idle reader,' begins the Prologue:

Without my swearing to it you can believe that I would like this book, the child of my understanding, to be the most beautiful, the most brilliant and the most discreet, that anyone could imagine. But I have not been able to contravene the natural order; in it like begets like. And so what could my barren and poorly cultivated wits beget but the history of a child who is dry, withered, capricious, and filled with inconstant thoughts never imagined by anyone else.

Suddenly I find myself able to breathe. The air is clean. This may be a rhetorical gambit by the author to gain the reader's sympathy, but it is much more. It is a public avowal of the fact that this new genre, the novel, without the support of tradition or (the same thing) of genre, is reliant solely on the wits and skill of the novelist and that these are *always* and only frail, fallible, and confused – that is, *human*.

And a modern descendant of Cervantes:

In my childhood I was a fervent worshiper of the tiger: not the jaguar, the spotted "tiger" of the Amazonian jungles and the isles of vegetation that float down the Paraná, but that striped, Asiatic, royal tiger, that can only be faced by a man of war, on a castle atop an elephant. I used to linger endlessly before one of the cages at the zoo; I judged vast encyclopaedias and books of natural history by the splendour of their tigers. (I still remember those illustrations: I who cannot rightly recall the brow or the smile of a woman.) Childhood passed away, and the tigers and my passion for them grew old, but still they are in my dreams. At that submerged or chaotic level they keep prevailing. And so, as I sleep, some dream beguiles me, and suddenly I know I am dreaming. Then I think: this is a dream, a pure diversion of my will; and now that I have unlimited power, I am going to cause a tiger.

Oh, incompetence! Never can my dreams engender the wild beast I long for. The tiger indeed appears, but stuffed or flimsy, or with impure variations of shape, or of an implausible size, or all too fleeting, or with a touch of the dog or the bird.

This is Borges, a little narrative that grew from a much inferior poem. Though he talks of incompetence what he is really saying is that the human imagination is never up to the task and the more it tries to conjure a tiger onto the page the more it will find itself resorting to clichés and platitudes.

It is this I call 'honesty', this, I think, that gives me the feeling of being able to breathe freely, that returns me, in a sense to genuine possibilities. And it is this I feel listening to Stravinsky's *Concerto of Wind Instruments* or *Octet*, my ideals, I now realise, of what good art can and should be.

Honest/Dishonest? Cleansing/Sullying? I still find those words useful, not to praise or condemn the art I like or dislike, but as pointers to the way art is bound up not just with morality but also with the body.

21.5.2020

Yesterday the hottest day of the year so far, 27–8°C in London, but cooler here in Lewes. Made a cake in the morning (the old *quatre quarts*, with caraway seeds); then T tried to cut my hair in the garden, but too timid to make much headway; then a 'distanced' walk with Dick and Ally in the afternoon: Mt Harry and back by the west side of the valley, through the wood – I think I prefer the other, where the valley and sea are in full view all the time and there isn't that climb at the end. Birdsong in the wood at the foot of Mt Harry, trees down everywhere, overgrown, sense that you are in deepest African jungle!

Finished A.B. Yehoshua's latest, *The Tunnel*, in bed. Very disappointing end – and actually the whole book, which I thought would be humane and interesting on the subject of memory loss, seems imprisoned by its conception – perhaps the death of his wife and her dementia too raw. Terrible ending, trying to make good on the title and to link literal and metaphorical – but whole plot around it unconvincing and not wittily enough done for us to accept that.

Hörspiel

The Germans have a word for it: hearing-game. In English it is banally called a radio play. The Germans have half a dozen radio stations; RBB (Rundfunk Berlin-Brandenburg), NDR (Norddeutescher Rundfunk [N.German Broadcasting]), WDR (Westdeutscher Rundfunk – [N. Rhine Westphalia Broadcasting]) etc. Each commissions on its own; and English-language plays used to be bought by individual stations, so often selling a play to one meant selling it to the lot. Each broadcasting centre has a study room, where one can request to hear or read a play. By contrast, when I used to suggest to MA students of mine that they might like to write their dissertations on the radio plays of Beckett or Pinter or Stoppard the BBC was not helpful and they had a lot of difficulty getting hold of tapes and scripts and sometimes could not get hold of them at all.

Yet in the post-war decades the BBC drama department was the envy of the world. Under a series of great producers it brought to the public such classics of the genre as Louis MacNeice's *The Dark Tower*, Dylan Thomas's *Under Milk Wood*, Samuel Beckett's *All That Fall*, Pinter's *A Slight Ache* and Stoppard's *Nude Descending the Stairs*. Readers of Beckett's *Letters* will know that it employed a scout, Barbara Bray (who became Beckett's lover and to whom he wrote his most impassioned letters), for the sole purpose of discovering good European plays.

Such days are long gone. But when I started writing for the BBC in the early 1970s I was enchanted by the atmosphere of friendship and collaboration that reigned in the Drama Department as producers called in on each other in their adjoining rooms along one corridor or consulted the Director, Martin Esslin, about some knotty point of planning. Esslin himself would choose scripts solely on whether he thought they were good enough. The script might, like the first of my plays, be 35 mins. long, or it could, like David Rudkin's *Cries from Casement as his Bones are brought To Dublin*, last for many hours. When I went to talk to the new people at the Drama Department in the early 1990s, after my two wonderful producers, Guy Vaesen and John Theocharis, had both retired or 'been retired', and Martin Esslin had long since gone to work in America, I was told that if they were to commission a play from me I had to submit a synopsis first, and that it must be timed to run for either half an hour or an hour or an hour and a half. Shocked and insulted that after writing award-winning plays for them for twenty-five years I too would have to submit to these 'rules', I left and never wrote another. Later I was somewhat mollified to learn that they had treated Stoppard in just the same way. Oh the ravages Thatcher wrought.

Yesterday, for the first time since T arrived on 22 March, we changed our routine. T needed to get her car moving and thought a fine day was the right time to see if we could look in for a 'socially-distanced tea' at Jimmy and Nicolette's. Haven't seen them since J diagnosed with dementia but both seemed in fine fettle, though clearly it's a strain on her. We had a walk first along the top to Mt Caburn and back, leaving the car by the new wind/electricity generator above Glyndebourne. Hot but breezy, hang-gliders out in force over Mt Caburn. Then down to Ringmer to see them. Jimmy brought out tea and we sat in the warmth of the late afternoon. Jimmy: I walk and my piano-playing is a great source of comfort. But Nicolette tells us he fell recently and hurt his face badly. And that he is convinced he will drive again. No way! she says, not with his dementia! But he tells me: They are making such a fuss about giving me back my licence, it's taking forever. I don't ask when they took it away and who 'they' are. Both clearly very pleased to see us and beg us to come again soon.

In the evening, as we are outside clapping for the NHS, Emmanuel, my neighbour, comes running up the road (he has recently run the Athens marathon). It's as if we are applauding *him*. He arrives at the house and stops, covered in sweat. He has run his usual ten K, he tells us. T, in admiration: You're a real runner.

Whether it is the taking out of the car or the walk or the visit to Jimmy and Nicolette or the sudden change to cold and blowy weather – but sluggish this morning, sleepy and can't really get going. I will have to leave my next thought/memoir till tomorrow. Rules are there to be broken.

Who would have thought all the features that characterised the Brexit campaign – the flouting of the rules, the blatant hypocrisy, the ghastly sanctimoniousness, the tarring of all opponents as enemies of the people, the Little Englander mentality, the fetishisation of 'this island nation' – that all would survive intact and be on daily show in this government's handling of a real national crisis, the coronavirus pandemic? The liberal press keep saying: Do they not realise that we are living in a different world from that of the Brexit debates? I wonder if we are. The Tories who cheered the resignation of Neal Ferguson, whom they saw as their bogey-man because he scuppered the plan that would, in their eyes, have saved the economy (even at the cost of 250,000 lives – dispensable, they felt), now hurry to insist Dominic Cummings was only doing what was right when he and his family drove from London to Durham, ostensibly to allow their child to be looked after by grandparents if they both felt ill (they had symptoms), but now, it is emerging, because that was simply more salubrious than London at the height of the pandemic. Interestingly, there is so much anger on social media, such a sense of unfairness, of 'one rule for you and one for us', that some conservatives, as well as all the opposition parties, are starting to ask for his resignation. Will this build up into an irresistible tide? It might do. After all, Cummings is not exactly a Tory favourite, though they are grateful to him for masterminding Brexit and their election victory.

And then there is the shame and horror of Rees-Mogg convening the House of Commons for 2 June, flouting the government's own safety rules. How is that going to play out?

Caught by the rain on our walk yesterday. We were soaked but T wonderfully cheerful as we returned.

Tried to write I, You, He, but got nowhere.

Try again today.

I, You, He

Why have I always had such an aversion to first person narratives? I think precisely because of their dishonesty – they start from a falsehood and can never recover. The falsehood that 'I' can talk in such detail and so smoothly about what has 'happened' to 'me', or even, sometimes, what is actually happening as 'I' write.

Not that I mind reading first person narratives – I am as happy as the next person to 'enter' a novel written in the first person, whether it's *David Copperfield* or the latest thriller. There are good and bad examples, just as there are good and bad examples of third person narratives. It's that I object to it when I do it, – though it's much more than mere objection, more like trying to walk along a narrow ledge in the mountains with a sheer drop on one or both sides, when my legs turn to water and I cannot stand up. Why this should be the case was made a little more comprehensible when I got to read Kafka in depth and discovered that he only found himself as a writer when he moved from the first to the third person. An early story like 'Description of a Struggle', which peters out and which he never published, shows us an omnipotent first person who can conjure stars into the sky just because he likes seeing stars in the sky, but who, for that very reason, soon loses any sense of the world or of himself. Just because I can say and do anything in a story I invent is precisely the reason why I can't bear doing it. What I have to do if I am to feel justified in what I write is to find ways to limit myself – and Kafka did this, dramatically, in the first spate of great stories he wrote the following year, 1912: 'The Judgement', 'The Stoker' and 'Metamorphosis'.

But if Kafka found his writerly salvation in turning from the first person to the third, Proust found *his* through precisely the opposite trajectory, from the third person narrative of the Jamesian *Jean Santeuil*, which he too abandoned before completion, to the first person of *À la recherche*. Clearly the story is more complicated than I have been making out. The key, I think is that Proust's narrator, 'Marcel' as he is called throughout the novel, does not know everything from the start. He does not tell his story from some secure vantage-point above the fray. He manages to give us the sense of discovering as he goes along, revising his views and then revising them again all the way through the giant novel.

We all have to learn the hard way, by trial and error, that there is no way to make art these days that automatically confers authority, validity. What I discovered in the early years of writing was that my body responded to the writing of dialogue and the rejection of any authoritative voice, whether first or third person. Later I felt the need to allow one voice to soar, as it were, even though I have remained conscious of the fact that that soaring must be anchored in reality, often (usually?) in a deflationary or semi-deflationary way – as with the driven speaker of *Moo Pak* or the often absurd Tancredo Pavone of *Infinity*. In that book in particular I also found that filtering Pavone's voice through his manservant/chauffeur was not enough – I had to find my way to the human in the preening peacock and only when I had got there could the book get finished.

There are times when I cannot read most novels – including highly touted ones like *The Great Gatsby*, and *American Pastoral*, at all – I do not want to enter their false worlds. Why they feel false while a few – a very few – do not, has always been the puzzle – I've tried to explain it to myself and others, but I'm not sure I've succeeded. Those who 'get it', like George (of course), Steve or Dick, or, often, Rosalind, just 'get it'; others, even those I feel close to, like Tim and T, just don't. Our tastes may coincide here and there – but then the gulf suddenly widens again and becomes a chasm – as when Tim recommends Iris Murdoch's *The Red and the Green* as 'a remarkable novel'.

I found myself, in 'Second Person Looking Out', writing at least part of a story in the second person. An interesting experience. But too artificial to do anything longer – though Butor's *La Modification* manages to carry it off. But even that feels like a wager: can it be done? Can I do it? And I find books like that less than riveting. But then I seem to have very little tolerance and it grows worse rather than better with age.

25.5.2020

Feeling in the country that Johnson has finally crossed a line in his backing of Cummings against all the evidence. In a press conference wretchedly poor even by his recent low standards, he stood up and said that while he understood that the country might feel that there was one law for the mighty and one for them, he had surveyed all the evidence and found Cummings had broken no law but acted responsibly at all times and as any parent would. The question of law is a tricky one because the government had not, as in France and Italy and Spain, actually made it illegal not to follow its guidelines. But the rest of it was nonsense and he seemed to know it was nonsense and that by backing Cummings he was showing his disdain for the country. Even supportive papers like the *Daily Mail* accuse the government of living 'on a different planet'. Clearly Johnson hopes the thing will simply blow over, but will it?

Gertrude, Bea's mother died in the home she was in after actually recovering from the virus. But her dementia rapidly got worse and she died in her sleep.

Intimacy

OED: *intimacy*: the quality of being intimate, close.

Intimate: L. *intimatus, inter*. Inmost; within; close (1632); *euph*. Illicit sexual intercourse (1676).

Not to be confused with the verb *to intimate*: L.*intimare*, to put into: to make known indirectly, hint. (1590)

Evidence of Intimacy was the title I gave to the first stage play I ever wrote. That was in 1971 or '72 in response to an invitation from the students at Sussex for a play for them to enter for the Sunday Times Student Drama competition. At the time divorce by consent was unknown in England; the grounds for divorce were, if I remember correctly, desertion, cruelty or – the one most often used – proof that 'intimacy' had taken place between one of the spouses and another person (see definitions above, 'illicit sexual intercourse', 1676). This led in many cases where couples wished to separate to what one might call 'arranged divorces', and Evelyn Waugh and other novelists made great comic play with this. It struck me that I could write a serious farce by taking the phrase 'evidence of intimacy' literally. A detective would come to the house of a couple and, presumably sent by the spouse of one of them (although at one point I floated the suggestion that the couple might in fact be married), set about examining everything from the crockery to the sheets for 'evidence of intimacy'. Thus, I hoped, the play would make the point, comically, that intimacy leaves no evidence. That is why it is so difficult to talk about.

George Steiner, however, in an early essay in *Encounter*, had no difficulty discussing the subject. Ostensibly reviewing an anthology of erotic fiction edited by Maurice Girodias, the founder of the Olympia Press, responsible for bringing to the public not only such 'serious' but at the time deemed unpublishable books as Nabokov's *Lolita* and J.P. Donleavy's *The Ginger Man*, but also a turbid mixture of pornography and pseudo-avantgardisme, Steiner is scathing about the book and about pornography in general. 'Since the Empress Theodora resolved "to satisfy all amorous orifices of the human body to the full and at the same time"', he writes, 'human beings have striven to add new elements to both the activity of sex and to its depiction in literature.' The trouble is, he goes on, that there are only a limited number of orifices, and he dismisses as nonsense the belief seemingly held by Sade and many of the contributors to the anthology, 'that one can double one's ecstasy by enjoying coitus while being at the same time deftly sodomized.' The plain fact is, he concludes, that these books are all maddeningly the same: 'The stuff is as predictable as a Boy Scout manual.'

He ends his polemic with a remarkable peroration: 'Sexual relations are, or should be, one of the citadels of privacy, the nightplace where we must be allowed to gather the splintered, buried elements of our consciousness to some kind of inviolate order and repose. It is in sexual experience that a human being alone, and two human beings in that attempt at total communication which is also communion, can discover the unique bent of their identity. Then we may find for ourselves, through our imperfect strivings and repeated failures, the words, the gestures, the mental images which set the blood flowing. In that dark and wonder ever renewed both the fumblings and the light must be our own.'

As always with Steiner, this is so eloquent it almost persuades. Why then am I so resistant to it? I think it is that by fetishising 'the nightplace' as he does, Steiner glosses over the complexities of human relations, even in the bedroom. I wonder what he would have made of Kundera, who, in his novels, so brilliantly explores the way we tend to bring so many of the clichés we live with into that which would seem most natural, the sexual relations between people?

And how would Steiner explain the visceral revulsion we see in Kafka and Beckett towards 'the nightplace', their sense that intimacy of this kind robs them of something precious, in some sense *violates their privacy*? Kafka's ideal of intimacy, it would seem (and all the indications are that Eliot's twenty-year long correspondence with Emily Hale, only just made public, will show him to us in the same light) was to write daily letters to the women he fell in love with but to keep them physically at bay. It is easy to become an amateur psychoanalyst in the case of these writers, but does it do them justice? Better surely to recognise that the greatness of their work is in some way bound up with this hatred or terror of 'the nightplace' and to try and understand it.

I have loved women for as long as I can recall and I have never doubted that getting into bed with those I desired was the natural culmination of any initial attraction and, in most cases, a deeply satisfying experience. But it has also been clear to me that, central as it has been to my relationships, it cannot be their be-all and end-all. Again this is difficult to put into words, and again I reach towards another to help me formulate my thoughts. Towards Peter Handke's wonderful book-length poem/meditation, *Gedicht an die Dauer*, translated (very beautifully) into English by Scott Abbott under the title *To Duration*.

'Even "the astonishing, miracles of the moment,"', writes Handke, quoting Schiller, '"do not engender the blissful,/ The calmly powerful durable."' Even the daily joys of a boat trip he took along the Turkish coast with two friends one summer, were not pure:

they were darkened by a melancholy, by a pain
that turned me to stone.
It was as if I were
forever cast out of the world,
as if in these moments I had
lost the right to be alive.
I felt like dying,
and not, by the way, of happiness.

'No,' he goes on,

even on the day of the experience I was aware
that the miracle would not endure.
I could indeed record the moment,
But I had, even then,
no right to it.
Home, get back home, those were my thoughts,
back to the humble garden I had abandoned.

His conclusion at this point? 'I realised once again: / ecstasy is
always too much, / duration, however, just right.'
    And lest he has got himself out of one Romantic dream into
another, he hastens to point out – to himself, to the reader:

But the appeal to the domestic garden
is not a claim
that a fixed abode
and routines
are paths to duration.
True, it arises from
repeated daily events,
but it does not depend on staying put
and on the familiar.

But this too needs qualification: 'Yes, duration is the adventure of the year-in, year-out, / the adventure of the mundane, / but not the adventure of idleness, / not the adventure of (however active) leisure.' 'Is it then related to work?' he wonders, 'to effort, to duty, to constant preparedness?' And again the answer is no. 'No; for if duration had a rule, / it would demand a paragraph perhaps/ and not a poem.' No, for 'Duration cannot be relied on: not even the pious / who attend mass daily / not even the patient, the masters of waiting... / can be assured of its lifelong presence.'

Now he is getting close to it:

> I know, perhaps,
> that it becomes possible only
> when I am able
> to stay at my task
> and to be vigilant at it,
> attentive, unhurried,
> presence of mind to the tips of my fingers.

'And what,' he asks, 'is the task / that demands my persistence? / It will manifest itself / in affection for the living / – for one of them – / and in the awareness of an attachment / (even if only imagined).' 'This task,' he goes on, 'it is not large, / not special, not unusual, not superhuman, / not war, not a landing on the moon... / I share it with millions, / and with my neighbour as well as / with the dwellers at the ends of the earth.' 'Yes,' he repeats,

> this task from which, over the years, duration springs,
> it is fundamentally inconspicuous,
> not worth talking about
> but worth holding on to through writing:
> for it must be my main task.

It must be my true love.
And I must,
if the moments of duration are to spring from me
and give my stiff face a form
and insert a heart into my empty breast,
practise, year in and year out,
unconditionally,
my love.

'The poem to duration is a love poem,' he insists. Love for a woman, for a child, even for yourself. For 'Affection for yourself over time / can also grant duration. / To be able to look into my own eyes amicably / can liberate me. / To think about the child / I once was / means to find him again.' But it can also be brought about by 'the presence of some small things, / the less conspicuous, the more poignant: / that one spoon / that accompanied me through all the moves, / that one hand towel…' And, after meditating on events in his past life:

Duration does not approach
the sitter-at-home,
but the walker towards home
… But it also often accompanies me at home
when I walk up and down in the garden,
in snow, in rain in storm.

And he brings it all to and end with:

Duration does not enrapture,
it forms me anew,
from the bright light of daily activity
I flee, determined, into the uncertain camp of duration…
Not to be counted on, not to be asked for,
not to be bidden

jolts of duration:
you are now joined
into a poem.

Occasionally even this cautious tiptoing into these mysteries
falls into the predictable patterns of Romanticism, though
Rilkean rather than Wagnerian. But on the whole I can say that
I have never come across a piece of writing which so accurately
reflects my innermost feelings about what life is about, mine
in particular, what its pitfalls are and what brings it joy and
fulfilment. Handke is so careful to balance the idea of practice,
of daily routine, and the idea that nothing is given, that, unlike
sport, say, hard work is not necessarily rewarded and what has
been gained is lost and has to be gained again and again. The
poem itself, its form, like Eliot's *Quartets*, which it resembles
(minus the Christianity) mimics the slowness, the constant
qualifying and backtracking, which, he brings out, is the path
to and the fruit of duration.

Intimacy, then, to return to my subject, is a sharing, indeed,
has to be a sharing, but not always with a beloved person. It
can also be with what for want of a better term we can call
the Muse. But that can make it difficult if there is another
person sharing one's life. I know it was difficult for Sacha at
times, she worried that my lack of response was a lack of love,
and is difficult for T, who worries when I am distracted that
somehow it is she who is at fault. It is impossible in words –
impossible for me at any rate– to express to them the truth
that in their different ways they are and have been have been
the ground of my being.

There is no way for me to express this in words, but perhaps
I can express it in what comes naturally to me, the writing of
fiction. As (I now see) I tried to do in *Contre-Jour*, taking as
starting point the idea that while for Bonnard his work was
the centre of his life, it was also rooted in his partner and later

wife, Marthe. Bonnard could not articulate it in words but it is there in all his art, suffused as it is with Marthe's presence and with what his life with her entails as it unfolds in time. Because I did not want to write a van Gogh's-ear type of biographical novel I transferred what I intuited about the two of them to an English couple living in the South of France closer to the time of the novel's writing, the 1980s. That allowed me to write *my* novel, not biography of any kind, however fictionalised. Tim was perceptive I think when he said, on reading it: 'It's about you and Sacha, isn't it?' I hadn't thought of that once when writing the book, so obsessed had I been with getting what I felt about my characters and their relationships down on paper, but when he said it I knew that even if 'about' wasn't quite the right word, my own relationship to my mother, so close, so loving, occasionally so fraught, must have fuelled it. I had always thought I harboured a particular affection for the book because it had come so quickly and so easily, almost as though I was copying something already written, but now I see that it must also be because it managed to encapsulate a truth about something central to my life, the nature of intimacy. It cannot be said 'in so many words', this difficult thing, but it can, with luck, be made into a novel, a poem.

26.5.2020

Beautiful day for walking yesterday and out to Mt Harry, then back along the East slope. Larks particularly loud.

In the evening, *shiva* on Zoom for Gertrude, Bea's mother. She died on Sunday in the nursing home, having, at 90, recovered from C-19, but her body and spirit already far gone with Alzheimer's. When Bea saw her on Tuesday she knew the end was near. She died in her sleep on Sunday. Moving tribute by Bea: her life – born in Slovakian village, survived the war, escaped to the West after 1956, Bea's father already out via E.Berlin – they ended up in Munich and she trained as a dentist. Bea grew up with her in Cologne. Very close relationship – she followed Bea to England in 1998 (when did I meet Bea? At Ralph's?). The rabbi from Malcolm's orthodox synagogue took the service on Zoom like a practised DJ. Moving prayer: Received into the bosom of her people.

Ridiculous press conference by Cummings in garden of Downing Street, with angry journalists. Explained his trip to Durham as 'necessary for the health of the child' and his sixty-mile round trip to Barnard Castle when there as intended to 'test my eyesight' before long journey home. As the Bishop of Worcester (?) said afterwards: 'They are taking us for mugs.' But now we learn that the Bishops who spoke out on this matter have received death threats – 'stay out of politics or we will kill you.' This is what Cameron's wretched Brexit referendum has brought us to.

Josipovici

In Cluj in central Romania in the late seventies, where I was based for a week during the course of a lecture tour of the country I had undertaken for the British Council, my hosts asked me if I would like to take a trip out to a 'traditional Transylvanian town'. I accepted gratefully as the Romanian visit had proved to be much more of a strain and to include far more days of sheer boredom than I had anticipated. I was told a car would come for me at ten the next day, and a further phone call asked me if I would mind being joined on the trip by 'a Polish professor' who was also visiting the University. Naturally I said I would be delighted, and after the car had picked me up we drove to the professor's hotel. As he entered the car the dapper little grey-suited gentleman stretched out a hand and asked: 'Do I have the pleasure of meeting a relative of Albert Josipovici?' I shook his hand and said that I was indeed his grandson.

In all my time in Western Europe – Britain, France, Italy, Germany – nobody had ever mentioned my grandfather. It took a chance meeting with an unknown Polish academic in a country strange to both of us (it was his first visit too as it turned out) for the connection to be made. Yet when the novel my grandfather wrote with his brother-in-law Albert Adès was published in France by Gallimard in 1919, with a preface by Octave Mirbeau, it caused quite a sensation and was short-listed for the Goncourt the year Proust won it with *À l'Ombre des jeunes filles en fleur*, and it has never been out of print since. *Le Livre de Goha le simple*, written by two young (both born in 1892) Francophone Egyptians living in France, is a curious book. Goha is the Egyptian folk-tale hero, the archetypal butt of many a joke. The brilliant idea of the two young men was to take the figure of Goha and insert him into what we would now call an orientalist vision of medieval Cairo, just at the time when orientalism was so fashionable. The book is moreover elegantly written and it is a tribute to their powers to say that it is still perfectly readable. It is not entirely surprising that educated Poles, still imbued with French culture, should have known it even in the seventies.

Last year, the centenary of Proust's Goncourt triumph, saw the publication of a fascinating book on the episode and on the usual jockeying among publishers and literati to get the prize awarded to their favourite. As it turns out Proust won it against the odds, which favoured a patriotic war novel, *Les Croix de bois* by the then well-known Roland Dorgelès. But of course *Goha* got a mention. Adrian Tahourdin, reviewing the book for the *TLS*, emailed me to ask if the Josipovici mentioned there was any relation, and when I affirmed it, said as much in his review. That is the only time, to my knowledge, that my grandfather and his book have been mentioned in the English press. Tim, however, a great haunter of second-hand bookshops, did once turn up at my door triumphantly brandishing an English translation. I have it still, a hardback entitled *Goha the Fool*, published in 1924 by Grant Richards. There is no mention of a translator, but Mirbeau's preface is included, with its comment that the style is 'as pure and austere as that of Flaubert,' and its assertion that 'Only on the day when I read "Goha the Fool" did I understand the East, did I live in it.' The jacket, a little faded but still striking in its muted red, green, white, blue, grey and black, shows a turbaned youth with an ear-ring gazing up at a large bird of prey. Inside I found a photocopy of two pages of the *Dictionnaire General de la Francophonie*, 1986, with an entry for Josipovici (Albert), which says that he studied in France before rejoining his parents in Cairo, where he worked in the Ministry of Justice, that he then collaborated with Adès on a novel, *Les Inquiets* (1914), and, encouraged by Maeterlinck, and both finding themselves in France during the war, they went on to write *Le Livre de Goha le Simple*. Returning to Egypt he published a further novel, written by himself alone, *Le Beau Saïd* in 1928, and died in 1932, leaving a number of unpublished works behind. My mother, who may have had this from my father, told me that my grandfather had the style and his brother-in-law the ideas, and that the book he wrote alone was a total flop. Though I got it from Gallimard when they published my *Contre-Jour*, I have never read it.

A few years ago my agent received an email, which he forwarded to me, from a woman who worked for Arte, the French TV channel. Was I, she enquired, any relation of Jean Josipovici? Indeed I was, I said, I was his son. Why? A further email explained that they were in the process of acquiring the rights of a number of post-war films, which they hoped eventually to show on Arte, and among them were two, for one of which Jean Josipovici had written the script and for another the dialogue alone. If I could prove I was his son and heir I might stand to receive some royalties when they aired. How do I prove that? I asked. I have a birth certificate which says I am his son but I have no idea whether he made a will or had any other children, though I suspect not. If you can send us a copy of the birth certificate, she responded, that is all we want. Clearly they wished to see the legalities wrapped up as quickly as possible and were not overly concerned about the finer points of inheritance rights. My agent saw the contract through, and when I asked what I might expect, whether we were talking tens, hundreds or thousands of pounds, he confessed that he had no idea but imagined it might be in the hundreds. I have heard nothing more from Arte.

My parents were introduced by a cousin of my father's, Stella, and this same cousin was living in London with her sisters and her elderly mother, my grandfather's sister, when we arrived in England in 1956. When we decided to move to London, after I had finished my schooling in Cheltenham in July 1957 Stella kindly offered to put us up until we could find somewhere to live. So my first introduction to London was a large house in Clarendon Road in Holland Park, in which Stella and her husband Didi, who ran the wine department at the Army and Navy Stores in Victoria, lived with her mother, *tante* Helene, who had the flat upstairs. While I roamed the streets and explored the park Stella had a number of serious talks with my mother. He's got to change his name, she said, if he's planning to make his life in this country. Why not Joseph? Or Josephson? But he has no wish to change his name, my mother protested. Stella, whose husband had changed his own name from Harari to Harcourt, was adamant. No one will be able to pronounce it, he'll be marked out as a foreigner for ever. I think we've got to leave that to him, my mother said.

Reluctantly, Stella took the hint. I think you should talk to him, she nevertheless said.

In the nineties, after my mother's death, when I went to Egypt to see my aunt, her sister, who, though a year older, only died at the age of ninety, I stayed with friends, an American academic who, after teaching for many years at the American University in Cairo had ended up as head of publications at the University, and his English wife. One day they announced that a good friend of theirs, an Egyptian ex-ballerina and her American archaeologist husband, were in the country and planning to drive out to the monastery of St Anthony's in the desert three hundred and thirty kilometres southeast of Cairo, close to the Red Sea, and would I like to join them? It seemed that medieval frescoes had been discovered there several years before, an American institution which funded restoration work in Egypt and of which the husband was a member had been responsible for the work, and he wished to see how it was going. The Egyptian turned out to be a ravishingly beautiful and charming woman who spoke multiple languages, while her husband, Jack Josephson, tall and powerful, was a man of few words. On learning his name and that his family had come from Romania I asked whereabouts, and when he said Jasz I told him my family had also come from there and suggested we might be connected. At first he dismissed this as preposterous. My great grandfather arrived in New York with nothing but a card round his neck with his name on it, he said, and in the archetypal American way he rose to become a rich man. But as we talked it through we decided that my suggestion might not have been as wild as all that. Jasz, on the Eastern border of Romania, and a great crossroads of migration, might have been a town of some 60,000 inhabitants in the 1880s. Of those perhaps a third were Jews. At some point the reforms instituted by the Austro-Hungarian Empire, of which it formed a part, had decreed that Slavic names should be Teutonised, and so

Josipovici or son of Joseph would have become Josephson. Yes, he said, it's not such a common name after all, we just might be related. Then he relapsed into silence.

It was a wonderful outing and the frescoes were spectacular, but I never saw the couple again and I have no idea if my hunch was correct. And genealogy, of the type undertaken with such passion by Nicolette, holds no interest for me. I'm happy enough with what I know, and I still find that people in England have difficulty with my name.

27.5.2020

Last night, second night of the Zoom *shiva* for Gertrude. Malcolm managed in his speech both to express genuine love and admiration for her and to hint at their many quarrels and disagreements. So good he did this. The rabbi at the end: *dor ve dor*, generation passes on to generation, and this is as natural as the growth and decay of a tree or a flower. *But*, he said, there is one generation where such a natural transition was not possible – the generation of the Holocaust. That caused such a breach, such a chasm to open up, that it is impossible to join up the *before* and the *after*. Holocaust survivors, such as Gertrude, he said, had the impossible task of bringing up their children to be conscious of this but not to be overly marked by it, marked as they themselves inevitably were. Gertrude succeeded magnificently in carrying out this impossible task, he said. And indeed, though she was pretty crazy all the time I knew her, and perhaps some of that was congenital but some was surely the result of her war experiences, she did manage to bring up Bea to be remarkably free of trauma, even though her professional life has been taken up with exploring those years in the form of her interviews and videos of refugees both from Europe and from the Middle East.

Of course I thought of Sacha. Gertrude was never in a camp, but she was in Slovakia in her teens and with her family hiding and dodging capture and deportation. Sacha was never in a camp but in her thirties, pregnant and with a small child, having to keep her wits about her to get us through it, with the added trauma of the death after ten days of my sister. Both Gertrude and Sacha were not afraid, after their war experiences, of taking further risks, Gertrude to get out of the Communist East and then to join Bea in London, Sacha to pack her bags and leave Egypt with me for an uncertain future. Both Bea and I were brought up solely by these strong women, though Bea did see her father. I too, I think, have to some extent managed the balance between recognising what happened and moving forward into whatever life may have to offer. Strange that we both ended up married to a Miller/Horovitz offspring. Perhaps both of us felt they offered, apart from their intrinsic qualities and looks, a wonderful blend of the rooted and English and the foreign and continental.

The Cummings soap opera continues to dominate. Johnson won't let go of him, clearly fearing he won't be able to get Brexit done and generally to govern without him. But the anger of the country at being taken for a ride shows no sign of abating, though of course BJ and his cabinet stooges keep asking us to 'move on'. The best comment on the whole Johnson/Gove/Cummings years came from a scientist interviewed on Newsnight yesterday, who said: 'Johnson is treating a national emergency as a party political issue, and no good can come of that.' The same of course was/is true of Brexit. A wise leader in 2016 would have seen this was a moment to reach across the parties. May was broken uneasily trying to balance party and country; Johnson triumphed by the simple expedient of making the success of himself and the party the only issue. And it goes on into the new pandemic reality.

Kurtàg

I must have heard the name Kurtàg and perhaps even heard a piece or two of his before 2006, but it was the series of concerts put on in London that year to celebrate his eightieth birthday that brought him fully into my consciousness. And how. In their expressive brevity, in the way he made the most complex music out of the simplest means, in the sheer beauty of the sounds, I felt what I had not felt since I fell in love with the music of Stravinsky, that here was a composer who, however different our worlds, was after the same things as me. There have been many pieces of music written in the second half of the twentieth century that have bowled me over – pieces by Stockhausen, Berio, Ligeti, Maxwell Davies, Birtwistle – but I always felt that in the end the artistic goals and trajectory of these composers were very different from my own. I was, so to speak, overhearing them. In this my relationship to them was different from my relationship to the music of Stravinsky, where from the start I felt that if I had the talent I would like to write fiction as he wrote music. And now, in 2006, I felt it again with Kurtàg.

I loved the way he made quite lengthy works out of the accumulation of very short pieces. The *Kafka Fragments*, for example, lasts for 55 minutes and consists of forty fragments. *Játékok* (Games), for piano (two and four hands) is an open-ended work to which he has kept adding new pieces all his working life, and which is now so long that only selections are ever played. I loved the fact that so many of his pieces are either homages or memorials to friends and fellow composers. What has so moved me in Stravinsky over the years, the mixture of brevity, wit and plangency, I found again here, though their sensibilities and the traditions they draw on are so different. Kurtàg, while obviously owing much to Bartok, is drawn to Schubert and Schumann and is not averse, in his piano music, to using the pedal; Stravinsky to baroque music with its roots in dance and he looks for clarity at all times. And so on.

Kurtàg shares with Britten a remarkable ability to use great literature in his vocal music and actually to add to its significance. Usually composers set great literature to music at their peril – we all know the dissatisfaction we feel when listening to most operas based on Shakespeare (to my mind even Verdi's *Falstaff* falls into this category). Yet Britten could set Eliot's 'Journey of the Magi' and actually illuminate it, first and foremost by the simple but brilliant expedient of setting it for three voices. I had always somehow taken the 'we' with which it opens: 'A cold coming we had of it', as a sort of generalised singular but Britten's setting made me understand (what of course should have been obvious) that the 'we' are the three magi, speaking as one. And who would have thought Hölderlin and Beckett, of all people, would be enhanced by being set to music? Yet Kurtàg has such a deep understanding of Beckett's work in particular that he has found ways to use both 'What is the word?' and *Fin de partie* without leaving us feeling: 'Why bother?'

28.5.2020

The fine weather continues. The country seems already to be out of lockdown, though I doubt the R figure has gone under 0.5, which is what all the experts say it should be before lockdown starts to be eased. The independent scientists nearly all predict a second spike, a second run on hospitals, multiple more deaths – all because of the ineptitude of this government. The pitiful Cummings saga only the latest and most blatant example of that. Now the government is changing the guidelines so as to include travel 'if there is good reason to do so'. In the *Guardian* today the Lancet editor, himself a doctor, Richard Horton, has a scathing attack not just on Johnson and Cummings but on all their stooges, *including* the scientific advisors. These men and women should not be standing up beside government ministers at the press briefings, far less mouthing their lies and evasions, he says. And where, he asks, is the Royal Society and the College of Medecine? Why are they not speaking out?

Kurtàg (cont.)

György Kurtàg was born in 1926 in the Banat region of Romania, but moved to Budapest in 1945 and became a Hungarian citizen, Wikipedia informs us. What the entry does not say is that he (like Ligeti) is Jewish and it is silent on what he and his family went through in the war years. It tells us he studied music at the Franz Liszt Academy in Budapest, where he met his future wife Márta as well as Ligeti. In 1956, when Ligeti fled to the West, Kurtàg and Márta stayed put. In 1957–8, though, he managed to get permission to study in France, where he worked with Messiaen and Milhaud and came across the music of Webern and the plays and novels of Beckett, both of which marked him for life. But, for reasons one may easily imagine, he fell into a depression, found himself unable to compose, and in the end had to seek help. He was fortunate to find the psychologist, Marianne Stein. One note is just a note, she said to him, but two notes are already a composition; start with the small things and build on that. In that way, returning to Hungary, he began to compose again, but now in the pared-down style which has become his hallmark. For the extraordinary thing about his music is that one just has to hear a bar of Kurtág to know it's him and no one else.

I love the thought: one note is just a note, two notes are already a composition. Kurtàg's music is often compared to

Webern's because of its extreme brevity, but their temperaments are entirely different. Webern, like his master Schoenberg and his fellow disciple Berg, operates at the extremes, always on the edge of hysteria. Kurtàg, by contrast, can move from the high tension of the *Kafka Fragments* and 'Samuel Beckett What is the Word?', his setting of Beckett's last tiny work, to the warmth of his homages to Boulez or to some of his Hungarian friends, and the quiet perfection of the Bach transcriptions in Jatékok. So much at one with the central strand of European literary Modernism from Hölderlin to Beckett, he, like Stravinsky, is also a great opener-up of the past, a humanist in the best sense of the word. Since that memorable Kurtàg season in 2006 he has been part of my inner world, a source of comfort and inspiration in my life and in my work.

It must have been in 2011 or 12 that I saw him for the last time. He and Márta came to the Wigmore Hall to perform a selection from *Játékok*. They performed on an upright piano, with their backs to the audience. In the pieces for four hands the audience looked at two square, drab, elderly Hungarian backs, quite still, shoulders just touching. When he played alone she stood back and gazed at him as though to say to the audience: 'Look at him, my husband the composer'. When she played alone he stood up close and protective. That, at least, is how I saw it. T, I have to say, saw it as more authoritative, even threatening, more master than life-partner. Who knows which of us was right? But I will never forget that concert, the music they played and the two of them, sitting there, backs to us, side by side, producing those ravishing sounds.

Márta died in 2019, at ninety-two. The previous year Kurtàg's first opera, *Fin de Partie*, premiered at La Scala. He too was ninety two, the last survivor of the great generation of composers who came to prominence after the war, Boulez, Stockhausen, Berio, Nono, Ligeti, Xenakis – and quite possibly the greatest of them all.

Johnson now subtly trying to turn the Cummings debacle into a story of a political witch-hunt. I doubt if that will wash. Too many people, from all parts of the political spectrum, have been shocked more by the spectacle of the Prime Minister putting his crony above the public good than by Cummings' actual breach of trust and refusal to resign. What all of us could see for years has suddenly seeped into the general public's consciousness. Whether that is a permanent dent or not only time will tell. No doubt Johnson will drive the country on to a no-deal Brexit and then blame the ensuing problems on the EU and the pandemic – but will the country buy it as more services are cut, jobs lost and a new austerity bites?

'My get up and go has got up and gone', T tells me her cockney grandmother used to say. I'm beginning to feel, after this healthy interlude, that my get up and go has returned – I hope to take up permanent residence – for a year or two at least. How it will be when the weather turns and the trips to London resume remains to be seen. For now, after a morning at the desk absorbed in this, I can't wait to get out onto the Downs for a walk with T. And lack any real passion for reading – always a sign that the work is going well – or at least: going.

Larry

Larry was one of the reasons I ended up teaching at Sussex. When, in the early '60s, I was a graduate student looking for my first job, it was difficult, if one was interested in literature, to avoid the name of Laurence Lerner. If it wasn't a poem by him in among the book reviews it was a review or even the review of a book *by* him, a new volume of poems or a critical book. When I discovered that he had recently moved to the new university of Sussex from Queens, Belfast, I thought: if they have someone like him on their books they might look with sympathy at someone more interested in writing fiction than scholarly works.

When I got to Sussex I found someone very different from how I had imagined him. Small, wiry, dark, gypsy-like, extremely friendly and without an ounce of conceit. He and his wife Nat were South Africans, Larry half-Jewish, but both staunch Quakers. Right from the start I had been puzzled to find that though we liked and admired each other and were happy to discuss books, we hardly had any common interests. I loved the Middle Ages and much of the twentieth century, but most nineteenth-century writing left me cold, while Larry's centre of interest was precisely the nineteenth century. Yet, like me, he had no time for a notion of Eng. Lit. that was confined to English or to literature. Our witty and intelligent friend and colleague, Gāmini Salgado, once introduced a lecture by Larry at the annual conference of the Association of Teachers of English thus: 'Professor Lerner will now speak on one of his minor areas of specialisation, Literature and Society'. The same Gāmini once quipped that 'Lerner is a Cavalier masquerading as a Roundhead; Josipovici a Roundhead masquerading as a Cavalier.' I knew what he meant about me, a certain desire to make others see the truth of my position and a certain intolerance for other views – but Larry always seemed to me a Roundhead proud of being a Roundhead. He was concerned with morals and hardly at all with metaphysics, pragmatic, at times fiercely Utilitarian. He was genuinely puzzled by me, I think, both by my fiction and my criticism, and even myself. That we remained friends all his life is a tribute to his generosity of spirit.

But also to the fact that I admired his poetry. I once said to him: 'You write such good poetry, Larry, why do you do so many other things – extra-mural teaching, critical writing, reviewing, even examining?' 'If I only wrote poetry,' he replied, 'I probably wouldn't write any more or any better.' And he was probably right. But what he didn't say was that his Quaker conscience drove him to want to do as much good as he could in the world.

30.5.2020

Why do I sleep so much, wake up so late? And feel so sleepy when I wake up? Is it age? The walks we take every day?

Yesterday Sir David King, the government's chief scientific advisor from 2000 to 2007 and now head of an *ad hoc* committee of top scientists who have formed in the wake of the pandemic, feeling that SAGE is too politicised and does not give the impartial scientific advice so desperately needed, on Chanel Four News: 'The government's bungling incompetence has led to 40,000 more deaths than we should have had.'

Larry (cont.)

In his heyday, when most of the poetry editors in the publishing houses and on the weeklies and Sunday papers were friends and fellow poets, he had been labelled a 'Movement' poet but, like most labels this one does not really fit. This early poem is perhaps the nearest he got to it.

Raspberries
Once, as a child, I ate raspberries. And forgot.
And then, years later,
A raspberry flowered on my palate, and the past
Burst in unfolding layers within me.

It tasted of grass and honey.
You were there, watching and smiling.
Our love unfolded in the taste of raspberries.

More years have passed; and you are far, and ill;
And I, unable to reach you, eating raspberries.
Their dark damp red, their cool and fragile fur
On the always edge of decay, on the edge of bitter,
Bring a hush of taste to my mouth.

Tasting of earth and of crushed leaves
Tasting of summer's insecurity,
Tasting of crimson, dark with the smell of honey,

Tasting of childhood and of remembered childhood,
And now, now first the darker taste of dread.

Sap and imprisoned sunlight and crushed grass
Lie on my tongue like a shadow,
Burst like impending news on my aching palate

Tasting not only of death (I could bear that)
But of death and you together,
The folded layers of love and the sudden future,
Tasting of earth and the thought of you as earth

As I go on eating, waiting for the news.

In 1974 he brought out *A.R. T.H. U.R. The Life and Opinions of a Digital Computer*, a volume like no other in contemporary poetry in English, yet recognisably Larry's. The introductory poem runs:

There are two kinds of people: metal people
And movers. Movers are much more supple
But are easily torn and hardly reparable.

Movers are constantly bending and running
Through a world of edges and obstacles. Cunning
Their reflexes, but cannot eliminate mourning.

Those who can print need neither move nor shout
They get along without getting about.
There are certain talents one is better without.

Movers are very slow-witted; need a day
To work out a graph or a mode or an orbit or pi,
And make what they call mistakes (e.g. twice two are three).

Movers use words like 'bad' and 'ought'
And 'purpose' and 'envy' and 'why' and 'hate' and 'God',
And hundreds of others that impede clear thought.

And look at the way the world is run,
It's always the movers decide what gets done,
And even how many metal people are born.

It took movers a thousand years to make up chess.
They still need five minutes a move, and often lose.
But who decides when the games take place?

Metal people aren't allowed to procreate;
All their decisions are questioned; they can't even vote.
Movers have all the power. Do you think that is right?

This need to impersonate, to speak 'from the other side', to
find words for those without words, became a central feature

of his poetry and led to some of his most profound and moving poems. My favourite is *The Merman*, which, at ninety-one and having just lost Nat, to whom he had been married for over sixty years, and having more or less lost his memory, he read at a public reading John Agard and I organised for him in Lewes:

The Merman

It was because I swam into their net
Because the net was there
The water thickened, there was no way out,
It was because it tangled in my hair
Because it caught the water it caught me,
I left the wet and came to live in air.

I learned to stand on two legs in the dry,
I learned to look at day, at brown and red
Till they went dark. And then I learned to die
And wake when dark was dead.
I learned to change the place I was, with legs,
Learnt to drink air, but never learnt their talk.

They gave me hungry needing fish to eat
And called it 'fish',
Then after needing nothing fish to put
And called it 'fish'. Fish, fish; as if the same
That same, that difference, they call that a name.
I couldn't talk like that. I couldn't talk.

When humans talk they split their say in bits
And bit by bit they step on what they feel.
They talk in bits, they never talk in all.
So live in wetness swimming they call 'sea';

And stand on dry and watch the wet waves call
They still call 'sea', only their waves don't call.

Strange are their pleasures, living in the dry,
Build a long finger on an empty house
And in it sing, four times a moon, and kneel,
And talk sea talk at last, talk what they feel
Not words, not names. I heard their holy song
It said belong, belong.

So one day in the finger house I stood
And sang of wet and swimming in the was,
And happy sang of happy singing till
They all came running noise and sticks of wood
And shouting devil kneel
And devil and that day I found out hurt.

That dark I did not die but ran away
To where the wet and swimming call and wait
And joined myself to swimming. This was back,
It did not hurt to change the way you lay,
It did not hurt to breathe. Just swallowing hurt
At first, till water washed the words out.

I must have tasted too much dry up there
I must have got a taste for words, or air,
Or hurt, or something. Now
I follow ships from far,
I climb on rocks and sit there till they see
Till they put off in boats to bring me words
And nets, and hurt. Wait till they're close and then
Almost reluctant, slip back in the sea.

I think now that everything that his Quaker moralism kept under in his daily life, in his dealings with others, emerges in his poetry. Perhaps it could only be let loose in fictions written within the tight confines of metre and rhyme. I wish though I had managed to break through to it while he was alive, on the many walks we took, both before he went to America and, much more frequently, when he came back and settled in Lewes, round the corner from me. But it never happened.

31.5.2020

Sunday.

The Cummings saga is not going away. Almost unbelievably, a German fact-checker has discovered that when he threw out in passing in his press conference last Saturday that he had predicted the pandemic in 2019 (and so implied he was always on the side of science and of good), he had in fact done nothing of the sort, but rather had, on April 14, altered a 2019 blog in order to insert a phrase about the pandemic. What a pathetic cheating schoolboy he is.

And MPs of all stripes are up in arms at Rees-Mogg's attempt to get Parliament to reconvene in person from Tuesday, a move designed only to bolster Johnson in his weekly clashes with Keir Starmer, but which the vulnerable among them fear will simply stop them, elected representatives, having their say,

And the sight of beaches – Brighton at the front of course – packed with visitors on these sunny May days when the scientists are warning that the virus has not been suppressed nearly enough to ease the lockdown even by a fraction – fills one with fear for a second spike, many more deaths, including those of doctors and nurses. And all because the Tory right are baying for action on the economic front even at the expense of 'a few lives', and Johnson is desperate to distract from the Cummings saga.

But the days go on being perfect for walking and we go on walking. The ninety-three-year-old man we've met two days running, turns out to be a neighbour of Anne-Marie's called Norman. Walks at least twice a day onto the Downs, he tells us, once during the day and once in the evenings to watch the sunset. A-M says he told her he was one of the two boys who found Virginia Woolf after she drowned herself – is that true?

Limits

Why does my heart leap when I see a sculpture (Giacometti) or a painting (Bonnard, Hammershøi) of a figure in a closed room? For leap it does. It's happened too often to be chance.

On the other hand too insistent a focus on the closed room leads to boredom, claustrophobia (for me at any rate). I can't read those Beckett prose pieces where he describes in detail the size of a closed room and the changing light inside it, or some of those late plays which consist entirely of the depiction of sealed rooms with or without figures inside them. I need a human element, as in *Footfalls* and *Rockaby*.

So my heart leaps (I think) not because it responds for some mysterious reason to images of a sealed room but because it responds, in art, to a depiction of *limits*. And I think that is because I feel then that this is an honest art. An art that puts in front of you what it legitimately can and cannot do. In *Company*, perhaps my favourite work of Beckett's, the narrator sits alone in his room and out of that solitude imagines/remembers episodes of his childhood. We watch him imagining/remembering and we watch him distancing himself from his imagining/ remembering, and the combination, for some reason, is overwhelming.

In *Tristram Shandy* we watch Tristram trying, always in vain, to piece his life together, to make the kind of book that was so popular in the eighteenth century, *The Life and Opinions of –* . And what I love about pieces like Stravinsky's *Octet* and Stockhausen's *Contra-Punkte* is how each note is clear and distinct form the others, each phrase is simple yet all add up to something rich and complex. What did Marianne Stein say to Kurtág? One note is just a note, two notes are already a piece of music.

So that my equally visceral dislike of the piano music of Schumann and Chopin and the symphonies of Mahler may be explained by the feeling they evoke in me that they are trying to lull my spirits rather than awaken them. And the same with so many novels and realistic paintings and sculptures. But also with abstract art like Pollok's and Rothko's, however different they may be, and with purely OULIPIan creations like the novels of Harry Mathews.

What moves me then is the depiction of the outside world, of human beings, which *at the same time* recognises that it is depiction and not 'life itself' and is prepared to press hard to see how far that brings freedom and how far enslavement.

For me the central problem with each new work, novel, short story, play, radio play, is finding the limits, finding the borders, beyond which it is impossible (for me) to go, but which can be pointed to, pointed at: Over there, another world. Or perhaps: Over there, the world.

Once I find those limits, those borders, the work often gets written quite quickly.

One of my mantras: John Berryman's: 'Write as short as you can / In order / Of what matters.' All three components are important. The first is obvious enough. The second is perhaps the most difficult thing to get right when linearity is no longer the driving factor. The third means, I take it: Of what matters to you. If it doesn't, however clever, subtle or powerful, the work will be dead.

Official summer time and the Government has used the date to 'start easing the lockdown', 'strictly following the science', say the ministers, as more and more public health experts and officials plead with them not to do it. Even their criteria have not been met, since the number of infections shows no sign decreasing, the R rate is still well above 0.5 (between 0.7 and 0.9 apparently), and the test and trace strategy, by their own admission, won't be fully ready before the end of the month. All due, as becomes more and more evident, to the Tories' long built-in reliance on outsourcing everything to private bodies with no expertise in the field and a hopelessly centralised system where what you need is local experts.

Meanwhile the US is engulfed in what are more than protests but seem to have the potential of turning into outright revolution or civil war, as black men and women in every part of the country feel that the death of a black man, George Floyd, at the hands of the police, caught on video begging for his life and saying 'Let me breathe!' as a policeman presses his face into the pavement – feel that this is the final straw. Trump stokes up the anger, partly no doubt because his gut instinct is to side with 'law and order', especially against the black community, but also I'm sure because a civil war would delay any election and lead to his remaining in office – and, among other things, avoiding the prison he would probably end up in once he has no longer got the immunity of the Presidency to protect him. Rather like Natanyahu really, but the repercussions for the world of a new American civil war don't bear thinking about.

Literature and Life

Kafka tried to explain to his fiancée Felice that 'I do not *like* literature, I am made of literature and am not able or willing to be anything else'. By that he meant that he did not think of himself as writing books for public consumption like his friends Max Brod and Franz Werfel, but that writing was, as he saw it, his life and his only road to salvation. In effect he was throwing out a hint that he would never be able to live with her, but since at the same time every one of the almost daily letters he sent her in the intense period of their courtship cried out his need for her, the poor girl failed to grasp this. On the whole I shy away from such pronouncements, as from the sort of 'dedicated' life artists like Maxwell Davies and Frank Auerbach have chosen for themselves. Or the kitsch American equivalent, the 'I am unique and if I hurt others that's because my art requires it' kind of attitude. I warm more to the Bonnard and Beckett way of being in the world, their work central to their lives but hardly exclusive of all else, their behaviour not always exemplary but always imbued by compassion and understanding. I think the idea of cutting oneself off from the world to concentrate on one's art can turn out to be as detrimental to the art as trying to live a full and rich social life can be. Max produced wonderful work when he first went to live in Orkney – *Ave Maris Stella*, *Image Reflection Shadow*, strange, taut, miraculously quiet pieces after the frenzy of *Eight Songs for a Mad King* and *Vesalii Icones*– but soon, I feel, lost his way as he went on living in Orkney isolation, and eventually turned himself into what he imagined as an Orkadian Haydn, churning out symphonies, quartets and concertos at an alarming rate – a hopeless ambition, even if one can understand the temptation. Yet it's hard, probably impossible, to get the balance right, harder still no doubt if you're a woman. Something gets lost somewhere, some people are unnecessarily hurt. But few human lives are perfect and few can say as they get older that they regret nothing.

2.6.2020

Drove to Crowlink yesterday to have a walk on the Seven Sisters. Wonderful light, sea blue to the east, turning into a burnished mirror as the eye moved west. Hardly a soul except on the actual Seven Sisters trail. Yet both T and I felt strangely disappointed. Before the lockdown this would have been a highlight but now the feeling that the drive was too long and, actually, unnecessary – we were happier, we agreed, setting out on foot towards Mt Harry and walking on that Western side of town, even though we'd been doing it for seventy-one days. So the lockdown – and of course the weather – has taught us a lot – about ourselves, about the surrounding countryside.

We might try the golf course today, no driving – but still, less good, I suspect, and more road walking, than the usual.

We hardly bother with the news any more – America descending into chaos, death toll rising in Brazil, and here any pretence by the government to be 'relying on the science' has been completely discredited How can we have moved so quickly from being a reasonable middle-of-the road country to being this island run by hopelessly inefficient ideologues?

Menhir

I had always been drawn to megaliths, those prehistoric standing stones to be found everywhere in Britain and Europe, and I had for as long as I could remember wanted to visit Carnac in Brittany, one of the greatest neolithic sites, where, so I had read, they stand not in circles but in long lines stretching for kilometres through the gorse and the bracken. An additional incentive, always somewhere at the back of my mind, had been a confusion between Carnac in Brittany and Karnak near Luxor in Upper Egypt. Even after our trip to Brittany the sound 'carnac/karnak' in my head still conjures up a combination of ancient Egypt and ancient Europe, something utterly mysterious, never quite to be grasped, and for that reason all the more desirable.

Stephen of course was the person to consult and he did not disappoint. 'Take this with you,' he said, thrusting a well-worn hardback into my hands, 'it will tell you all you need to know'. I looked at the title and laughed: *The Hungry Archaeologist in France and Brittany* it was called, and the author was the renowned archaeologist Glyn Daniel. Stephen had a great many passions, but high on the list were archaeology and food, and here they were brought together in one volume by a world famous authority on prehistory – and, as I discovered, someone with something of Stephen's passion for good food.

So, armed with *The Hungry Archaeologist in France*, Sacha and I took the ferry from Newhaven to Dieppe and set off West. As we stopped in one little fishing port in Brittany after another what I remember above all are two sets of noises: as we entered each restaurant we would be greeted by the brittle sound of cracking bones as the diners broke into the lobsters they had come there to eat; so difficult was this feat, except for the most experienced, and so eager were they all to get at the delicious flesh so carefully guarded by nature, that the pleasant sound of human conversation, normally such a feature of French restaurants, was almost entirely absent, replaced by the crack crack crack of hard bones being broken by specialised tools. The other sound was the tinkling of the pennants on the masts of the yachts and sailing boats moored in each little port as we took a stroll round the town after our own struggles with the varieties of shellfish always on offer.

But we did eventually get to Carnac, at the Western edge of Brittany, close to the Gulf of Morbihan and the town of Quiberon. We found, with the help of Glyn Daniel, a pleasant hotel/restaurant nearby and set out the next day to explore. We were not disappointed.

The site consists of three extensive rows of *menhirs* or standing stones, running for several kilometres through flowery gorse and bracken. There are over three thousand of these, ranging from four metres to 0.6 metres high. Archaeologists date the site anywhere from 4,500 to 3000 BC. The stones are man-made, that is, the local granite has been roughly cut and shaped, but over the millennia they have weathered and become covered with yellow-green lichen, so that they blend with the countryside and you feel as though you are walking along immense quiet natural avenues of stone. Close by are a multitude of tumuli or earth-covered graves, *menhirs* or giant single sanding stones, and *dolmens*, huge stones supporting a capstone such as one sees at Stonehenge. There is a giant *menhir* of six and a half metres, standing tall above the landscape, but what we were most moved by was the so-called *Grand Menhir Brisé*, a twenty-metre monster that has fallen or been somehow toppled over and is broken into four pieces. As we climbed over it I was reminded of one of my favourite bicycle excursions into the desert when I was growing up in Egypt, to what was called a petrified forest, but consisted in reality of just one or two trees, turned to stone by time and the climate, lying broken on their sides, compelling and mysterious. The mystery I suppose resided in the sense one had, looking at them, not so much of time passing as of Time itself, present and visible – and even touchable. The Carnac *menhirs*, at the border between nature and culture, captured that for me as well, the *Grand Menhir Brisé*, at once grand and pitiful, most of all.

That feeling of something present and palpable and yet incomprehensibly other, is more powerful than any artefact

I have ever encountered. I came across it again in a great exhibition at the British Museum some years ago of art from Western Nigeria. It is usually the Benin bronzes that attract all the attention, but on my several visits to the show what drew me were two or three far more ancient, massive, barely formed stone pieces. At the time I was writing *Infinity*, and I was so overwhelmed by these that I managed to get them into that novel, allowing me, through the medium of my composer/protagonist Tancredo Pavone, filtered through the words of Massimo, his amanuensis, to explore them and the feelings they evoked in me.

I have been back to Brittany since that trip with my mother, but never to Carnac. It is as if I know those *menhirs* too well and do not want to disturb them as they lie there in my memory.

3.6.2020

Overcast but hot, though it's supposed to get colder and rainier this week.

The large man (and his small wife) we often meet on the Downs, yesterday: 'We could do with a bit of rain.' And for once I don't feel like contradicting him. It's been too unreal, this non-stop fine weather. As if the pandemic had to be played out in glorious technicolour, not drab English greys.

Dreadful novel I've been reading in bed recently: Elizabeth Bowen's *The Death of the Heart*. Never read her before and don't think I'm going to finish this. In the *LRB*, a fine long essay on Simenon by John Lanchester. In it he says: Anyone who has been brought up on a diet of the classic English novel is in for a big surprise when he turns to the French classic novel. Austen, Dickens, Eliot, the Brontes all essentially write children's books, in which the bad are bad and the good are good and good triumphs and it ends in marriage. Balzac, Stendhal, Flaubert and Proust, by contrast, write realistic novels in which good and evil are inextricably mixed up and endings are rarely happy. Obviously, easy to quibble, but he's essentially right. And, thinking about the Bowen and that previous dreadful book with a wonderful title I tried to read, Dorothy Whipple's *Someone at a Distance*, and Jean Rhys etc., it struck me that so many 'women's novels' in the last century have been written by people who, raised on a diet of the classic English novel, howled with anguish when life did not, for them, turn out as they felt it should. The kind of English and American innocence James both admired and was so good at puncturing. Of course it's not so much the result of a diet of the classic English novel as that the English novel is itself a product of a Puritan tradition which cannot tolerate the idea of complexity, needing everything to be either good or bad.

Ivy Compton Burnett, who it seems was a friend of Elizabeth Bowen, is said to have remarked: 'Everyone keeps writing to her about the deaths of their hearts.' I.C.B., like Virginia Woolf, is splendidly free of that tradition.

Novel, novella, *récit*

'What you write are novellas.' Or: 'You know, what you write are really what the French call *récits*.' Or: 'What you write are really radio plays.' I have heard those comments numerous times, and each time I want to say: 'Well, no.'

To start with the last point, that what I write are not novels but radio plays. When this was first put to me I had difficulty in rebutting it. After all, my novels – or those I had written at the time when I was writing radio plays – make great use of dialogue, and two of my early novels had been adapted for radio with the minimum of change. And yet, from the inside, as it were, the writing of a radio play and the writing of a novel feel like quite different endeavours. Writing a radio play you can trust the listener to 'fill in', as it were. But often in my novels what I want is for the reader to empathise with characters who are themselves struggling to 'fill in', to anchor themselves in life in some way. That seems to me very different and to lead to very different end results.

In my novels I seem to be wedded to the phrase 'he said', 'she said'. This is partly a rhythmic thing, but I feel it is deeper than that. I want the reader, I think, to be subliminally reminded, all the time, that this is not 'reality ', but, inevitably, 'reality filtered through narrative fiction'. And yet I don't want to try and convey through adjective and adverb the way he or she is speaking, because I feel that, however you elaborate the description you won't really be able to convey it – better put it down starkly and allow the reader to work out how it is said. So: not 'he said, sighing deeply' or 'he said in a low growl', or 'she answered calmly', but simply: He said, she said. Let the reader work.

But it goes deeper than that. Often I am struggling with the desire to express the feeling, which sometimes presses strongly upon me, that when we are gone all that is left are our words – and that they can hardly be said to be 'ours'. They are simply what is said, the common currency of speech, spoken by this person at this particular moment. Can we get at 'who they are, or were' through this, all we are left with?

And, last of all: allowing characters to speak and allowing the narrative to develop through speech feels more honest to me, since words after all are the currency writers deal with. So: to find a way to make that currency redeemable. As Duras does so beautifully in *Le Square*. That is the task as I see it.

I'm not sure I've managed to express it, but it will have to do for now.

As to the first two remarks or accusations (they are usually made in an accusatory tone), I have no idea what a novella is.

In popular parlance a novella is shorter than a novel and longer than a short story. And in popular perception a novella is for that reason less than a novel. But not in my experience. I find *Bartleby* more meaningful than *Moby Dick*, *The Death of Ivan Ilytch* than *War and Peace*, *Seize the Day* than *Humboldt's Gift*. And when flicking through the reviews of novels in the *TLS* I look first at the number of pages and skip the review of any book over 250 pages. That isn't of course a hard and fast rule. After all, I would put *À la recherche* and *The Devils* among my top five or six novels of all time, and they are hardly short, and (now I come to think of it) neither are *La Vie mode d'emploi* and *Tristram Shandy*. Would I put Büchner's 'Lenz' and Kafka's 'Metamorphosis' as among my favourite short stories or my favourite short novels? The point is, *it doesn't matter*. It may matter to publishers and booksellers but not to the ordinary reader whether you publish Kleist's *Michael Kohlhaas* or Melville's *Bartleby* by itself or in a collection of their short stories – though I prefer to handle such works singly and relish the German and French traditions of printing small books – now taken up by such publishers as Melville Books.

As far as my writing is concerned I know from the start whether what I have is a short story or a novel. And my short stories tend to be very short even for a short story and my novels very short for a novel. That's the way it is and there's nothing I can do about it. I once heard a composer say his 'length' was around fifteen minutes, and that even if he started out thinking a piece would be much longer it always ended up around that length. It's the same with me. Occasionally I've thought, when I'd got a novel going, this is it, this is the big one, perhaps it will be my *Vie Mode d'emploi*, my *Extinction*, but in the end it never is, the length remains constant, take one or two dozen pages.

The exception to my rule that a short story is a short story and a novel is a novel (unlike Thomas Mann, who began *The*

Magic Mountain thinking it would be a longish short story) is *The Cemetery in Barnes*. I had written a story in the 80s, when I wrote a lot of them (they tend to come in batches, with long periods when no short stories come at all), which even I, who relish compression, felt was perhaps a little too compressed – or rather, felt, for once, that it could do with expansion. That story was called 'Steps', and I liked the title, felt it caught very well (and succinctly) what I was after. But the idea that I might expand it, from within as it were, stayed with me for the next thirty years and eventually I felt I had to see what an expansion would yield. By the time I had finished *The Cemetery in Barnes* I wondered if all I had succeeded in doing was ruining a good story – and I'm still not sure, now, a couple of years after it has been published.

The idea of the *récit* is more interesting than the idea of the novella. I will pursue that tomorrow.

4.6.2020

Grey. Much colder.

In a Channel Four *Dispatches* programme yesterday on the government's mishandling of the Covid pandemic Sir Paul Nurse, the Nobel prize-winning geneticist who now heads the Francis Crick Institute described how, at the heart of the crisis, when the shortage of PPE was a major anxiety, he offered the services of the Institute to help, but was rebuffed. 'It was like poking a blancmange,' he said. 'There was a vague indentation and then, after a moment, the blob resumed its shape.' His offer was never taken up.

Novel, Novella, 'Récit' (cont.)

In an essay entitled 'The Song of the Sirens', which opens *Le Livre à venir*, (1954) Maurice Blanchot discusses what he sees as the essential difference between the novel and the *récit*, using the allegory of Ulysses' encounter with the sirens in the *Odyssey*. He compares the novel to the cautious preparations Ulysses undertakes in order to resist the lure of the Sirens' voices, which tempt sailors to their deaths. Both Ulysses and the novel, suggests Blanchot, choose safety over submission to the beautiful but destructive song of the sirens, while nevertheless endeavouring to overhear it (Kafka adopted a different interpretation, as we have seen). Blanchot describes this as an 'entirely human story' (*une histoire toute humaine*), and contrasts it with the way the récit responds to it: The novel pursues its course as a tale, while the *récit* gives itself up solely to the sirens' song, even though it will lead to its own eventual destruction.

The fixation of the *récit* on the lure and the lure alone does not mean that it simply chooses one novelistic episode over the others. The lethal appeal of the song of the sirens is not used as material for story-telling and its depiction is therefore not just another episode in a long sequence of events. Where the novel turns away from the devastating lure and busies itself elsewhere, the *récit* seeks to express the very nature of the lure.

This has nothing to do with length. Blanchot's examples of works focussed on the lure are *Moby Dick* and *À la recherche du temps perdu*, neither of them exactly short works. But his most helpful remarks about how the *réci*t works in practice come, I think, in his wonderful brief essay on *The Turn of the Screw*, though it makes no mention of the sirens and their song. Where English and American critics have long debated whether to read James's story as a ghost story, as it purports to be, or as an exploration of the fantasies of the governess/

narrator, Blanchot argues, convincingly to my mind, that it is the ultimate expression of James's constant search, in later life, as described in his *Notebooks*, for 'the one true story', that which will free him from bondage to endless description of characters and events and allow what he feels he has it within himself to speak to finally emerge. The governess is shown relentlessly trying to force the two children in her care, and particularly the little boy Miles, to 'tell her the truth'. In the end she succeeds. He utters the words she wants him to utter – and dies in her arms. You reach the sirens at your peril.

To read *The Turn of the Screw* as either a ghost story or a Freudian narrative of repression and fantasy is to read it as a novel. It is to assert that there is 'a story' which it 'tells', and that this story was dreamed up by James (based as so often on an anecdote he heard at one of the innumerable dinner parties he attended) and then written down. But, says Blanchot, in 'The Song of the Sirens', as far as the *récit* is concerned there is no prior story, only a story always in the process of emerging, as the writer gets to work, a story which will never, can never, be fully realised and which is both always in the past and always in the future yet also always in the now of the writing. It is the reason why a Melville, a James, a Proust, felt that only by writing could they fulfil themselves and knew also that the quest was both endless and doomed to failure and yet also strangely joyful.

5.6.2020

Today the news from Britain is that the 'world-beating' test trace and isolate system Johnson trumpeted as being 'up and running' by 1 June, may not be ready before September! (The CEO of one of the component parts of this in the Downing

Street 'plan', boasts in a leaked email that this will solidly entrench private firms in the NHS.) And as for the notion that 'lockdown will only be eased when we have a reliable TTI system in place', that, of course, belongs to yesterday's pronouncements.

Walked over the golf-course yesterday, for a change, and again found there is no beating the Mt Harry and Black Cap walk, *du côté de la petite école*. But interesting to walk back through a mainly deserted and boarded up Lewes. In the evening got back to *Brothers K* and felt again how Dostoevsky, uniquely, along with Shakespeare, seems able to capture in his work a vivid popular idiom, an idiom saturated with religious language and feeling, so that, seemingly effortlessly, they seem to tap into age-old popular wisdom without, like Agnon, say, feeling antiquated. Other writers of the time had the same opportunities and occasionally in the other Elizabethan play-wrights and the other Russian novelists one gets a glimpse of it, but with them it's central.

Proust's correspondence with his mother. From fifteen (1886) to her death when he was thirty-five (1907). How his asthma kept him a child throughout her life. And how close she is to Marcel's mother and grandmother in the novel. That combination of Jewish warmth and Enlightenment education and values – very similar to Sacha (much more confident, of course, entitled almost), which is part of the reason, no doubt, why when I read him at seventeen I at once felt Proust was speaking to me.

Optimism

Ever since I read Bacon's remark that 'I am a pessimist by nature but I have an optimistic nervous system' (another brilliant *mot* of his was: 'Champagne for my true friends, true pain for my sham friends') I've felt that described me pretty well. Especially in the past decade I have lost any faith in progress and the betterment of society. I've become more realistic I suppose in my feeling that social democracy, greater equality and the improvement of living conditions for all round the world is a dream which is never likely to be achieved. Where before, however pessimistic I was about many things, I still believed that in time tyranny would give way to democracy, however flawed, now, with the examples of China, Russia, Turkey, Egypt, Syria, Brazil, the UK and the US before us, that seems like a pipe-dream. As in the thirties the world has stood by and watched how Assad, with the help of Iran and Russia destroyed Syria and its (his!) people, and been powerless to stop it. How Iran and Saudi Arabia have helped ignite and then fuel Islamic extremism. How Xi has returned China to totalitarian intolerance and an aggressive stance *vis à vis* the world. And so on.

And then there is global warming and the growing sense that there is no way the nations of the world are going to join together to fight it, the only way. The Covid-19 pandemic offered a brief glimmer of hope in that direction, with the evidence before us of what even a few months without carbon emissions can do to help nature recover, but we just don't have the world leaders prepared to face down all the vested interests in keeping the status quo ante in order to institute the reforms that would be needed. Someone once compared global warming to smoking: it is so difficult to give up smoking because the costs are so obvious and immediate while the benefits are long-term and intangible, so why should we give up? That strikes me as the best description of the problem besetting the tackling of global warming I have come across. With individuals who smoke, of course, there are societal pressures to give up, various medical aids, such as Nicorettes, which were of such help to me, supportive friends.

Unless there are world leaders who can provide the equivalent of some of these things how on earth can nations, or rather, the governments of nations, be pressured to give up? The pandemic should have helped, redirecting jobs and resources towards green energy and the like, but I don't see it happening, not with Trump, Xi, Modi, Erdogan, Putin, and the current rulers of Iran and Saudi Arabia in power.

So: every reason to feel pessimistic, yet I wake up most mornings when the weather is good and feel joy in my heart at being alive, looking at the trees now in full leaf, the roses everywhere, the vistas on the Downs, the thought of getting down to work.

Stravinsky dedicated his *Symphony of Psalms* 'To the Glory of God and the Boston symphony Orchestra,' a wonderful yoking not exactly of God and Mammon but of what is practically necessary to music as to any art – someone who wants what you do and is prepared to pay for it – , and what is indispensable to good music – innate talent and the god-given powers to persevere in its realisation. Does this mean then that to find joy in your art in the modern world, in the era of the disinherited mind, you need to be religious? Perhaps, but the term covers a wide range of meanings. It does not mean only a Christian believer, like the Orthodox Stravinsky or the Roman Catholic convert, Muriel Spark (and of course Greene and Mauriac are evidence that being either a cradle or a converted Christian does not automatically entail joy in creation). For both Spark and Stravinsky it seemed to provide a bulwark against depression – indeed, I sometimes feel that in Spark's upbeat tone there is just a hint that 'the lady doth protest too much'. Stravinsky confessed to Robert Craft that even he, with his notorious work ethic, needed often to 'trick himself' into sitting down at his desk, and this makes him, for me, that much more human than Spark (in her novels, for in life as I knew her she was the most warm and human of people, though one was always aware of her steely determination, her ruthless streak). A firm religious belief no doubt helps but it is not necessary. I doubt if Bacon believed in anything and I certainly don't.

So is Bacon's 'optimism' to be reduced to a nervous system – or, in my case, I suspect, to bodily health? When I'm feeling well I sit down to work with enthusiasm, when not so well it's harder. I am very dependent on my body and wonder how I will cope when it starts to give way. But what of the sickly Proust, who, though in his novel he describes the frustrations of the writer in the time of the disinherited mind only does so in order to prepare the way for the joyous discovery of his vocation? What of the firmly secular Maxwell Davies and Georges Perec, both of whom have expressed much the same optimism as Spark and Stravinsky when it comes to the pleasure they take in their work?

I think the answer must be that even the most 'pessimistic' artist, a Bernhard, a Shabtai a Kafka, finds a powerful joy even in the expression of pessimism. The pleasure of creation trumps even bodily pain and relentless gloom about human motives and possibilities. We know how Kafka enjoyed reading his own work out loud to his friends, and one cannot understand Bernhard unless one recognises the childish prankster behind even the darkest work. This is where he is utterly different from writers like Krazsnahorkai or Knausgaard, touted by their admirers as the true inheritors of modernism. Bernhard, on the other hand, in his last great works, *Cutting Timber*, *Old Masters* and *Extinction*, actually seemed to find a way to combine his notorious expressions of horror at all he saw around him with a joyous zest that comes close to what emanates from Shakespeare's comedies.

So perhaps there are more ways of being 'religious' than being a cradle Russian Orthodox or a Catholic convert; it may be that a Tikhon or a Father Zossima would intuit in a

Kafka, a Bacon, a Bernhard, a profoundly religious spirit. It may be that you cannot be an artist without believing in God, whatever that means.

6.6.2020

Broke regular routine by having to fetch Dick from Haywards Heath Hospital, where he had been kept overnight for a check-up and to get rid of the stones that always build up where he was operated years ago for cancer. Just back. Trying to settle in.

Trump was always weird, a psychopath, but now, what with the pandemic, which has already notched up 100,000 deaths in the US, 40 million unemployed, and national fury, which shows no signs of abating a week after the George Floyd incident – 'Let me breathe!' has become a rallying cry– all this has finally sent him round the bend. How middle-of-the-road Republicans can still back him is a mystery, he is clearly a danger to America and the world. Joe Biden finally speaking up, trying to calm things down – but the elections still five months away and Trump has plenty of time to do even more damage.

Johnson and co. not mad, not out-and-out white suprematists, but still bungling bigots. Now their eyes are set on their goal of a Brexit solely on their terms, which will probably mean a no-deal Brexit, they are even more incompetent than usual – today it's face-masks, which a week or two ago they said were unnecessary, then said should be worn on public transport, now they say must be worn by all those going in and out of hospitals (and, I think, though not clear, by all over 60s) where they will be handed out to those who don't have them – but the hospitals have not been alerted to this or consulted and of course don't have the requisite supply. And so it goes on. The independent scientists who have been criticising the response for weeks have now banded together and have issued a set of recommendations and warnings: there will be a spike in September, they think, and the government absolutely needs to be prepared – not just *say* they are prepared. Will the Government pay attention? Don't bet on it.

Perec

I will break my rule not to write here about anyone or anything I have written about extensively before. Except that I am not really breaking it, because I do not want to write about the work but about my (shadowy) relations with the man and his work.

In the seventies Stephen rented rooms from the historian Malcolm Kitch in Southover High Street where on Saturday mornings he would often give little sherry parties. At one of these I found myself sitting on the floor of the crowded room with a young Frenchwoman. We got talking and it came out that I wrote novels and plays, some of which had been performed in little theatres. She said: 'I have a friend in Paris who writes novels and plays. From what you say about your work I think you'd like what he does.' We talked on and as I got up to leave she said: 'Give me your address and I'll send you one of his books.' I had more or less forgotten the encounter when one day a parcel arrived and, on opening it, I found myself staring at the white cover of a book with a large red pattern on it. I opened it and found that it was called *La Disparition* and was by someone called Georges Perec. There was no letter and no return address on the parcel. When I next saw Stephen I asked him who the young Frenchwoman had been to whom I had talked that day. He said he knew of no young Frenchwoman, she must have been a friend of Malcolm's. However, when I eventually asked Malcolm he too said he had no idea there had been a young Frenchwoman at the party and that she must have come with someone.

I began to read the book. It was written in a strange style that seemed vaguely Renaissance-y but clearly wasn't. Nor was it at all clear what was going on in it. And the blurb was no help, for it was written in the same strange style and was equally enigmatic. It was easy to read though and I liked the rhythms, so I kept going. About halfway through I said to my mother: 'I'm reading this book that arrived so mysteriously the other day and I can't really make head or tail of it. It seems to be about these twenty-six sons, the fifth of whom is missing.' My mother loved crosswords and nearly always completed the *Times* and later the *Guardian* crossword in an hour or two. She immediately said: 'It must be about the letter *e*. Look and see if it's missing.' I looked at the page I'd reached and indeed there were no *e*s. I looked at the blurb and there were no *e*s there either. I examined the cover again and realised the red pattern was the letter *e*, filling the surface and seeming to want to burst out of its confines. I dipped into the book near the start and towards the end: no *e*s. And as I glanced at different passages I realised that the quaint style was the result of this lack, for *e* in French is even more ubiquitous than it is in English – think of *et* 'and', and *est*, 'he is', and all feminines, so that in order to accomodate an *e*-less vocabulary you have to perform some strange contortions.

Needless to say, I went back to the beginning and read the book almost in one go and with a growing sense of pleasure and disbelief. After that I read everything by Perec I could lay hands on. His work never gave me the feeling that he was opening up fruitful avenues for me to follow, as I had felt in my twenties with Robbe-Grillet, Simon, Duras and Pinget, but rather that he was a kindred spirit, setting about solving problems I was always encountering in his own way and with a brio and panache I could only envy – and enjoy.

On a visit to Paris in 1978 I saw that every bookshop window carried copies, prominently displayed, of a new book by Perec: *La Vie mode d'emploi*. The trouble was, it was enormous and I've always been suspicious of big books. Every novelist in his forties, I thought, imagines that he has to write a masterpiece and too many confuse quality and size. Besides, I thought, it will never get into my suitcase. However as the time for my departure approached I found myself going up to bookshop windows more and more and staring at Perec's book, always prominently displayed. Finally I ventured inside and actually opened the book and glanced at the first pages, which were full of funny little diagrams or figures, I could not tell which. But I began to read and understood they were the pieces of a jigsaw puzzle, and as I read on I found I was hooked. This, clearly, was no American-style blockbuster but consisted of innumerable very short chapters which seemed to be both strange and funny. I decided to buy it.

Even as I was reading it, on my way back across the channel, I sensed that it was a great work, the kind of book every writer dreams of, when all their interests and concerns come together in an irresistible tide and the world opens up to them in a way it never had before – think *Lolita*, think *Augie March*. And subsequent re-readings have only made me admire it more and more. When I had finished it for the first time I wrote Perec a fan letter and sent it to the publisher. He did not reply but the following New Year, and for several years after I would receive a little, hand-printed booklet from him consisting of varied types of puzzle and word-play. When I showed one of these to Marcianne Lebovitch, with whom I used to stay when I was in Paris, she said: 'But one of his friends belongs to the gym class I attend. Shall I see if I can arrange for you to meet him?' I was shy, though, and held back, thinking that sooner or later we would be bound to meet and such a meeting was best left to chance. And then, in 1982, I heard that he had died, at forty-six, of cancer of the liver.

In 2002, when I was in Paris teaching for a semester at the American University, I got to know his great friend, the mathematician and poet Jacques Roubaud and of course the conversation turned to Perec. 'One of the great pleasures of my life,' Roubaud said to me as we had tea in a pleasant café in Abbesses, where I was living, 'has been to witness his ever-growing reputation. There seems to be no end to the interest even the slightest of his books elicits.'

7.6.2020

Sunny again today. Yesterday the first really grim day since the lockdown started almost three months ago. Drizzle, cold, windy, grey skies. We thought of waiting for it to clear, as promised in the forecasts, then took a chance. By the river and then straight back past the allotments on the Lansdown estate. Always good to be out but the Downs would have lifted the heart more. As we walked the drizzle stopped and by the evening it had all pretty well cleared. Good evening reading and the elusive novel again swam into view.

Huge numbers of people, here as well as in America, young and old, black and white, marching to protest against the killing of George Floyd.

In this week's *TLS*, which I was reading in bed this morning, a quite-good piece by Elizabeth Lowry on re-reading *A Passage to India* during lockdown. She quotes from the book:

Most of life is so dull that there is nothing to be said about it, and the books and talk that would describe it as interesting are obliged to exaggerate, in the hope of justifying their own existence. There are periods in the most thrilling day during which nothing happens, and though we continue to exclaim 'I do enjoy myself', or 'I am horrified' we are insincere. ... A perfectly adjusted mechanism would be silent.

This, she suggests, is what the novel is 'about'. Everyone tries to explain 'what went on' in the Marabar Caves, both the characters within the book and, subsequently, the critics, and the answer is – nothing. The novel is like John Cage's *4.33* – four minutes and thirty three seconds of silence (she says 'like a John Cage piece', but this is clearly what she is thinking of).

She quotes from *Aspects of the Novel* the famous remark: 'Yes... oh dear yes, the novel tells a story – and I wish that it was not so, that it could be something different – melody, or perception of the truth, not this low atavistic form.' And she suggests that it was the full realisation of this that led Forster, though he lived for another forty-six years, dying at ninety-one, never to write another novel.

I think both Forster and Lowry touch on something crucial about both life and fiction, but that the conclusions they draw are wrong, unless you want to distinguish between 'the novel' and 'fiction', which I don't think either of them does (Lowry describes *Aspects of the Novel* as 'his chatty study of the art of fiction'). It is not that life is so dull that there is nothing to be said, but that life is – just life. That is why the most interesting art of our time seeks to catch within the web of fiction or painting precisely this 'what cannot be said'. Not so as to turn fiction into music, or melody, as both Forster and Lowry tentatively suggest *A Passage to India* does, but in order to give us access to that most elusive thing – life. Allows us, in Claude Simon's case, to 'see the grass grow'; in Bonnard's, to give us a sense of what a long shared life consists of.

Forster and Lowry share with other English writers, such as Graham Greene, both a sense of what the novel cannot do and which they would so like it to do, *and* a premature shrugging of the shoulders at this impasse. If one reads Graham Greene's *A Burnt-Out Case* and then his notebooks for that novel, *In Search of a Character*, one is struck by the way a fascinating and powerful idea is ruined by the instinct of the old pro for a good plot to 'bring it to life'. If one compares it to another novel set in colonial-era Africa, Robbe-Grillet's *La Jalousie*, one sees how a turning away from the normal novel's way of going about its business, a refusal of the 'oh dear yes, the novel tells a story', makes not for silence but for a gripping narrative about time, jealousy and colonialism, while Greene's acceptance of it turns the fascinating and universal idea of 'burn-out' into just another page-turner. At least Forster, in *A Passage to India*, stayed with his instinct and produced by far his best novel – though both before and after, in commenting on the book, he misunderstood his own creation.

Piers Plowman

I have grown to love Chaucer. It really is the case that, like Shakespeare, he can bear countless revisitings, and his combination of wit, humanity, sense of structure and acuteness in the depiction of the world, will always enlarge our horizons. And I have always loved *Pearl*, that poem tucked into the *Gawain* manuscript, and, like its more famous companion, almost lost for ever in the fire in the Cottonian library – the burn marks are visible even in facsimiles. I found it more touching than *Gawain* in its depiction of loss, and more beautiful (and of course more highly wrought), though

Gawain is more varied and I suppose more 'exciting'.

But the poem I most fully responded to as a student was *Piers Plowman*. This may sound surprising as it is so dense, so long and so complex than even the scholars cannot agree as to which two of the three existing versions, the so-called B and C texts, is the last and best. Yet, all that said, it is often breathtaking in its directness and simplicity, and nowhere more so than in its opening:

> In a somer seson, whan softe was the sonne,
> I shoop me in shroudes as I a sheep were,
> In habite as an heremite unholy of works,
> Went wide in this worlde wondres to here.

It is puzzling that he should clothe himself 'like a sheep' in the summer, one would have thought a woolly coat would be more appropriate for the winter, and the scholars seem to steer clear of the puzzle of line three: Why a hermit *unholy of works*? And yet all these questions evaporate under the force of that first person narrative and the wonderful first line, as they do at the opening of Dante's *Commedia*:

> Nel mezzo del cammin di nostra vita
> mi ritrovai per una selva oscura
> che la diritta via era smarrita.
> [In the middle of the path/journey of our life I found myself in a dark wood, having lost the straight/true way.]

In Dante there are eleven syllables to every line and the rhyme scheme (obscured here where the second line also rhymes) is abacbcdcd etc., an unbelievably strict and yet flexible system that produces thirty-three syllables to every tercet, echoing the thirty-three cantos to each of the three canticles (plus the prologue canto at the start) and a kind of ever-moving chain. Langland, unlike Chaucer but like almost all Chaucer's contemporaries, who worked far from the Frenchified court, wrote in the alliterative line of old Germanic poetry, with four strong stresses and a caesura in the middle, able to accommodate a varied number of syllables. Yet in both poems we are drawn by the combination of first person and powerful steady rhythm into instant acquiescence.

As with Dante, the poet has not finished with his proem:

Ac on a May morwenyng on Malverne hilles
Me bifel a ferly [marvel], of Fayrie me thoughte.
I was wery forwandred [from having wandered] and went me to reste
Unde a brood bank by a bourne syde;
And as I lay and lenede and loked on the waters,
I slombred into a slepynge, it sweyed so murye.

More than in Dante we breathe the air of the countryside, here the Malvern hills in Worcestershire on a hot summer's day. The scene is utterly realistic and yet also on the border of the mystical. I can think of no other writer who conveys this so simply and so powerfully, apart from Thomas Traherne in his prose *Centuries*. I marvel now as I did when I first read it as an undergraduate sixty years ago at the simplicity and speed with which Langland moves from 'I was wery forwandred and wente me to reste', which conveys in its dragging rhythm the pleasant tiredness of a day's walking, to the lying down by the side of the stream, the leaning over and looking at the water flowing, and finally to 'I slombred into a slepyng, it sweyed so murye.' We don't use 'merry' in this way anymore but we know at once what he means, and if we are momentarily held up by 'sweyed' and think that perhaps it means he felt dizzy rather than 'the stream made such a merry sound', that is not terrible.

In his sleep the poet has a dream. He sees 'a field full of folk', which is nothing less than the world. But if we are expecting the steady progress towards understanding of Dante's poem we will be disappointed. The B-text, in the excellent Everyman edition, edited by A.V.C.Schmidt and published in 1978, runs to 263 closely packed pages, and even an alert reader has difficulty remembering how many times the 'I' figure falls asleep, wakes up, falls asleep again, dreams again. The poem is as full as Dante of theological debate and exposition, but, lacking Dante's lucid structure, this is often difficult to follow. This makes it closer to Proust's *À la recherche* than to Dante's poem, for the final set of revelations emerge not in a steadily increasing clarity but out of the rubble of failure.

8.6.2020

Everywhere in the world the immediate question is how to ease the lockdown without risking an immediate second spike and the longer-term question is how, if at all, the pandemic will change forever our way of doing things. The left-leaning optimists see the pandemic as a dry run for the climate crisis that is looming ever nearer and hope the industrial nations will radically rethink not only their energy strategies but also the entire economic structures that underpin them. They see the devastation the pandemic has caused, to lives, to jobs, to each country's economy, as a last chance the world has for radical reorientation, for a final putting to bed of the models of Progress and Growth that have dominated thought since the industrial revolution and specifically the Friedmanian economics that have dominated economic thinking in the West for the past forty years. For the right it is a chance to implement an ever more draconian nationalist and free-market agenda, claiming the dire state of the economy after the pandemic will not allow the luxury of investment in schools, libraries, leisure centres and so on, and that even investment in schemes to relieve deprived areas will have to be put on hold.

Piers Plowman (Cont.)

There are twenty sections or *passus* in the B text, and here is how the climactic Passus XVIII starts:

> Wolleward [shirtless] and weetshod [shoeless] went I forth after
> As a recheles renk that recceth [cares for] of no wo
> And yede forth lik a lorel [wastrel] al my lif tyme,
> Til I weex wery of the world and wilned eft to slepe,
> And lened me to a Lenten [idled till Lent] – and longe tyme I slept;
> Reste me there and rutte [snored] till *ramis palmarum* [Palm Sunday]
> Of *gerlis* and of *Gloria, laus* gretly me dremed
> And how *osanna* by organye olde folk songen,
> And of Cristes passion and penaunce, the peple that ofraughte [extended to].

As Proust's narrator, defeated by life, has a breakdown, enters a rehabilitation clinic and only eventually (it is impossible to say how much time has passed) resumes his old life again before the final series of revelations rush in upon him at the *soirée* he has reluctantly agreed to attend, so here the footloose wanderer, haunted by his many dreams of Piers Plowman and the impossibility of ever making sense of them, goes about the world 'like a wastrel' for a long time ('al my life time'). Then, as in the opening, he grows weary, but this time not as a result of a wholesome hike on a warm spring day but (we sense) out of despair. He lies down and goes to sleep.

But, unlike Proust, Langland is able to set his protagonist in a world which, for his first readers at least, has firm and familiar landmarks. He sleeps, we are told, till Lent. And in his sleep he seems to grow aware of what is happening around him: Lent is over and it is Palm Sunday, when clergy and people process round the church carrying blessed palm-branches and on re-entering sing the Palm Sunday hymn, clergy and adults ('old folke') chanting the verses and children ('gerlys', choir and others) the responses.

And again as in the opening sequence, a second panel is now added as a figure appears:

Oon semblable to the Samaritan, and somdeel [somewhat] to Piers the Plowman

Barefoot on an ass back bootles cam prikye [came riding],

Withouten spores other spere; spakliche [lively] he loked,

As is the kynde [nature] of a knight that cometh to be dubbed,

To gete hym gilte spores on galoches ycouped.

   Thanne was Faith in a fenestre, and cryde '*A! Fili David*.'

As dooth an heraud of armes when aventurous cometh to justes [to joust].

Olde Jewes of Jerusalem for joye they songen,

Benedictus qui venit in nomine Domini.

   Thanne I frayned at feith [inquired of Faith] what al that fare bymente [meant],

And who should just [joust] in Jerusalem, 'Jesus', he seide,

'And fecche that the fend [Fiend] claymeth – Piers fruyt the Plowman.' [the fruit of PP]

All of the poem is here, its greatness, the speed with which it moves despite its massive size, its slipperiness, and its rich embeddedness in the Christian liturgy and therefore in a communal experience which counteracts the dreamlike and intensely personal experience of the protagonist narrrator. To unpack it even a little is to see both how close it is to Dante's poem and how utterly different, how close to Proust's novel and yet how utterly different.

The Gospel for Palm Sunday is Matthew 21:1-9, and it tells of Christ entering Jerusalem. This is the context in which this scene plays out. It is difficult to tell whether the narrator is still asleep or wide awake. Having heard the people cry 'Osanna!' he now sees a figure come riding in, looking like the Good Samaritan of Christ's own parable, but also like Piers the Plowman, who has been appearing throughout the poem to the narrator in different guises. As Schmidt notes in his edition: 'Christ rides "without boots" but not "without a remedy for man's sin"; without spurs to "prick" his mount, he is yet the knight par excellence, seeking the supreme battle against Death (personified a moment later when, quoting Hosea, the knight says: "*O Mors, ero mors tua*" – "Oh death, I will be thy death.").' In all this the Jerusalem of old is embedded in fourteenth century England, the ancient narrative, as in the liturgy, re-enacted in the present. This becomes even clearer as the scene undergoes a new transformation. Just as the weary sleep of the protagonist was interrupted by that joyous 'Osanna!' sung by 'the old folk', so now a window is thrown open (rather as in *Guernica*) and someone cries out 'O son of David!' We are told this someone is Faith, but it would be wrong to feel we have to allegorise the scene; on the contrary, we have to allow its realism to work on us, helped by the Latin of the liturgy. The 'old folk' have now metamorphosed into the 'old Jews of Jerusalem', who sing joyously 'Blessed is he that cometh in the name of the Lord', Matthew 21.9, which ends the Sanctus in every mass and also ends the second Palm Sunday antiphon, *Pueri Hebraorum*. When the narrator asks Faith what all this activity means, Faith explains that the knight is Jesus and, mysteriously, that he has come to fetch the fruit of Piers Plowman which the Devil claims as his own.

In some sense the climax of the whole poem is the ensuing fight between Jesus as knight and the Devil, where the poet successfully calques the Christian story onto the old pagan notion of a final contest between hero and antihero, light and darkness, but even then the poem is not done. Overwhelmed by what he has seen the narrator withdraws into 'that derknesse to *descendit ad inferna*' where he sees not images of horror but 'a wenche, as me thoughte / Cam walkynge in the wey'. This is Mercy, and she is joined by her sisters Justice, Truth and Peace. After another brief excursion into the central tenets of Christianity, Truth cries out: 'Clippe [embrace] we in covenaunt, and ech of us kisse other', enacting the words of Psalm 84: 'Mercy and truth have met each other; justice and peace have kissed.' The scene reaches its climax with the four of them singing the *Te Deum* and the words of Psalm 132: 'Behold how good and how pleasant it is for brothers to dwell together in unity.'

Unlike Dante, though, the poet does not want to leave us in heaven but in the England of his time. It's a special day in the Christian calendar, Easter Sunday, a week after Palm Sunday:

> Til the day dawed [dawned] this damyseles carolen
> That men rongen to the resurexion – and right with that I wakede,
> And called Kytte my wif and Calote my doghter:
> 'Ariseth and reverenceth Goddes resurexion,
> And crepeth to the cros on knees, and kisseth it for a juwel!
> For Goddes blessed body it bar [bore] for our boote [salvation].
> And it afereth [frightens] the fend – for swych is the myghte,
> May no grisly goost glide there it shadweth!' [where its shadow falls]

For the whole of this long poem the narrator has awoken from one glorious dream or another only to find that the reality of the world he wakes up to is sadly distant from the one he has witnessed when asleep. But now, as though his whole life has been a preparation for this, dream and reality coincide in the moment of Easter Sunday. We had not heard of a wife and daughter before, but there they are, as much part of the narrative as they would be in any nineteenth century novel, and the Passus ends with his joyous exhortation of them to come with him to celebrate the Easter Mass. Yet even this moment of supreme joy ends with the hint of something else in the apostrophe to the fiend, that grisly ghost, to keep away, and the last word of all is not 'light' but 'shadow'.

There are two more Passus to go, but this is the heart of a poem I will always treasure as giving me a taste of an England deeply entwined with both the Middle East in the form of the Bible and Europe in the form of Christianity, and no less England for it.

9.6.2020

Headache.

Robert Pinget

I've always had a soft spot for him, the quietest, the most retiring of the Editions de Minuit so-called *nouveau romanciers*. Beckett certainly did. He even translated Pinget's play, *La Manivelle*. Yet I never got on with the early books – *Graal Flibuste* and the rest. Too whimsical for me. Then two books which really hit me hard: *L'Inquisitoire* (1962) and especially *Passacaille* (1969). I was touched by the late M. Songe books too, but only mildly. The other two, though, are remarkable.

I love that opening line of *L'Inquisitoire*, out of which the whole huge structure develops: 'Oui ou non répondez.'

['Answer yes or no.'] It says so much (everything?) about what a novel can and cannot achieve. For three centuries it has pretended it can answer that question while knowing all the time that it cannot. Here Pinget calls it out.

Passacaille is the masterpiece towards which all his work had been moving and after which there was really nothing left for him to do. So harrowing; so funny; so beautiful; so impossible to describe:

> Le calme. Le gris. De remous aucun. Quelque chose doit être cassé dans la mécanique mais rien ne transparaît. La pendule est sur la cheminée, les aiguilles marquent l'heure.
>
> Quelqu'un dans la pièce froide viendrait d'entrer, la maison était fermée, c'était l'hiver.
>
> Le gris. Le calme. Se serait assis devant la table. Transi de froid, jusqu'à la tombée de la nuit.

In Barbara Wright's fine translation:

> So calm. So grey. Not a ripple in view. Something must be broken in the mechanism, but there's nothing to be seen. The clock is on the mantelpiece, its hands tell the time.
>
> Someone in the cold room must have just come in, the house was shut up, it was winter.
>
> So grey. So calm. Must have sat down at the table. The house was shut up, it was winter.

Every time I read/internally speak those words, they work their old magic on me. Like Alain Resnais' film, *Muriel*, it remains, for me, lodged in my body somewhere, a kind of ideal every work of mine secretly wishes to replicate in its own way – or so I think.

Not as varied or as great as Beckett, nor, in his life, as fierce in the protection of his privacy – it was not of course as much under siege as Beckett's was – he was nonetheless quite as reticent, gliding through life as if unwilling to impose himself on it in any way – altogether admirable, both as man and as writer.

10.6.2020

Headache. Hence slowness of progress.

Statue of seventeenth century Bristol slaveowner and philanthropist Edward Colston torn down and dumped in the river. No one knows quite how to react. Tories do the age-old thing of trying to separate 'the thugs who will be brought to justice' and the 'many peaceful protesters with whose pain we empathise'. They don't want to acknowledge what the (black) mayor of Bristol expressed so eloquently, that these things spill over into one another. All politicians hate mobs, unless they are on their side, because they feel they are losing control. All want to show that 'they understand'. But they don't. Only those who have felt the force of that 'I can't breathe', those resonant last words of the murdered George Floyd – the looked down on, denigrated, sneered at, condescended to – can understand. Jews I think have it in their bones. Old Etonians might have problems.

On the other hand of course no one wants to see crowds simply deciding on a whim what statues to topple, or even being incited to do so by a few with long-term ambitions to do just that. I wrote in *Forgetting* about the problem that arose in Oxford over the small and not very visible (I can't remember it) statue of Cecil Rhodes and whether it should be pulled down or not, and I asked there where, once one started, one would stop – what about all those saints on Oxford colleges? Surely an oversensitive Protestant or Jew could argue for their disappearance? At least we need the question of statues to be debated and resolved by Parliament, even if, like early debates about hanging, say, or homosexuality, this proves abortive at first and only the continued insistence on bringing the subject to the attention of the House leads to its finally being properly debated and voted on.

Plays

Fired partly by Max's willingness to try his hand at anything and everything – music for the very young, large works for orchestra, chamber music, operas, music-theatre – I was keen, in my early years, to see what I could do with radio drama, with theatre, even with film if the opportunity came my way, as well as with fiction. Poetry I was never drawn to, for some reason I have yet to understand, though as a reader poetry is as important to me as fiction and Yeats, Eliot, Rilke and Stevens have given me as much as Kafka, Proust and Mann.

You can write a novel in the seclusion of your own home and even a radio play can be explored 'in the head', as it were, but a play? Some playwrights have perhaps written their first plays with no idea where or if they are going to be staged – I think Joe Orton and Shelagh Delaney fall into that category – but I can't work like that. Perhaps that shows I'm not a natural writer of plays. So when the students at Sussex came to me in 1971 to ask if I would write them a play to be performed by them at the newly-built Gardner Centre at Sussex and to be entered for the *Sunday Times* National Student Drama Festival, I eagerly accepted the challenge. I had written a monologue, 'One', for Nick Woodeson, at his instigation, and been excited by how well he did it and how satisfying it was to see/hear it with an audience, so I had him in mind from the start. The play was *Evidence of Intimacy*, and though the students – who did it brilliantly I thought – didn't win anything that year, the play did, and we managed to fill the Gardner Centre every day for a week. But it could not have been written had I not had a specific space in mind – the Gardner Centre – and at least one of the actors, Nick. I sent it up to the Royal Court, who turned it down but said they'd like to see more work of mine. So when the opera whose libretto I was trying to write for (and with) the Australian composer Peter Sculthorpe came to nothing after several months of intense work, I salvaged it with a play, *Dreams of Mrs Fraser,* which I duly sent the Court and which they accepted. It was then put on at the Theatre Upstairs in a dire production which was rightly panned by the critics, though Harold Hobson, who had been enthusiastic about *Evidence* when the students did it at Edinburgh for the Drama Festival, and who was the only critic to ask to see the script, was full of praise. Alas, this was not sufficient (as it had been with Pinter's first full-length play, *The Birthday Party,* which was also panned by all the critics except for Hobson) to save it from oblivion. A pity. (It had a brief afterlife in a touring production by a young company and then a rather good one at the Studio Theatre of the Derby Playhouse, but that was it.)

Evidence was then put on at the Soho Poly but did not succeed in attracting either many reviews or much of an audience. I don't think it's that bad, though obviously influenced by both Pinter and Orton. The trouble was that my work was not commercially very viable and the little theatres, which had sprung up everywhere in the early seventies tended to be more interested in overtly political theatre than what I was providing. That didn't stop Stoppard's rise of course, so perhaps that's a poor excuse.

I have talked above about my play *Flow* and about my need, in order to write plays, to have the stimulus of a commission, the more precise the better. A few more came my way over the next decade, but not leading to any wider interest in my work for the theatre. Bernard Gallagher and his wife Sheila got in touch in the late seventies or early eighties. They were the spearhead of a Brighton-based group of experienced actors with many parts in West End and TV plays behind them, but wanting in their spare time to do something a little more adventurous than the roles they tended to be offered or the voice-overs they were hired to do and accepted in order to feed their families. The Brighton Combination, as they called themselves, were keen to commission new plays and I collaborated happily with them for a number of years, producing a variety of plays, some good, some indifferent. But I enjoyed writing for actors and a space I knew, and in Bernard, who had appeared in William Gaskill's original productions of Bond's *Saved* and in Orton's *Ruffian on the Stairs* at the Royal Court in 1967, and in plays by Stoppard and Caryl Churchill, as in Nick Woodeson, I found someone with an instinctive understanding of my work.

There was one more, surprising, commission. John Russell Brown, the Shakespeare scholar and advocate of the study of the playwright in performance rather than on the page, had come to teach at Sussex in 1971 and a short while later he was invited by Peter Hall to act in an advisory capacity at the National Theatre, looking out for innovative new plays. Whether it was he or Hall who conceived the notion of the Platform Play I'm not clear. The idea was to put on a short play with no props on the platform of the Lyttleton an hour or so before the main play started, and John asked me to write one, preferably a two-hander. I was excited by the possibility and, inspired by a poem by the Israeli poet Lea Goldberg, 'Twenty Years', produced a play in which a man and a woman recall contradictory narratives of their affair twenty years previously. The play lasted roughly half an hour and required great concentration from the two actors as it moved from past to present and back again. In the five Platform performances we were allotted the two (very fine) actors lost their way on four occasions and on the one occasion when there were no slip-ups from them something went wrong with the lighting. A shame as it was quite a good play.

I wrote one more play for a commission, though it was not exactly that. A friend of mine and Sacha's, Pamela Gravett, was friends with Paul Scofield and his wife – they had all been young actors at the Birmingham Rep in the forties. She saw Nick Woodeson in *One* and liked it so much that she asked me for the script and showed it to Scofield. Oh, she reported him as saying, I'd like him to write a companion piece for me to perform. I was thrilled and spent a summer turning over possibilities.

11.6.2020

Lindsay Halsey: 'All the way through this pandemic the government insisted on treating a national crisis as an exercise in political management.'

Grey. Cold. As a result aches and pains all over.

Bea and Malcolm almost came down for a walk, we had prepared a wonderful lunch for them, but they cancelled at the last minute. Disappointed, yet it made me realise how little I want to see people or change my present way of living.

Plays (cont.)

The trouble was that all the monologues I tried to imagine were only variants of the little piece I'd written for Nick. But that is the advantage of a commission or of someone like Paul Scofield being interested – one sticks to the problem longer than one might if it all came solely from oneself. I changed tack and started thinking of Scofield's impressive appearance and stature. What could I write that would suit *him*? And then I woke up one morning hearing a voice seemingly giving me directions: 'Left and then turn left again.' And I at once thought: Borges says somewhere that the way out of a labyrinth is to turn left at every junction – and on the heels of that came the thought: Virgil in the underworld. And then: this is my play for Scofield! Virgil, dying, we are told, asked for his manuscripts to be burned. I recalled reading a novel by Hermann Broch, *The Death of Virgil*, a large and (when I had read it as a young man) interesting though rather boring book. I had no desire to re-read it, but it gave me the confidence to pursue my idea. Since we were in the middle of the summer holidays I packed all of Virgil and some light reading and went down to S's place in the Brecon Beacons, where I had written my first radio play.

It was a wonderful few weeks. As I read, thinking of course of Kafka as well as Virgil, the shape of the play began to emerge. I started in on it and before I knew it had written not a little companion piece to *One* but a 90-minute monologue. I knew Scofield had Peter Hall's ear and imagined him performing the piece in the Cottesloe – after all, Peter Hall had recently directed Barry Collins' brilliant and disturbing play-length monologue, *Judgement*, at the ICA, after Peter O'Toole had given it a stage reading at the Bristol Old Vic. I sent the play to Scofield and waited in trepidation. Eventually he got back to me. He loved it, he said, but felt it would be wise to try it out first on radio. As so often with these things, this was not quite what I had hoped but it was better than I had feared.

Guy Vaesen, who had produced all my radio plays with immense tact and skill, came out of his recent retirement to produce it and Scofield found a few days when he was free. Of course he was superb. He has given some memorable radio performances, quite as good as his best stage performances, which are of course amongst the greatest there have ever been, and it was an honour to have him perform in a play of mine. But as the recording went ahead and we had the chance to talk about it it became clear to me that he had reservations about performing it on the stage. Whether that was something to do with the play itself I don't know; he was always too courteous to say. Perhaps it was that he belonged to an older generation of actors, who were much more averse to taking risks than younger ones. I will never know. He may have thought of the sound of theatre seats going up as audiences rose and left in mid-performance and felt he did not want to take the risk. I quite understand, though of course I go on feeling disappointed that he never went for it.

When the play was broadcast the *Radio Times* mistakenly billed it as lasting for two and a half rather than one and a half hours. One of the critics who reviewed it commented that 'though fascinating, at two and a half hours it rather outstays its welcome'. I did not bother to call him out on this, being sure that his response would be: 'Well, it felt like two and a half.'

12.6.2020

Unsettled weather. Cold. We are paying for glorious April and May.

Sir David King the other day, in answer to the question: 'Was the Government taking a gamble when it stopped following WHO advice on 12 March and went for a "herd immunity strategy"?' 'Yes.' Devi Sridhar, the Edinburgh epidemiologist, in answer to the question: 'But is it the Government's fault that it wasn't fully prepared in early March? No one, after all, knew what this new virus could do.' 'It was known as early as January and it's no use the Government hiding behind the mantra that they followed the science at all times. The WHO were warning countries then and by February the evidence from Italy was overwhelming.'

Repetition

You never know till you've plunged in just what it is you really want to write. When I started writing *The Inventory* I had no idea repetition would play such an important role in it. And so it has been all through, right up to *The Cemetery in Barnes*. If I was a poet I would no doubt use refrains – I love the way the same thing becomes different the second time round – like the aria in the *Goldberg Variations*.

The other aspect of it: how a perfectly innocent phrase, such as 'The laburnum's in flower,' the first line in my radio play, *Playback*, can grow threatening when repeated – not said again but repeated in its precise timbre and intonation, easy to do in radio, though when we put it on in 1972 'cutting' still meant a technician using a razor blade. And how it can grow more and more threatening the more it is broken up and meaning completely disappears. I suppose *Comedy* and *Playback* written fairly close to one another in the early '70s, treat this aspect of repetition most fully. I so enjoyed the way the 12-minute *Hamlet* in *Comedy* grew more and more wild and threatening as it was broken up, fragments were spoken by two or three characters rather than one, then in chorus by the cast. It was too wild for the first (and only!) audience, at the Gardner Centre, and I was rounded on for 'desecrating the classics', etc. Please.

It all stems I suppose from my feeling, as I write, that *of course* I am not transcribing 'life', I am only writing a novel, a play – which can have its own life, reveal much about our life, but is other, made up by one person. From that it follows that it will often take the form of the dramatisation of the fantasy (or fevered imagination) of one person – the mad kings of Maxwell Davies or of Ionesco, the hammy king of Beckett's Hamm in *Endgame*. For a king or tyrant, by definition, has it in his power to bend reality to his imagination – up to a point. The task of the artist is then to show us what happens when the tyrant's imagination comes into conflict with reality (Picrochole in Rabelais). In much modern art it is the respect for reality rather than (the usual accusation) a disrespect for it, which leads to narratives about mad kings and the like – for what the mad king does is to refuse all limits to his absolute power, and the artist, by revealing that there is indeed a limit, even if it's only what all must endure, death – the artist brings us to a new understanding of and respect for, the reality that lies beyond. In *Comedy* it is not a mad king but a mad ape-Devil (the image found (from a medieval Psalter) in D.W. Robertson's unpersuasive *A Preface to Chaucer*). In writing *Comedy* I only knew that the trajectory of the play would be the gradual disintegration of the absolute authority of the ape-Devil. At first the cast fly to it when he shouts out his commands: 'Comedy!' 'Tragedy!', 'Melodrama!', but gradually (I remember I thought of it as the electricity supply gradually being shut off) his hold loosens, first one character than another will not obey, does his or her own thing instead, until in the end all turn on him and, maenad-like, tear him to pieces.

More difficult than verbal repetition (and physical repetition in the theatre) is the repetition of events, an event in the past encountered as if for the first time in the present and gradually revealing itself to be identical to the old one, with all that implies. I struggled with that for years and eventually made a not entirely successful attempt to nail it in *The Echo-Chamber*. It goes on haunting me.

I recall reading Kierkegaard's *Repetition*, excited by the title, but, by the end, feeling disappointed that the thinker who had opened so many doors for me seemed, here, to be confused and confusing. But I probably did not understand the book. Peter Handke's novel of the same name, *Die Wiederholung*, is a beautiful book, his best novel, I think, but its title is something of a misnomer. It's true the narrator goes in search of his lost brother by following in his footsteps from their village in Lower Austria into Slovenia, but the repetition is – how to put it? – light, even minimal.

From Marx's *Eighteenth Brumaire*, with its famous opening, 'history repeats itself, the first time as tragedy, the second as farce', to Freud's development of repetition compulsion, to Deleuze's *Difference and Repetition*, the modern era has not been short of meditations on repetition. Obviously there are links between forgetting and repetition which have some bearing on my own compulsions to repeat in work after work, but I have no wish to explore them here. Another time, another place, perhaps.

More interesting to me, at the present moment, is the modern artist's need to create series, whether within a poem, as in Stevens' 'Eighteen Ways of Looking at a Blackbird', or in a tight sequence of variations, as in Picasso's *Las Meninas*. Thomas Mann in *Doktor Faustus*, if I remember right, in Wendell Kretschmar's great lecture there on why there are only two movements in Beethoven's last piano sonata, has some wonderful remarks on why sonata form, with its powerful sense of forward momentum, belongs to a particular era, which is no longer ours, and so variation form becomes the only alternative. And of course one can see how Schoenberg's serialism and then the kind of total serialisation of every aspect of music in immediate postwar works like Stockhausen's *Contra-Punkte*, and the use of magic squares by Maxwell Davies and Perec all follow from that. Already in the 1840s Kierkegaard had grasped this in that wonderful essay in *Either/Or*, 'On the Rotation Method', ostensibly a discussion of agricultural methods of maximising yield but in fact the response of the young man who supposedly writes the essay to his sense of the pointlessness of all forward movement. More illuminating by far for me than *Repetition*, and one of the seminal essays of modernism.

13.6.2020

12 weeks since T came down – 86 days!

Weather clear again and set to be warm – 23/24°C. they say. And what a difference it makes to wake up to sunshine. A lovely breeze too.

Interesting piece in the *Guardian* yesterday about link between Grenfell and Covid-19 and how the Tories have responded to both: failure to heed repeated warnings beforehand, muddle and obfuscation after the disaster has hit. It's that whole entitlement thing, with Brexit horribly intertwined with ludicrous pseudo-patriotism and jingoistic dislike of 'foreigners'.

Repetition (cont.)

The most moving exploration I know of the theological and ethical implications of repetition at the same time as it is an apologia for what had been his way of composing from the time of *Le Sacre*, occurs in Stravinsky's late opera, *The Rake's Progress*. But probably it would be fairer to describe it as Auden's gift to Stravinsky, for it is there in the wonderful libretto Auden and Kallman wrote for him.

We are at the centre of the opera: the Rake has risen high on the tide of Fortune and then fallen, his bubble burst like the South Sea Bubble in the 1720s. Now, a year after he has fallen into the clutches of his servant/master, Nick Shadow, comes the reckoning. In a cemetery close to midnight (shades of *Don Giovanni*) the two meet and Nick, revealing who he is, claims his master's soul. Toying with Tom, he makes him a gentleman's offer: They will play a game with a pack of cards. Nick will cut and Tom has to guess what card it is. He has to do it three times if he is to be saved.

Nick cuts: 'Come, try!' he exclaims. 'I cannot think,' says Tom to himself, 'I dare, I dare not wish.' Nick teases him with hints:

Let wish be thought
and think on one to name.
You wish in all your fear
To rule the game
Instead of Shadow.

To himself Tom mutters the name of the fiancée he had left behind in the country when he so foolishly followed Shadow to London: 'Anne!' And then to Shadow:

My fear departs.
I name the Queen of Hearts.

Nick shows him the card, which is indeed the Queen of Hearts. The clock strikes once. Nick congratulates him.

'Again, good Tom,' he says. 'You are my master yet.' He shuffles. Tom asks himself what card he should go for as Shadow presses him: 'Come try!'

Suddenly a nearby spade falls down noisily. Before he has time to think Tom says: 'The deuce!' And, to Shadow: 'She lights the shades and shows the two of spades.' The clock strikes twice. 'Congratulations,' says Shadow, 'the goddess still is faithful.'

There is one card to go. 'Oh God!' wonders Tom, 'what hopes have I?'

Shadow picks up the discarded Queen of Hearts and surreptitiously reinserts her into the packet. He explains to the audience:

> The simpler the trick, the simpler the deceit.
> And there is no return.
> I've taught him well. And repetition palls him.
> The Queen of Hearts again
> shall be for him the Queen of Hell.

He shuffles. Tom, in despair: 'In his words I find no aid. / Will Fortune give another sign?' Shadow echoes him in an aside: 'Now in my words he'll find no aid. / And Fortune gives no other sign.' He teases Tom: 'Afraid, love-lucky Tom? / Come, try!' 'Dear God,' exclaims Tom, looking down, 'A Track of cloven hooves.' Shadow taunts him: 'The knavish goats are back/ to crop the spring's return.' But the rhyme and the concluding word trigger something in Tom and he cries out: 'Return and love! The banished words torment.' Shadow repeats his mantra: 'You cannot now repent.' But Tom is on another trajectory: 'Return, Oh love!' he cries out, and in answer, miraculously, comes Anne's disembodied voice: 'A love that is sworn before Thee / Can plunder heaven of its prey.' That is all the spur Tom needs. He cries out:

> I wish for nothing else.
> Love first and last
> Assume eternal reign.
> Renew my life,
> Oh Queen of Hearts again!

At this the clock strikes twelve and Nick Shadow sinks back into the ice and flame of Hell from which, so long before, we now know, he had come. But not before he has had some sort of revenge on Tom, ensuring he lose his reason for the rest of his life.

This is not perhaps the greatest poetry Auden ever wrote but it is one of the greatest things. Playfully, lightly, he covers ground already marked out by both Judaism and Christianity, where return, *teshuvah*, and repentance are seen as the key to salvation, to an acceptance of both oneself and God. Dante anchors this beautifully in both psychology and theology when he makes the pivotal difference between those in Hell and those in Purgatory turn on this question. In Hell the souls cling to their identity ('As I was in life, so am I now', as Capaneus says in Canto xiv), and remain locked in their respective circles. In Purgatory by contrast, we find those who, even if it was at the last moment, repented in life, and now, in death, can move, can spiral up the great mountain towards salvation. Throughout the canticle the key words are *tornare*, often linked to *amore*, love, and to *verde*, green, the soft and pliant green shoots of the plant. Auden and Kallman have used the tradition and given it new life, as Tom, who had felt for so long that he was so far into his dissolute life that there was no possibility of return to Anne and the time before Nick Shadow appeared, hears her voice at the end and finds the strength to repeat and return and so, in the end, bring release to his paralysed spirit, though at terrible cost. As is stressed in both the Jewish and the Christian traditions, the spirit cannot find it in itself to turn and return except with the help of God or the tradition or the liturgy (the concept of *teshuvah* is central to the liturgy of Yom Kippur, the Day of Atonement). With the communal hearing of the words, the communal saying of the words, return becomes possible, repetition, far from being a sign of compulsion, becomes both the sign and the springboard for rebirth.

Thus do the ancient and the modern, the religious and the secular, find common ground.

14.6.2020

Clashes between police and far-right protesters and football hooligans yesterday, mainly round the (boarded up for its own safety) statue of Winston Churchill in Whitehall. Strange sight on TV news channels of men giving Nazi salutes and shouting taunts to the police, ostensibly to protect the statue and 'What Churchill stood for'. One wonders what Churchill himself, for a while the only leader of the free world prepared to take his nation to war against the Nazis, would have made of it all.

The whole statue thing will only be worth it if it leads to a prolonged debate about how Britain faces up to its past. Absurd to take down Churchill's statue because in the course of his long life he made comments that can be construed as racist and even acted in ways that can be so construed, or even that probably were. Iconoclasm is never something I can be happy with, it comes too close to book-burning, though I would not care one way or the other if all the statues put up since 1800 were taken down – nor do I mind if they remain. Those who care deeply should think hard about what they really want: wider understanding of the past, such as has occurred by now in most West European countries, and an acceptance of differences, or a long battle over what should stand and what should be toppled and a continuing xenophobia.

Robbe-Grillet

To write a novel in which nothing happens and yet everything happens: a secret dream of mine ever since I began to write – and there was Robbe-Grillet doing it even as I was dreaming! I read *Le Voyeur* in 1961 I think, just after graduating, and I could not believe what I was reading.

When I first read Beckett, or Duras, or Simon, I immediately thought: yes, this can help me find my way. Sometimes (Beckett) that was extremely dangerous and seductive and I saw many of my contemporaries succumb: what had looked like an enabler had turned into a treacherous disabler. But with R-G it was different. I knew from the start that I did not want to imitate that style and, moreover, couldn't even if I had wanted to. It did everything I disliked about novels – it relied on description, it had no dialogue, it was flat. And yet all this was at the service of a vision I perfectly understood but had never imagined could be realised. What vision? What did it mean, a novel in which nothing happens and yet everything happens? Flaubert said that *his* dream was to write a book 'in which nothing happens', but I found and still find, that I do not respond to Flaubert, that there is something willed, relentless, certainly without humour, but also without humanity, about him, which turns me off – though of course I can admire aspects of his achievement. Exactly Proust's response, of course, in the wonderful essay he wrote in defence of Flaubert against his academic detractors and which I only read much later.

But Robbe-Grillet was different. What you have in those early novels is obsession. Not just his admirers but RG himself completely misunderstood his purpose in those novels, the purpose of his novels at any rate – just as Dostoevsky misunderstood his own purpose in his later work. The obsession, in *Le Voyeur*, is that of a child-killer, though the beauty of the novel resides in the fact that the silent and anonymous protagonist through whose eyes the reader is made to look, and who therefore takes the place of a first-person narrator, may not in fact have murdered the little girl we learn has been killed on the island, may only imagine that he has – no, the beauty resides in the fact that the reader/viewer too may only imagine the protagonist/viewer has killed, or may only imagine he imagines he has killed.

Why is this so exhilarating? At the time I didn't particularly want to tease that out. Since then I think I have, but don't want to go into it all again here. Suffice it to say that it has to do with understanding what the novel can and cannot do, what fiction, made up of words which are then printed and bound as a book, can and cannot do. What does 'in fact', as used above, *mean* in a novel? RG forces us to ask. Sterne had a great time, two centuries earlier, exploring precisely this, in comic mode, but Sterne's lesson is a hard one for both novelists and their readers to take on board, hard not because it is complicated but because it goes deep down into the heart of why we read fiction in the first place. Is it to transport us into 'other realms', or to bring us face to face with ourselves and how we relate to the world? In the twentieth century the question grew urgent again, though still not among the wider reading public. Beckett made his work out of agonising over it; Nabokov, a great admirer of RG (it was mutual), explored it in one way; Bernhard, in the next generation, in another. All four of them loved their craft and loved the language they wrote in, whether (in the first two cases) it was their adoptive or their native language, but Beckett and Bernhard also hated it, hated the way it tended to elide our imaginings of the world and the way the world really is. By forcing the reader to respond to the sensuality of their language and rhythms while at the same time distancing themselves from its connotations, they learned how to use the poverty of their means to explore the world of obsessive imagination.

And that is just what RG does. A *jalousie* is a blind, and *jealousy* is blind, while at the same time it is obsessed with the other, with the cause of jealousy. RG joyfully welcomes the pun in the French word and constructs a fiction in which a man in a bungalow on a north African banana plantation sits or lies in his room, overhearing and trying to see through the bars of the *jalousie* his wife and a male friend sitting talking on the verandah outside. Nothing happens and yet everything happens. RG has no need of an Iago or a handkerchief or a *crime passionel* to convey obsessional jealousy and to convey as well how, in a novel, we only 'see' as much as the novelist wants us to see. We have learned, through RG's contemporary and admirer, Roland Barthes, that what the novelist wants us to see is never unmediated, but always comes (for the novelist as well as for us) filtered through the slats of convention – the conventions of the novel at the time the novelist is writing, the conventions of society and the language it uses at that time. RG makes that plain in non-discursive prose, through the beautiful pun in the title. Just as, of course, a *voyeur* is both one who simply sees *and* an obsessive peeker into what should not be looked at – English, at a loss for its own word for this condition, has adopted the French. Perhaps the English translation of *La Jalousie* should have been not *Jealousy* but *Blind*.

After I had read those two novels in quick succession I went back to the first, *Les Gommes*. I'm sure a perceptive critic could have told from a reading of the two later ones what that novel was likely to be 'about', and in hindsight it was almost inevitable: a modern take on the story of Oedipus. That was another dream of mine, again barely acknowledged: a man goes in search of the murderer of his father and discovers that it was none other than himself. RG does it beautifully but it feels a little too contrived, unlike *Le Voyeur* and *La Jalousie*, which seem as natural as water. He said later that he wrote as he did because he was trained as a scientist, an agronomer, not in the humanities or as a painter, like his friends and contemporaries, Michel Butor and Claude Simon. Of course that is another way of deflecting questions and it does not explain his obsession with obsession, but it perhaps helps us understand the sense the early novels convey of care and absolute precision in the making, the refusal of ideas, big or small. That reaches its apotheosis in the fourth novel he published, *Dans le labyrinthe*, in which a soldier is desperately seeking in a snow-bound city to deliver a parcel. Despite the subject, it is the most lyrical and abstract of his novels. That is to say it is closer to Stevens' 'The Snow Man' than it is to Hans Castorp's venture out into the snow in *The Magic Mountain*:

> For the listener who listens in the snow,
> And nothing himself, beholds
> Nothing that is not there and the nothing that is.

We never learn what is in the parcel, and he never gets to deliver it, but it is, strangely, much more dreamy, far less nightmarish, than the previous books.

I was in the middle of my absorption in RG, my attempt to grasp what he was doing and how he was doing it, when a visit by the man himself was announced on the notice-board of the Maison Française in Oxford. He was to give two talks, or perhaps seminars. I remember nothing about them except that he had a fine moustache and spoke with calm authority. I suspect he was as candid and unilluminating about the books as he proved to be in subsequent published interviews. His visit neither impressed me nor turned me off the books, but it did seem providential, and gave me a sense that, unlike Proust and Kafka, who had meant so much to me in my teens, he was my contemporary, or at least shared the world with me (he was born in 1922, so by then he was about forty). He went on to write innumerable novels, all of them second-rate in my opinion, and a number of interesting critical essays. His finest work by far lies in those early novels and the volume of very short pieces he published at the same time as these, and of which 'La Plage', which inspired a beautiful piece of music by Birtwistle, is the most fully realised. Sacha, I recall, loved *L'Année Dernière à Marienbad*, the film he made with Alain Resnais, but I found it stilted and bordering on the parodistic rather than – as it was clearly meant to be – haunting and beautiful. He died in 2008, the most enigmatic of all the *nouveau romanciers*.

15.6.2020

Closing in on the Summer solstice. On Saturday we walked to Kingston via Ian Littlewood's and then past the windmill and up Kingston Hill, taking the steep right-hand ascent. Windy on top but wonderful sunshine. Longest we've done, three and a half hours, but though tired at start of return (on the Green in Kingston), I soon picked up and was fine by the time we got home. Then we had tea and sat down to watch *Goodbye Christopher Robin*, interesting film, if a bit shmaltzy (especially the photography and the music) about A.A. Milne, his ptsd (as it was not called) after fighting on the Western Front, his pacifism, his intolerable stupid wife, how he wrote the Christopher Robin Books and, in the world-wide craze for them, sacrificed his child to publicity. The boy wants to assert his independence of 'Christopher Robin' by going to fight in the next war and begs his father to help, insisting it is his one way of making amends for lost childhood. Milne does so with heavy heart. Wife furious with him. Inevitable telegram: 'Missing, presumed dead.' The parents and the nanny (the one good adult in the piece) mourn, but then, one day, he turns up. He wasn't dead after all. Cue stiff upper lip reunion and all past ills forgotten. Ah.

Not just C-19 maelstrom now and debates about easing lockdown to 'get the country back on its feet' (easy to see which side the government is on), but whole racism issue and England (yes, England) finally being forced to look at its past. Not sure about tearing down statues and wholesale reform of school curriculum, but there should certainly be the type of debate, exhibitions, etc. about Britain's imperial past that Germany has had about its Nazi past – though of course in some ways it's much easier to deal with ten years of very obvious atrocity than four centuries of complicated history. Johnson clearly still doesn't get it though, with his promise to set up a commission to 'investigate the perceived racial injustices in this country'. Critics have rightly called him out on that 'perceived' (very like what has tended to be said to women who have complained over their lot recently) – he and his ilk cannot acknowledge that there is any substance in the inequality/racism charge. There's about a 10 percent truth in that view.

Routine

How I enjoy it. How I need it. F, many years ago: 'Why do you lay the table for breakfast the evening before? You might want quite different food, or maybe no breakfast at all.' I tried to explain that when I come downstairs to make breakfast I don't want to have to think, just to make it automatically, since I don't feel properly awake till I've had my cup of tea. But I knew even then that that wasn't the only or perhaps even the real reason. I like things to be regular because it's only then that I can function. And, even more deeply, after Sacha's death I think I felt that if things weren't in exactly the order I was used to everything would crumble and I would end up in bed all day, unshaven, the house filthy, and so pass away – the Bartleby syndrome. So routine is a survival mechanism.

Of course there are other ways of looking at it: some artists like, need, a disorderly life – Dostoevsky, Giacometti – others an orderly one – James, Stravinsky. In fact composers tend to sit down at their desks every morning while writers are more wayward, Painters? Auerbach only takes Christmas Day off every year and most of them are the same even if not quite so rigid. Yet Andrzej will have long periods of emptiness, as I think did Schoenberg. For myself, though the books come in bursts of intense work, rather like Muriel's, I hate the ridiculous waste sad time between. I long to be at the desk, with a project unfolding slowly, day after day. And even when I don't have such a project or have one but it's not working, I like to give myself a chance every morning. It need be no more than an hour or two but it's the difference between a sense of misery for the rest of the day, a sense that there is both too much time and no time at all, and a sense of peace and joyfulness, the sense that there is plenty of time to do all the other things I want to do – walk, read, listen to music, see people.

There are dangers, I can see, in both the fanatical commitment to routine and in the lack of any routine. The danger that one starts to mistake routine for achievement, that one loses that sense Kafka had so keenly – but did he have it too keenly? – that one is in the lowlands most of the time, when a recognition of the fact might lead to change and improvement. I think of Josef towards the end of his life, still getting up at 5.30 every morning and spending the day, till lunch at any rate, in the studio, drawing, painting. And the later work, it has to be admitted, repetitive and often disappointing, after the glorious 1940s and '50s. I thought at the time: Why doesn't he stop, take stock, try to change direction? But in recent years I've thought: Why be hard on him? Part of what drove him was the desire to banish the thought of the horrors that befell his family back in Poland. Nini told me he dreamed more about those things in his old age. Can one blame him for working feverishly day after day, doing what he enjoyed doing and knew he did well? And Max in *his* later years, the comforting idea that he was Haydn *redivivus*, producing what was required with exquisite skill, acclaimed by his public (but dismissed by most younger composers I've talked to, however much they admired the earlier work)? He didn't have the excuse of the Holocaust, but why judge? I suppose because I loved and admired the early work so much.

Did they both know in their heart of hearts that their work was indeed 'in the lowlands'? But what does that mean? No doubt at some moments they did, but then we all at moments, even when producing our best work, have those feelings. And at other times they must have felt that what they were producing was great.

And what of Pinter? When he sent me the first of his later political plays – was it *One for the Road*? – and I wrote back to say that I was less than enamoured of it, he cut me off for ever. Was it because he had surrounded himself with admirers and felt he was above criticism? That he really believed that this was the right direction for him? That 'the situation of the world' demanded it? Or that he knew deep down that he'd lost it and couldn't bear other people confirming that? Or all of these things?

But I've wandered from the topic, routine. How it can hide doubts which should have been allowed to surface, but also how it can help one past the difficult moments. I was amazed to discover that Stravinsky, whom I consider the most regular and disciplined of composers, an artist who has said that it is the work that satisfies, not the finished product unless it is the result of such work, had, every morning, to coax/trick himself to sit down at his desk. This shows I think that the moment of transition from idea to work, from potential to realisation, is the hardest of all. And routine helps with that.

I think of Philippe Petit in *The Walk*, the film about his walk on the high wire between the Twin Towers with no safety net beneath (the walk was clandestine, he would never have been given permission) saying: 'Once I'm on the wire it's all right. It's the moment of transition from the solidity of the building to the wire that's frightening.'

And even for a student essay the story is the same. I used to say to students: 'Just start writing. I know it's scary, but no matter how much reading and thinking you've done, unless you start to write you won't have anything to show me. And what you'll find when you do start is that it will be both much worse than you imagined as you were thinking about it and, in places, surprisingly better.'

There is another aspect of routine, of my routine. I remember Sacha saying, when I complained once about the rigidity of our eating times: 'I have always felt, because of the traumas of your first five years, that I had to provide you with as stable an environment as possible, and that regularity was important for that.' And of course while I chafed at times when she was alive I internalised it after her death. As a result I grow unnecessarily anxious if meal-times are delayed. T has gradually weaned me from this, mainly by recognising the reasons for my anxieties and respecting them, so that it has not felt like a disaster if we now eat at 7.30 instead of 7 or 1.30 instead of 1. And I now begin to think that perhaps Sacha needed the routine not just for me but for herself as well, though she did not recognise this, because of the traumas *she* had been through.

The lesson of all this is that, as with everything else, there are no hard and fast rules, even in individual lives. Randall Jarrell once wrote a glowing review-essay of Wallace Stevens's last poems. He had, he said, been highly critical of Stevens's long middle-period poems, such as *Notes Towards a Supreme Fiction* and *An Ordinary evening at New Haven*, feeling that

Stevens had lost his way. But now, he said, faced with this last volume, he understood that, deep down, the poet knew best; without those middle period poems we would never have had the glory of the late ones.

In this case – but was Jarrell right? I happen to agree with him, but we might both be wrong – the artist knew better than the critic and perhaps better than he knew himself, for of course his poetic life did not develop according to any preconceived plan. But what of later Hockney? And, sadly, for every Yeats or Bonnard, there is a Wordsworth, a Chagall.

16.6.2020

Yesterday up to Mt Harry and then back along the Eastern edge of the valley. Two and a quarter hrs. It's become our standard walk on a fine day. Felt my legs stronger than for a long time. Pushing off from the heel when I'm beginning to feel tired. Result of nearly ninety days of walking on the Downs.

Today seems to be fine again. But a two-hr walk leaves very little time for anything else if I've spent the morning at the desk. Never mind. Time enough for that later.

Deeply, deeply depressing sight of people queuing at all the 'non-essential shops' which have re-opened, as though all this had only been an extended bank holiday and 'life' could now resume. I had hoped the experience of the lockdown and the daily dose of deaths would have given people the chance to reflect on what they really valued in life and that it would not be GDP and clothes. Of course the English are lambs, to be led wherever the politicians wish, despite their profound belief in themselves as independent-minded. And where Johnson leads… And here he was in the Westfield Centre, encouraging 'everyone' to 'come shopping', for all the world like the owner of Sports Direct – which is what he essentially is. But still, very very sad to see that this kind of thing is what my fellow-Britishers most want out of life.

Spiral

Was it Michaelangelo who said that in the spiral resided 'the whole beauty of art'? I seem to recall this from my reading of Georgio Melchiori's fine book on Yeats, actually entitled *The Whole Mystery of Art*. But it may have been Leonardo or even Hogarth. It doesn't matter. Even a cursory glance at Yeats and Eliot will show the importance of the image for them, in the form of spiral stairs – literally for Yeats as well as imaginatively, via Dante, for Eliot. Was Dante the first to make extended use of the image? It would be interesting to know.

I am not looking for origins and don't want to think of specific examples, for clearly Dante, Yeats and Eliot all use the image because it corresponds to or is the externalisation of a *form* they find their work needing. Freccero is very good on this in his lovely essay on *terza rima* in Dante: *aba bcb cdc* etc. two steps forward and one step backward. The idea of the coiled spring. It can be coiled more or less tightly, but it combines return with advance, as opposed to the forward thrust of the traditional plot-driven novel and of sonata form. Variation form is of course a version of this return/forward rhythm.

Jill Purce, once one of Stockhausen's muses, wrote a book in the seventies called *The Mystic Spiral: Journey of the Soul*, very much a book of its time, with its many images of oriental religious art, but suggesting, as Dante, Yeats and Eliot of course all do, that the journey of the soul is upward and spiralling. I want to talk here, though, strictly about the spiral as an artistic means, not so much a line of beauty as a 'way forward'.

It was this that so moved me when I first read *Ash Wednesday*:

Because I do not hope to turn again
Because I do not hope
Because I do not hope to turn
Desiring this man's gift and that man's scope
I no longer strive to strive towards such things
(Why should the agèd eagle stretch its wings?)
Why should I mourn
The vanished power of the usual reign?

I had no idea what the poem was about, and as the stanza progressed, less and less (what's this eagle got to do with it?), but what filled me with joy and with a sense of something opening up for me was the way the return ('Because... because... because...') seemed to allow something new to be released ('Desiring... I no longer...'), which itself seemed to lead to further release ('why should I mourn?...'). Of course it's not just the content of the opening but the rhythm, so that the new development appears, again, to be somehow embedded in the old.

In Part VI, the final section, 'Because' is transformed into 'Although':

Although I do not hope to turn again
Although I do not hope
Although I do not hope to turn

Wavering between the profit and the loss
In this brief transit where the dreams cross...

Later I learned that Eliot was merely (merely!) translating a line from Guido Cavalcanti: *'Perch'io non spero di tornar gia mai'*, the opening of a poem lamenting exile much admired by Rossetti and Pound, and that the Italian may be translated as either *because* or *although*, a possibility which Eliot so beautifully exploits ('Because I have no hope of ever returning' / 'Although I have no hope of ever returning'). Bad poets imitate, good poets steal. Eliot, stealing Cavalcanti's line, transforms it from a literal to a spiritual exile, brings out the possible ambiguity of 'because' and 'although' in '*perchè*', and builds his poem upon it. But for me, though I did not know it at the time, it showed that an art of language, like the art of music, can employ the spiral, the repeat, half-repeat, advance, return, advance, advance, return, and carry the reader with it. And I found that mould there for me when I realised I needed to move from the staccato juxtaposition of fragments of dialogue, which I had used in my first novels, to something with a longer breath, something continuous yet not linear, in *Migrations* and then again, more consciously perhaps, in *Moo Pak* and in *Infinity*.

Much later I discovered that both Thomas Bernhard and his disciple W.G. Sebald had also found out how to use the spiral in prose fiction. But for me it was already there in *Ash Wednesday* and *Four Quartets*.

17.6.2020

Now there is the suggestion from scientists that it was not only the government that was slow to act but the initial scientific advice that was flawed, imagining that Covid-19 was only a version of flu – though contact with their Chinese and east Asian counterparts would quickly have put that right and shown that this was much more like Sars than flu, easy to catch and potentially far more lethal. Nothing though excuses the lack of PPE for front-line staff, the woeful disregard of Care Homes, the lack of any preparation for Test and Trace, and now the schools fiasco, when a merely competent Education Secretary would have spent the intervening weeks developing an all-encompassing plan for primary and secondary education. And now it takes a twenty-three year old black footballer from Manchester to shame the government into providing free school meals for those who need them throughout the summer – though it was obvious from the start to those who watch football that Marcus Rashford was no ordinary footballer. The way he bided his time under Mourinho, never complaining when left out, but, when he was finally given his chance, seizing it and proving he was indispensable to the team. Contrast that with the shameful government response to the surge of sympathy for the Black Lives Matter movement and you see the two faces of modern England.

Trace

Why does the idea of the *trace* excite me so much? As though all my writing can do – and what my writing *wants* to do – is to record the trace of a life. It was there after all in my first novel – the dead reconstituted out of the inventory of their belongings and the memories, however distorted, of the living. But that did not put the idea to bed, because it clearly was more than an idea, it was something very close to my heart, to my whole being as a writer. In a way all my books are both 'about' that and the trace itself. Very clearly in *Contre-Jour*, where you never 'see' the protagonist, the Bonnard figure, but you reconstitute him through what the two women, the daughter and the wife, say about him and the remarks of his they quote. In contrast to their rambling monologues all you get of him is the brief, heart-stricken but formal letter he writes to his friend after his wife's death, copied more or less verbatim from the letter Bonnard wrote to Matisse after Marthe's death in 1942. He never speaks and there is no narrator, no 'I', purporting to give him to us 'as he really is' – only the traces of him, to be reconstituted by the reader. And then, in more comic mode, in *Infinity*, Pavone only seen (heard) through the words of Massimo, his amanuensis and chauffeur, a man patently ill-equipped and yet through whose words Pavone, I hope, emerges in all his vanity, pretentiousness, genius and pathos.

Sciascia, now I come to think of it, does something similar with his meticulous accumulation of 'objective' reports into, say, the disappearance of the physicist Majorana (I adapted his novel *La Scomparsa di Majorana* for radio in the seventies, and Sacha later translated it) and the death of Raymond Roussel in Palermo (*Atti relative alla morte di Raymond Roussel*). I prefer my versions (more human), but I realise now that I am drawn to LS partly because of our common aims, and I do love the way he does it, that coolness, objectivity, laying the documents before us without intruding.

The itch to write a novel about the traces we leave behind is still strong, and the failure to ever find an adequate objective correlative for it. (I have never forgotten that youthful reading of, I think, an Ellery Queen mystery in which the clue lies in the trail left by a snail – is it that at one point that trail is interrupted and Ellery realises a body must have been dragged through the path? I can't remember, only the snail's trail as central.)

I suppose it's linked to what Monika Fludernik picked out as central to my work: echoes and mirrorings. The original is lost, irretrievable but we can reconstitute it (tentatively) through the traces it has left, or hear the echo, or see it in a mirror. And so it's another aspect of the profound sense I have always had (since I came to consciousness as a writer with *The Inventory*) that I cannot give 'life as it is lived' (*I* cannot and it's my firm belief that art *tout court* cannot) but can be *true to* that life provided I make it clear that the book is not 'it'. But that makes it sound too mechanical, too cerebral, whereas I know that when I think of traces, of echoes and mirrorings, it's a gut feeling, even a feeling in my loins. What a strange thing this is that has been so dominant in my life. Who would ever have imagined it beforehand? Why me?

18.6.2020

Grey. Drizzle. We walked along the beach at Tidemills yesterday – ninety-plus days here and T had not yet touched the sea. Heavy clouds. Very still. Sea like a lake. Hardly a soul. A few children with wet-suits playing in the water close to the beach, two upright paddlers (what are they called?) further out. Water so clear the shingle visible under it for a long way out.

Then tea with Bet in her little garden at the back. Kitty looked in. Left a copy of *Forgetting* with Bet, I had hesitated to give it to her fearing the first chapter would re-awaken the pain of the last years with Tony. We'll see.

Strange sense of not-quite-lockdown and not-quite-normal-life. Premier league football resumed and normality was restored as Arsenal lost 0–2 to Man City. No spectators of course.

Johnson retreats, like Trump, to his little-Englander base with decision to merge Foreign Aid department with Foreign Office and to paint official plane with Union flag at cost of £900,000. Wasteful, as it will soon have to be repainted with only the English and (?) Welsh flags.

The Twittering Machine

The months, years even, wasted struggling to find a fictional or dramatic form for the idea. I say 'idea' knowing well enough that it's the title of a Paul Klee painting, now in MOMA, a painting I love. But as so often in Klee it's the title almost as much as the image that is evocative. In German *Die Zwitschern-Maschine*. I look it up in the Oxford Duden and it tells me that *zwitschern* means 'to chirp'. But *The Chirping Machine* wouldn't have the resonance of *The Twittering Machine*, and I wonder who came up with that inspired translation and take off my hat to him or her. It sounds right for the picture in a way that 'chirping' just doesn't – too chirpy, while the other just catches the mechanical, the aimless, the repetitive, which is there in the Klee picture.

He painted it in 1922. It's a watercolour and pen and ink oil transfer on paper, roughly 48 by 63 cm. It depicts in cartoon form four birds with big white faces and big black tongues sitting on a wire singing their hearts out into a greeny-blue sky bordered by pink to the left and a darkness to the right. The wire, though, is attached to a pulley or handle, and the whole contraption is held up by a rod on a sort of transparent table, suggesting that these are not birds on an electric wire but rather a parody of one of those mechanical musical machines that were so popular in the eighteenth century. E.T.A. Hoffman devoted a story/essay to them in 1814, entitled 'Die Automate', and he was very critical of them for distorting the true purpose of music, which, he says, is like the reflection of 'God's own inner music' that can only be conveyed by a 'feeling musician'. Thus Klee's troubling and enigmatic picture would take its place alongside *The Ghost of a Genius*, also painted in 1922, as Klee's complex response to Romantic idealism. Today, he is suggesting, there can be no such thing as 'a feeling musician' who bodies forth the pure sound of 'God's own inner music', no Beethovenian genius who can convey to multitudes the undiluted ideals of the Enlightenment and Romanticism. Yet the artist is still drawn to such ideals and still, against the odds, believes in his or her mission – for otherwise what would be the point of art? – but it must be one that is fully aware of the dangers to precisely those ideals from importing debased versions of them into the public domain – a web of feelings and ideas that would be explored in fiction by Thomas Mann in *Dr Faustus* during the Second World War and the terrifying tyranny of the Nazis over Europe, two decades after Klee painted those pictures by Thomas Mann.

The Twittering Machine has generated quite a few musical compositions of its own, including a tiny piece by the young Peter Maxwell Davies, the third of his *Five Klee Pieces* written in the late '50s when he was teaching at Cirencester Grammar School. The whole work only lasts for ten minutes and the individual pieces are miracles of wit and precision. The third uses a form of repetition that gathers new elements to itself as it proceeds, then gradually sheds them, the whole underlaid with an ostinato on cellos and double-basses, brilliantly conveying both the troubling nature and the toy-like quality of Klee's masterpiece. It surely prefigures another and much larger and more complex exploration of eighteenth century musical boxes and mechanical singing birds, the *Eight Songs for a Mad King*, a music-theatre piece 'about' how George III in his madness would try to sing to his caged bullfinches, with the musicians as the birds inside giant cages and the king (a part of extraordinary versatility which moves from moans to screams to the imitation of the sounds made by those who cannot hear their own voices) attempting to imitate and cajole them. Max has great fun distorting Handel.

Proust writes in a letter to his mother about a lady he has met at Evian, where he is on holiday: 'Quelle différence entre elle et le petit harmonica de province de la presidente où on sent dans le moulu des mots le movement de la manivelle qu'on fait tourner? Il y a dans le ronron de sa voix quelque chose de mécanique et de vulgaire comme dans une machine à moudre le grain.' [What difference is there between her and the little provincial harmonica of Mrs President, where one senses in the grinding of the words the movement of the handle being turned? There is something mechanical in the purr of her voice, something vulgar, as in a machine for grinding corn.] (16 September 1899) In his novel he is adept at letting people damn themselves simply by the way they speak, and, long before Barthes, explored with fascinated horror and amusement the societal and psychological pressures that turn speakers more or less into automatons.

I knew that I wanted something much more spiky, much more violent than Proust or Dickens, much closer to Klee and Maxwell Davies. Klee's painting and Max's rendering of the Twittering Machine bordered on the crazy, on something at the edge of language and representation. For several years I kept coming back to this notion of a novel or play which would not just give life to but would actually *be* a twittering machine. To no avail. Perhaps I got somewhere near it in that first radio play, *Playback*, where an innocent phrase like 'The laburnum's in flower' (the anodyne opening line, spoken by the wife as she draws back the curtains in the morning) grows more and more threatening as first it returns in another context, then is broken up, repeated, broken up still further, and so on. Repetition and fragmentation as the means of metamorphosis of the banal into the terrifying.

But that has not put it to bed. As with the idea of the trace, I still find, every time I hit upon a new idea for a work, that underneath it is the notion, there in the Klee, at once of rapturous singing and of crude mechanical repetition. In much of the work I am happiest with, such as *Contre-Jour*, *Everything Passes* and *Infinity*, those two contradictory feelings are in play. And it pleased me enormously to be able to put Klee's *Ghost of a Genius* on the cover of the Yale edition of *What Ever Happened to Modernism*?

More blunders to add to the litany of this government's blunders. First, Hancock has to admit that the tracking and tracing phone app he was touting a month ago as the answer to all the problems the easing of lockdown would cause is not fit for purpose and will be scrapped. The UK will now be doing what most countries did from the start, working with Google and Apple instead of, once again, trying to be different, wanting to centralise everything and hand contracts to its cronies. But four vital weeks, if not more, have once again been wasted. They never, but really never learn.

And then Raab in a radio interview showed not only his and his colleagues' crass ignorance, but the insolence of those in power not even bothering to find out stuff, easy enough in these days of internet searches. 'I imagine taking the knee,' he said, 'derives from *Game of Thrones*. To me it smacks of servility.' A minute's search would have led him to understand that it in fact derived from a gesture of Martin Luther King's, taken up two years ago by American sportsmen as a gesture of defiance to Trump, being unwilling to stand at attention before the American flag. Oh dear (but then this is the man who evinced surprise when Brexit Secretary that so much of the UK's trade with Europe passed through Dover. How do these people even get into parliament?).

Unity

In an earlier entry I wrote about my need to have a strong, even physical sense of where the boundaries of a projected work would have to be. Here I want to explore the question of when a book is finished.

Butor: The urge is to correct and correct and correct. When you realise the whole book needs correction then you know it is time to move on to the next one.

Valéry: A poem is never finished, only abandoned.

Both very suggestive, but not very helpful when one is actually working on a book!

Do we have to give up the idea that each work has its own unity and when you've achieved that, it's done? But what is unity? Is *Tristram Shandy* less unified, than *Bleak House*, because it is unfinished? Or Kafka's three novels and Musil's *The Man Without Qualities*, all unfinished, les unified than *The Magic Mountain*? Proust did not live to revise the last volumes of *À la recherche*, but is the novel less unified than *To the Lighthouse*? And does that matter? They are what they are and to have 'finished' them would not have made them any different. There is a difference, then, between 'unfinished' and 'incomplete'. And it may be that it is a characteristic of post-Romantic works to be abandoned but not unfinished – like Keats's *Hyperion*, Schoenberg's *Moses und Aaron*, Kafka's novels. But then are *The Canterbury Tales* and *Tristram Shandy* any different? Their authors did not abandon the work, it is true, but died before it could be 'brought to completion'. But would it ever have been finished? Had not Chaucer said enough? *Troilus and Criseyde* without the final book would have felt unfinished, but *The Canterbury Tales* is so set up that it does not much matter if it is finished or not. Again the question: What does 'finished' mean?

Are *The Waste Land* and *À la recherche* a unity? Both works recognise the problem: Eliot never sought to hide the extent of Pound's cutting of his first version and Proust acknowledged that his novel was not and never would be the cathedral he had dreamed of, only, at best, a patchwork dress. But then it may be this, the lack of 'finish' and the recognition of its inevitability, that 'unifies' (ah, those inverted commas coming to my rescue) each of them – as it 'unifies' Kafka's novels and *Tristram Shandy*.

Can we not say: We have enough; the rest we can imagine for ourselves? And that in a world where the notion of genre is no longer viable, 'finish' can become a means of avoidance, as Kierkegaard understood when he talked about the writer who puts in 'the last part' and 'thereby shows that he is not a writer'?

Nowadays only the most obsessive Shakespeare scholars worry about what bits of what plays are by Shakespeare and what are not. The majority are more relaxed about the issue, even in a play like *Pericles* where it is obvious that large parts are not 'by Shakespeare'. At the same time they are more obsessive about not presenting the public with some idealised notion of *Hamlet* or *Lear*, made up of the best bits of the quartos and the Folio, but instead giving us each version separately (as the Arden has started doing). It may be that each 'version' of *Lear* was conceived for a different public or with a different purpose, but are they really two quite separate plays, as the Oxford Shakespeare seems to imply? I still prefer to read some sort of composite *Hamlet* or *Lear* and not worry too much about the role the editor has played in it. That old scholarly obsession with 'what the author really said' has its roots in Reformation anxieties about truth and lies, authenticity and forgery, especially where the Bible was concerned, and I for one am happy to read the Masoretic text of the Hebrew Bible and not get bogged down in the arguments of nineteenth and twentieth century German scholars about the different 'authors' involved in the writing of Genesis or Exodus. Much of the Hebrew Bible and the Gospels were not written but oral in the first place anyway. And for Shakespeare too the important thing was the play being put on, not what the author had *written*. And the same holds for music, by and large, till the Romantic era, as Lydia Goehr among others has pointed out. For Mozart, she shows, what was important was the next *performance*, not 'the work', whereas for Beethoven it was quite the reverse. Hence the sense amongst the general public that Beethoven is 'a genius', whereas Mozart merely wrote delightful music.

On the other hand Dante and Virgil are fanatical about unity, completion, numerological patterning – even if the *Aeneid* ends with a (deliberate) whimper. And the *Iliad* and the *Odyssey* would be lesser works without the great twenty-fourth books. Just as the works of Virginia Woolf and Thomas Bernhard almost depend on the endings. Indeed, we know that Bernhard often had to have his last sentence in place before he could begin a book. How complicated it all is.

And me? I need to have a strong sense of the rhythm of the book, and especially of the rhythm of the ending, if it is to work. I may not know the exact words but I know 'where it has to go'. Not always but nearly always. Strongly in *The Air We Breathe* and *Moo Pak*, less so in *Infinity* and the *Cemetery in Barnes*. But – ah, I'm getting there – just as there has to be a quasi-physical feeling of what the boundaries of a new work are going to have to be, so there has to be, at the end, a quasi-physical sense that it has come to an end, that it has achieved its rightful form. Or, sometimes, that it hasn't, quite, but that I've done the best I could and there is enough there which I like to allow me to let it go out into the world.

20.6.2020

Tracey came yesterday to clean while we went for a walk, suggesting (to my sorrow) that 'things are getting back to normal' – even football on the TV, though sounding strange on radio, broadcast from empty grounds, like training sessions. I didn't even remember to look at the scores of Tottenham v Man U before going to bed – quite lost the old enthusiasm.

Victoria College

Edward Said hated his time there (a few years before I arrived), accusing the teachers, who were mainly English, of racism and colonialism. I may have been particularly insensitive, but I never noticed anything of the sort, although if they had been they would surely have treated a Jewish boy in the same way as a rich Palestinian kid. But then Said hated his father and seems to have had a chip on his shoulder from the start – though in my few personal dealings with him he was the epitome of urbane courtesy and charm. I never found any of his books particularly illuminating, though full of large assertions, a bit like Steiner in that. *Orientalism* obviously touched a chord and made a few good points powerfully, but like all polemics, lacked nuance. I found Elie Kedourie, a hard-headed Iraqi Jew, much more enlightening on Western misapprehensions in dealing with the Middle East.

The school had been founded in Alexandria in 1901, at the death of Queen Victoria. During the Second World War, when there was the danger of Alexandria being overrun by the Germans (until Montgomery turned the tide at El Alamein in October-November 1942) it moved to Cairo where it took over the Italian school (Italians were of course treated as enemy aliens and the men interned). By 1950 the Italians wanted their school back and Victoria College returned to Alexandria but decided there was enough demand to keep a Cairo branch, to be built in the desert on the outskirts of the town, Maadi, a few miles south of Cairo, where we were living. So it was that when it opened there in 1952 I was just of an age when I would have had to transfer from junior to senior school and my mother enrolled me there. Most of the students were bussed in from Cairo every day but those of us who lived in Maadi cycled in, and there was a smallish group of boarders, mainly from Saudi Arabia and the Gulf States. It was run on public school lines, tempered to the time and place, with uniforms, Houses, and a great deal of sport, and I can't say the teaching was wonderful, though I always did very well, and in the senior classes we did have a remarkable English teacher, David Humphries, who had been at Cambridge in the Leavis era, though I'm not sure if he was an actual pupil, and who encouraged us to think for ourselves.

The Houses were named after Britain's former colonial administrators and generals: Gordon, Allenby, Kitchener, Cromer. I don't think any of us was aware of who these men were or what their claim to fame (or, these days, infamy) might have been. In fact we were, as I remember it, remarkably ignorant. I recall the boredom of having to learn the names and dates of the Pharaohs and the English Kings, both equally unreal to me, and of having to read Wordsworth's 'Daffodils', never having seen a daffodil. On top of that the sensibilities of the Egyptian Government under Nasser (my years at Victoria College fell between the coup by the army officers which deposed King Farouk and replaced him with General Neguib in July 1952 and his successor Gamal Abdel Nasser's nationalisation of the Suez Canal in July 1956) meant that, for example, Shaw's *Caesar and Cleopatra* had to be replaced by another, less 'offensive' play (the sale of records of Handel's *Israel in Egypt* were banned) long after we had started studying it, and, for some strange reason, we found ourselves studying Shakespeare's *Julius Caesar* for three consecutive years. Our French teacher, who came from Malta and who had, as a young man, been secretary to my writer grandfather, was too obsessed with his own poetry (he wrote long poems with titles like *Le parabole de l'inconnu*, which he had privately printed on expensive paper) and, I later discovered, was too fond of gin (so that was the strange smell on his breath!) to be bothered to teach us, especially as most of us could speak French, and would merely intone: 'Révisez messieurs!' and spend the hour scribbling in his notebook or fast asleep. As a result I learned no grammar and so, while a fluent speaker, am an atrocious speller, so bad it embarrasses me to write even the shortest letter in French. Occasionally he would berate us for our ignorance, me especially: *'Vous, M.Josipovici, le petit fils de votre grandpère, d'écrire si mal! Quelle honte!'* Or he would call us up before him if he felt we had been up to no good while he slept: *'M.Josipovici, je vous connais comme ma petite poche!'* Or: *'Alors, messieurs, qu'est-ce-que vous voulez? Un verre de champagne et une femme sur un canapé?'*

In Nasser's new Egypt even English schools had to devote nine hours a week to Arabic, more even than to English. Unfortunately the Arabic teachers had never been taught how to teach non-native students, so that those of us who did not speak the language or had only the most rudimentary and oral acquaintance with it were shoved to the back of the class and not given any extra help at all. I remember one lesson in which the teacher could not believe me when I said I didn't know a particular expression. 'Then ask your servant!' he shouted. I retorted, truthfully, that we had no servants, but this was so inconceivable that I was promptly sent out of the classroom.

Despite all this I have nothing but happy memories of my school years. We seemed to have plenty of time to play marbles (the craze of the time), loaf around, or take part in sports, which I was lucky enough to be good at. Thus I remember, usually with pleasure, innumerable athletics and swimming Sports Days, and football and tennis matches, both at home and away at other schools.

The headmaster, Mr Elliot Smith, was a very tall, very distinguished, very grey man, who terrified us. He had previously been headmaster of Cheltenham College, where his pupil Lindsay Anderson conceived a particular dislike of him and portrayed him as the head of the school in his devastating portrait of public school life, *If*. Yet to me, though I was as afraid of him as everyone else, he was something of a saviour, advising my mother on what was best if she wished to get me into Oxford (her dream) and helping practically by finding a place for me as a day boy for my last A-level year at Cheltenham. He spoke always in the same grave and distinguished tones at School assembly, whether it was to reprimand us for not putting our bicycles in the proper racks or to announce that, because of the extreme July heat, we would be allowed to sit our O levels in our bathing suits. I was obviously a naturally happy child because I enjoyed almost everything about school, whether it was working hard or training hard on the sports field or fooling about with my Maadi friends on our bikes when – which was more and more frequently as the fifties wore on – there were anti-British riots in Cairo and the school buses could not get through and so school was cancelled for the day. Yet I was not sorry to leave and had no wish, half a century later, when (the internet having made it possible to trace almost anyone in the world) I was invited to a three-day jaunt in Egypt to celebrate the reunion of 'the last class ever to study at Victoria College', to accept he invitation. For shortly after I left to move to England, the Suez War erupted and in its wake the French and British were expelled (The Elliot Smiths were given a fortnight to pack their books and belongings and clear out). But, instead of closing, the school, by a nice irony, was renamed, by the simple expedient of substituting a 'y' for the final 'ia', Victory College. André Aciman, who attended the Alexandria branch of the school till his family finally left in 1964, describes the daily humiliations he underwent as a Jewish boy in an Arab school, albeit one that dubbed itself an 'English School', in *Out of Egypt* and I have to take his word for it. My experience of Victoria College from 1952 to 1956 was very different. I was lucky beyond words in my timing. Looking back now, of course, I can see that the school as I experienced it encapsulated in microcosm the last days of the British Empire.

21.6.2020

Summer solstice. Rain. But sun forecast later.

Yesterday tried a new route: up to base of Mt Harry, then veered right into the woods above Coombe Place. Caroline had told us there was a path back to Offham, but if there was we lost it. View of Coombe Place on N. face of the Downs. Impressive eighteenth-century house. Later, looking at Google Maps, we saw that if we had carried on down to the tarmacked road that passes in front of it and gone right we would have reached the Blacksmiths Arms in Offham, but I feared it would take us only to the main road, and after looking in vain for a stile over the barbed wire fence we retraced our steps, got back into the wood, and eventually found a way out into the valley leading down to Offham. Turned back uphill instead and rejoined our outward path. Two and a half tiring hours, but good to get to see Coombe Place. The lesson though is to stick to the western and south-facing routes and not venture down that steep slope towards the underhill road, unless one is making for the Jolly Sportsman at East Chiltington, or, further on, for Ditchling itself.

In the evening, Laura Spinney's engrossing book about the 1918 Spanish flu.

Walking

'I have two doctors,' the historian G.M. Trevelyan once remarked: 'my right leg and my left leg.' And it's true that if I manage to walk regularly I feel well but if the weather is wretched and/or I feel lazy and decide to skip my daily walk I feel that something is missing. Perhaps it's only habit, mingled with a sort of puritanism, but, whatever the reason, I know that daily walking, and the longer the walks the better, makes me feel well inside and out. And being out on the Down every day for the past ninety or so days has made us both feel better and even keener to get out every day.

How did I acquire the habit? Or rather, how did Sacha, for it was she who got me going. I know that there was a culture of walking in her family, I have photos of Chickie and Albert out with friends on long desert walks, though Sacha was always too busy looking after me to join them – or they may have been taken before or during the war, before we arrived in Egypt. It may have been their English nanny who gave them the feel for it in Helwan when they were small. I can't remember Sacha ever talking about walks she did with my father in Aix or Vence – car trips yes, but not walks.

Nor can I remember regular walks I did with her when I was a child, though she told me I used to walk with her regularly to the Ferme de la Fosse and occasionally to Le Mont D'Or when we were in France during the war, and there are even one or two photos showing me on those walks. In Egypt I was mainly too busy training in the pool or playing football or cycling with my friends. But we did take our dogs for walks and I remember walking with Chickie when she took her dogs out on summer evenings and passing the fields of sweet peas just before the dyke which separated Maadi from the desert, dug in 1945, before our arrival, after the flash floods that swept down the wadis and through the town – loo rolls could still be seen dispersed round the town for months afterwards, I was told. By the time I walked with Chickie, though, the desert immediately beyond the dyke consisted of the green playing fields and modernist buildings of Victoria College. The smell in the warm evenings of those fields of sweet peas.

In Putney Sacha and I would go for long walks on Wimbledon Common, and then later, in Woodstock, round Blenheim Park (a village entrance was on our doorstep) on the weekends, since Sacha was working during the week. During the week, if I was not in the Bodleian I would go by myself, trying to work out as I walked round the lake how to proceed with any story I was writing. We only got into the habit of a regular afternoon walk when we came to Sussex. I managed to condense my teaching into three days, leaving me four days to write, read and walk, and first in Kingston and then in Lewes we got up onto the Downs every day after lunch on the days I was at home. Sacha would go by herself the other days, or in the first years, when we lived in Kingston, would sometimes walk over to Lewes to shop and back. In later years she would go out every afternoon by herself when I was away, rightly maintaining that if one did not go out immediately after lunch in the winter it was hard to get out at all. And of course we took part in the many longer walks we organised with colleagues and friends.

I remember one memorable walk with Tim and Stephen Finer and many others from Lewes to Brighton via Rottingdean, when Tim, in his large coat, had difficulty getting over a style. You must realise, Gabriel, he said, standing astride it as I tried to guide his feet to the appropriate places, that I am the most physically awkward person there is. That did not stop him and Judith coming with us to Kabis and Bressanone one summer and joining us on innumerable Downland walks over the years.

I have written about the walks in the Dolomites in *A Life*. Sacha and I both felt, she when she rediscovered Bressanone, where as a young woman she had spent several holidays and once a whole year recuperating from illness, and I discovered it, that it was a place we wanted to return to again and again. We felt the walks there in the mountain air made us both feel so happy and so well – and that is the thing with walking, it is the easiest thing to do, it costs nothing, it is enjoyable and it is healthy. I would rather have a good walk any day than a good restaurant meal or even a good swim in the sea – we all discover our priorities.

I knew the end of something had come when, in Lewes, Sacha, more and more frequently, would say: 'I don't think I'll join you today', and I would set out on my own, trying to make the best of it, but knowing something was lacking. And still today, when I have had much practice at it, I find that, most of the time, I much prefer to go out with friends than by myself. Not always of course, but most often. What a blessing it has been that T shares this passion with me, nowadays often pushing me to go further than I might perhaps be inclined to go. As with everything, she starts slowly and reluctantly and hits her stride just at the moment when I begin to think of home and tea.

Walking has become as much a part of my life as writing. I can't think how I would survive without both.

These past wonderful walking days during the lockdown have freed me from what at times had become a slightly jaded feeling at going once again round what I call 'the little racecourse' (an hour's walk on the Downs above Lewes where there had once been a thriving racecourse that only closed the year after I arrived), my staple walk for as long as I can remember. I once calculated that I must have been on that walk for roughly 300 days every year for fifty years, which added up to fifteen thousand times. Now we spurn it as much too short and never, even on rainy days, go out for less than an hour and a half. And I have come to love that great Westward sweep of the Downs from Lewes towards Mt Harry and Black Cap in a way I never did before. Such luck to have ended up in Lewes, T keeps saying, if I was in London during lock-up I think I'd go crazy. We are indeed lucky.

Caught short during our walk yesterday, managed to get home without accident, but then felt drained and aching in every bone and muscle. By the evening it seemed to have turned into a bad cold and took a paracetamol with gloomy heart, sure I had finally caught the virus. But woke this morning if not as fine as ever, certainly well enough. Good to see such miracles can still happen.

Sunshine today and wind has dropped. Temperatures set to rise to 29 or 30 by mid-week, too hot for me.

Almost finished *The Ox-Bow Incident* in bed last night. Book I'd wanted to read for years and found it for £1 in the High Street just before shut-down. Not at all what I'd expected – though as always I don't know what I expected. Quiet and humane account of incident in the American Wild West in 1885 where three men thought to have rustled some cattle and killed one of the cowherds wrongly hanged by a group of men from the township. Very good on difficulty even for a group of taking life – now we think of what we have since learned about the *Einzatsgruppen* and stories of US soldiers taking drugs to kill in Vietnam and elsewhere (it was published in 1940). All I read about the author, Walter van Tilburg Clark, makes me like and respect him more.

What Maisie Knew

It's not among James's best-known works and not among those usually regarded as his greatest – *Portrait of a Lady*, *The Golden Bowl*, *The Ambassadors*, *The Wings of the Dove*. And there are other works of his – late short works like 'The Figure in the Carpet' and 'The Beast in the Jungle' – which touch me more deeply. *The Turn of the Screw* is perfect in its way, too. But none excites me so much as *What Maisie Knew*, perhaps because I feel that James is here doing what I would love to do and what in a sense I feel I *can* do – not in his way of course, but nevertheless I can sense at every turn that I know what he is up to and love the way he does it. And that is to tell a story rich in human interest without telling a story at all. How can that be?

The 'story', then, is easily told. Maisie is the child of recently divorced parents. Though the novel is told in the third person it is through her eyes that we see each parent trying to make a life with different lovers, not caring for the child yet competing for her affection and approval and attempting to use her and to win her to their side in the parental rift. And Maisie is more than an innocent spectator like the child in an apparently similar set-up in L.P. Hartley's *The Go-Between*. Somehow that novel, by comparison with James's, seems predictable, a though Hartley knows from the start just where his story will go. *What Maisie Knew*, by contrast, is never predictable, mainly because Maisie keeps developing, because what she 'knows' changes all the time, and our own sense of all the characters and where they are heading grows and changes with her. What we watch, and what makes the novel so wonderful, is, beyond the selfishness, the schemings and machinations of the parents, the growth of the child's understanding of the world. James sees this transformation as neither a curse nor a blessing, he simply shows it to us – and it is remarkable that he can do so because, though this is something we all undergo, we none of us really understand what it is that happens and how. I suppose that is because once we are on the other side we forget what the transition felt like. And though there are a myriad autobiographies in print, both fictional, like *David Copperfield*, and purportedly factual, like Rousseau's, none of them, the classics at least that I have read, ever really conveys that. Even *À la recherche*, wonderful as it is, does not really capture the *transition*, except for the great scene of the mother's goodnight kiss withheld.

The instrument James uses as his mode of narration, the strange style he developed as he grew older, both gives profusely and withholds. It gives sensation and withholds meaning, or at least envelops meaning in such a cloud of sensation that it more or less disappears. Here is a paragraph – one needs to give James space – in which we are told of the mother's impact on her daughter early on after the divorce. 'Ida' is the mother, though it's not clear if this nomenclature – 'Ida', not 'mother' – is how Maisie thinks of her or how the narrator does. Mrs Wix is the housekeeper, who is very much on Maisie's side, yet whose down-to-earth comments on the situation ('her explanation... was that her ladyship was passionately in love'), while accepted by Maisie are felt by us as not taken by her as the whole truth but as a provisional probability. So, Maisie is 'at last summoned into the presence of her mother.'

There she encountered matters amid which it seemed really to help to give her a clue – an almost terrifying strangeness, full, none the less, after a little, of reverberations of Ida's old fierce and demonstrative recoveries of possession. They had been some time in the house together, and this demonstration came late. Preoccupied, however, as Maisie was with the idea of the sentiment Sir Claude had inspired, and familiar, in addition, by Mrs Wix's anecdotes, with the ravages that in general such a sentiment could produce, she was able to make allowances for her ladyship's remarkable appearance, her violent splendour, the wonderful colour of her lips and even the hard stare, the stare of some gorgeous idol described in a story-book, that had come into her eyes in consequence of a curious thickening of their already rich circumference. Her professions and explanations were mixed with eager challenges and sudden drops, in the midst of which Maisie recognised as a memory of other years the rattle of her trinkets and the scratch of her endearments, the colour of her clothes and the jumps of her conversation. She had all her old clever way – Mrs Wix said it was 'aristocratic' – of changing the subject as she might have slammed the door in your face. The principal thing that was different was the tint of her golden hair, which had changed to a coppery red and which, with the head it profusely covered, struck the child as now lifted still further aloft. This picturesque parent showed literally a grander stature and a nobler presence, things which, with some others that might have been bewildering, were handsomely accounted for by the romantic state of her affections. It was her affections, Maisie could easily see, that led Ida to break out into questions as to what had passed at the other house between that horrible woman and Sir Claude; but it was also just here that the little girl was able to recall the effect with which in earlier days she had practised the pacific art of stupidity. This art again came to her aid: her mother, in getting rid of her after an interview in which she had achieved a hollowness beyond her years, allowed her fully to understand that she had not grown a bit more amusing. (Ch.9, pp.57–8)

There is so much here which, for the reader, is difficult to understand, yet the overall effect is quite clear: the overwhelming physical presence of the mother, the conflicting responses of the daughter caught between wonder and horror, and under it all the daughter's slightly detached, puzzled attempt to piece everything together. Ida is not the monster she would be depicted as by a Fielding or a Dickens, nor is she the embodiment of desire, as is the young woman who makes use of the boy for her own purposes in *The Go-Between*. In those books we feel the character has been understood and 'placed' by the novelist beforehand and then fleshed out, often brilliantly. In James the mother is as mysterious, overwhelming and destructive to the author as to Maisie, and both novelist and child need to be both utterly open and preternaturally vigilant if they are to get through it all. One way of putting it would be to say that in the other novelists moral judgements predominate while James is ultimately interested in how we acquire our knowledge of the world and how secure that knowledge is. Another is that James uses the fiction he has devised to discover what he, as well as Maisie, knows and can know, while the others know what it is they want to say beforehand.

And here, towards the end, is an interview with the father:

> She was conscious enough that her face indeed couldn't please him if it showed any sign – just as she hoped it didn't – of her sharp impression of what he now really wanted to do. Wasn't he trying to turn the tables on her, embarrass her somehow into admitting that what would really suit her little book would be, after doing so much for good manners, to leave her wholly at liberty to arrange for herself? She began to be nervous again: it rolled over her that this was their parting for ever, and that he had brought her there for so many caresses only because it was important such an occasion should look better for him than any other. For her to spoil it by the note of discord would certainly give him ground for complaint; and the child was momentarily bewildered between her alternatives of agreeing with him about her wanting to get rid of him and displeasing him by pretending to stick to him. So she found for the moment no solution but to murmur helplessly: 'Oh papa – oh papa!'

It is not so much that the father is less overwhelming than the mother – after all, he too wants something from the child and he too knows how to get it. It is simply that his method is less direct, aimed more to her feelings towards him than to her feelings *tout court*. But the bulk of the book has intervened between the two episodes and in the course of it Maisie has learned not only what is to be known, but how to distinguish it from what can never be known. She is also more open to the complexities of her own responses. And in this paragraph she is pushing those boundaries one step further: 'It rolled over her that this was their parting, their parting for ever' – but at the same time, even at this extreme point in their relationship, 'he had brought her there… only because it was important such an occasion should look better for him than any other'. She is now the adult and he the child, and her response to the impasse of finding it impossible either to play along with his version or to displease him by refusing, by insisting on her right – and her longing – to remain with him, is to speak and to utter words that are at once a reproach – she has to show she has seen through him – and a plea for him to accept this and to change: 'Oh papa – oh papa!'

The words and where they come are almost as powerful as Miles's last desperate: 'Peter Quint, you devil!' in *The Turn of the Screw*, after which there is nothing left for him but to expire. I prefer this, where life just goes on and the question remains: what to *do* with this hard-earned knowledge?

Of course if I had written the book I would have made dialogue, not the strange narratorial prose James uses, the main vehicle of exposition. Not the exposition of 'the truth', but the exposition of how one comes up against the limits of understanding and of words. For in a strange way it is by revealing this that one makes 'the truth' come alive, vibrate. And in that way I find that I as the explorer at the limits come alive. That, at least, is what drives me. And it is what makes me re-read *What Maisie Knew* when I let the rest of James sit happily on my shelves.

23.6.2020

Lockdown easing in all sorts of ways in England despite new cases still being reported dayly, and deaths too, and no tracking and tracing yet in place. All very well to talk of clamping down in isolated areas where it will certainly surge again, but what if one is one of the affected ones? Both of us nervous about going back to normal life before it's really clear how England is going to be affected by the massive easing. And this even though Lewes has, to date, only recorded 216 cases and no deaths for a population of roughly sixteen and a half thousand.

Not quite finished *The Oxbow Incident*, but my admiration for it continues to grow. The best kind of realist novel. On the other hand more and more convinced that *The Brothers Karamazov* is a mess, like *The Idiot*. A wonderful mess, but a mess. Dostoevsky clearly wrote two perfect masterpieces, *Crime and Punishment* and *The Devils*; two remarkable but flawed and uneven books, *The Idiot* and *The Brothers K*; two brilliant early works, *Poor Folk* and *The Double*; and several other novels I have found it hard to get into, including *A Raw Youth*, which I've had several goes at; and some fine short stories, as well as essays and polemics. Not bad for one life.

Suddenly we have a heat-wave. Apparently going to go up to 33 by Thursday and Friday. Not as good as the lovely Spring weather, around 20–24. Yet today seems lovely. Don't want to do an all-day walk till I've finished this – not much more to go.

Wise Women

There have been six in my life: my mother; my aunt Chickie; my Oxford tutor Rachel Trickett; Muriel Spark; Marianne Fillenz, the Oxford neuroscientist I got to know when, in the autumn of 1996 I was based at St. Anne's for a term; and Mary Douglas. Two of them, Muriel Spark and Mary Douglas, have been described by others as 'difficult women', but I never found them anything but charming and, more than that, immediately felt they were friends, despite the disparity in our ages and reputations. Three others, Rachel, Marianne and my mother, have been described by those who did not know them well as 'formidable' or even 'scary'. But again that was not my experience of them. They were opinionated, strong-willed women, but remarkably warm and loving with those they liked and trusted. With all of them I felt that there was an almost physical response to me: they liked me from the word go, it seemed to me, though with Rachel it took longer to move from a tutor-student relationship to a genuine friendship.

Why have I never felt towards men what I felt towards these women: that they were wiser than I could ever be and at the same time warm and caring? (That does not quite describe Chickie, but intellectually she had a great influence on me and even when I began to realise that her bent of mind did not quite coincide with mine I still marvelled at her passion for literature of all kinds. On my last visit to Egypt, with F, who was German, she again amazed me by starting to recite Novalis to her in German. I had no idea she knew the language.) I have known many brilliant and fascinating older men: Max; Pinter; Bellow; Golding; Kitaj. But I never felt entirely at ease with them, always felt they liked me and liked my admiration of their work, but were somehow distant, happy to let me do all the running but never themselves initiated anything. (Josef Herman and Aharon Appelfeld were exceptions, but I somehow can't attach the adjective 'wise' to them as I can to the women.) So I never felt wholly at ease with them as I did with the women.

Was that simply a result of their gender? Perhaps. Certainly I felt a warmth, an open and giving quality, which has on the whole been missing from my relationship with older men.

Perhaps too because I grew up almost exclusively in the company of women, first my mother and then my aunt and two female cousins I have always felt more at ease with them. (As I write this I think that perhaps there was one man I would characterise as wise in the sense I'm using it here, Aharon Appelfeld.)

I met Marianne when I had just lost my mother, and I suppose I felt at once that that mixture of powerful intellect, wide-ranging curiosity about art and culture and people, and that Jewish substratum impossible to define but immediately present to me, which made it almost inevitable that I would think of her as the kin of the mother I had known and loved. But our friendship blossomed precisely because she was herself and not someone else, not my mother. And grew as she became a vital support in the ten hardest years of my life, between losing Sacha and getting to know T.

On our first walk together this white haired lady, this eminent scientist, suddenly said: 'I need to pee!' and disappeared into the bushes. I loved that.

John, her Australian ecologist husband, was a vital part of it, though Marianne always made it clear I was *her* friend, not just theirs. John recognised and respected this, understanding, I think, how much, just then, I needed Marianne's wisdom and commonsense. I loved the way they each did their own thing yet also did so much in common: he worshipped her, feeling that she, born in Romania of Hungarian Jewish and Viennese non-Jewish parents, escaping with them to New Zealand in 1939 and coming to Oxford to pursue her studies, where she met him, a humble and monoglot Australian biologist, belonged to a different, culturally much richer world; she needed his solidity and dependability and also the way he had expanded his own horizons, becoming a passable pianist and a faltering Chinese speaker after an academic spell in that country. But how much she depended on him only became evident after his death when they were both well into their eighties. She became a different person, more withdrawn, though still outwardly as welcoming. She ceased to wish to have me stay overnight, so that visits to her in Oxford had necessarily to be fleeting, and I felt her turning away from life and so of course from me. And though it pains me still that

I could not see her for one last time with the knowledge that death was close – it came too suddenly – I realised then that in a sense she had died the day he had. But she has left a big emptiness in my life.

It was different with Muriel and Mary. Because I met them so late on in their lives I never saw either of them very much. But with both I sensed at once that a genuine relationship had been forged, that I did not have to stand on ceremony with them, however famous they were, however feted and admired. Yet both lived too far away, Muriel in Italy, Mary in Highgate, for any close friendship to develop. We corresponded, I wrote admiringly about their work to them – Mary was in her late 'biblical' phase, bringing her remarkable anthropological skills to bear on that most recalcitrant of biblical books for the non-religious reader, *Leviticus* – and they in turn, with their respect for my work, gave me the confidence to move forward; but I saw them only rarely and even then fleetingly – a couple of days with Muriel and Penelope in their house in Italy, the odd visit or party at Mary's in Highgate. Yet they remain, after their deaths, palpable, benign presences.

Rachel was different again. When I began to attend tutorials with her in my third year as an undergraduate, sent there by our regular tutor, Graham Midgley, I sensed at once that this was what I had come to Oxford for: here was someone for whom the English writers from Chaucer to Tennyson were not an object of study but simply old friends. Her bookshelves contained the complete works of them all, including their letters, when available, and the latest biography, but no criticism. Needing to refresh her memory as she made a point she would dart from her chair, always chainsmoking, and inevitably find the right volume and quickly open it at the right page. All of it was half-alien to me, but I was happy to drink from it as from a refreshing stream come straight down from the mountains (she was a great champion of the local and the rooted, a passionate admirer of Wordsworth). There was nothing provincial about her, though, despite her proud Wigan roots. She was an avid Proustian, having come to him through Ruskin, and was part of that Oxford generation of English tutors – John Bayley and John Jones were close friends – who took it for granted that if you were going to write about French or Classical or Russian literature you learned the language and learned it well. And on top of that she was an established novelist; though I had no wish at the time to read her novels I later discovered that a couple of them were rather good in a post-Jamesian manner. It began to dawn on me as the term went on that perhaps after all it might be possible to pursue an academic career in tandem with my writing.

I got to know her better when I came briefly to visit her in the flat by the Parks to which she had retired. We had started to become friends when, as a graduate student, I was living in Woodstock with Sacha. By the time she retired we had known each other for more than thirty years and when I visited her she began to talk to me, as she never had before, about her father and her childhood in Wigan. One conversation in particular has stayed with me. I had asked her how it was that she seemed to be equally at home with the great English historians, Clarendon, Gibbon, Macaulay, as with the poets and novelists. 'I'll tell you, Gabriel' she said. 'You see that round table in the corner? It was our dining table when I was growing up. After our evening meal our father would say to my sister and me: Now girls, do you want to go to bed or do you want to sit under the table and hear me read? Of course we said we'd sit under the table, so we crept in there and sat quietly, hidden by the overhanging tablecloth. And then our father would read out loud from the works of the great historians. He had been a Methodist lay preacher and he had a lovely voice. It must have entered our souls.'

When I graduated with a First I gave her, to thank her, one of my discoveries of the previous two years, a volume of

Maurice Blanchot's essays. She never commented on it. But what did that matter? She was what she was. And she gave me what I needed, like all the wise women in my life.

Not been too good these past few days. Stomach again. Or perhaps it is just unconscious letting go as I approach the end of this, after almost a hundred days of continuous writing.

Hot again today. Said to rise to 30 degrees or more. But, as nearly always here, a saving breeze.

Working, Writing

How I like those present participles: walking, writing, eating, listening, making love. And how impossible to convey in writing and what is involved, precisely, as Kierkegaard was the first to note, because writing, that is, writing fiction, autobiography, etc., is always *writing after*. You write to tell a story that has *already happened*, even if it is only in the writer's mind. But here I want to try and focus on its present, the writing part of 'writing a story, a novel'.

In an anecdote, now notorious, in *Worlds Within Worlds*, Stephen Spender, who almost made an art out of showing himself up for the second-rate hanger-on and name-dropper he largely was, recalls how, as a young man, he met T.S. Eliot and the great man asked him what he wanted to do with his life. 'I want to be a poet', said Spender, whereupon Eliot returned: 'I can understand someone wanting to write poetry, but I cannot understand somebody wanting to be a poet.' Yet Eliot was here being a little disingenuous. In our modern times, when saints no longer roam the earth, the idea of 'the poet' is a potent one. It surely informs every artist, no matter how enlightened or cynical, he or she is. We need to earn our bread of course, but many of us want something more than simply earning our bread, we want some kind of fulfilment, and we also want the respect of our peers. We see this at play in Dostoevsky, where what drives those ageing students and government clerks who people his books is the sense, which they can only get from other people, that they exist. And if people only laugh at their efforts at writing then they will even kill in order to prove to themselves that they are alive, that their lives mean something. Beckett can pour shit over his protagonists and even over his readers and his audience in an attempt to make them see that the idea of art itself is a con perpetuated by our culture, but he needs to go on producing it and even, as we see from his early years as a jobbing writer, needs to get it published.

And that is the thing. Though there is not quite the distinction between being a poet and writing poetry that Eliot suggests in Spender's anecdote, we who write or paint or compose know that, actually, there is one. Stravinsky, as so often, puts it succinctly in the course of one of his conversations with Robert Craft: 'I consider the work on the music to be such an essential part of my life that if it were given to me to receive it ready made I would feel cheated.' While we all feel when working on a particularly recalcitrant piece that we would love to wake up the next day and find it all sorted out, we also know that if it was given to us from the start we would feel cheated. And if we had discovered a way of producing all our work simply by opening a drawer or pressing a button we would feel we needed to find another way of life, however much the work that appeared under our name was admired. I am talking of course about those who have made the making of art a central part of their life, not the inveterate buyer of lottery tickets or the con man.

But it's a strange business, writing. Valéry called it 'this dizzying profession', because, however much we believe in ourselves and our work, there is no objective way of deciding whether it is any good or whether we have been fooling ourselves all the time. Some, like Mann, have a comforting sense of their own worth, others, like Kafka or Beckett, have a gloomy sense of their own terrible limitations (But what is that late novel of Mann's, *Felix Krull*, but his version of Melville's *The Confidence Man*, his novelistic confession of his doubts about writing and his own in particular?). How much does the admiration of one's public count? There are far too many known cases of artists who have started out producing good work succumbing to the view of themselves held by the public and turning, in successful middle age, into fatuous bores. Or turning to drink if they sense deep down that the public is wrong. Few indeed are those like Kafka who have, by and large, a clear sense of the value of what they are doing. Though for much of his life he felt that his writing 'remained in the lowlands' and failed to reach the heights he felt he had it in himself to reach, he knew, especially in that miraculous autumn and winter of 1912 when he produced in rapid succession 'The Judgement', 'The Stoker' and 'Metamorphosis', that *this* was what he had been put on earth to write. Yet of course this was the man who asked his best friend to burn his manuscripts after his death, manuscripts which contained his unfinished novels and such wonderful short stories as 'The Burrow' and such profound meditations on life as the 1917 aphorisms.

Harold Pinter, on being highly praised: 'I'm good, but not that good.' Perfect, though he did not always remember this. Or perhaps, in the privacy of his study, he did.

And Proust must have known that the huge novel two thirds of which he had written by the end of the 1890s, when he was approaching thirty, *Jean Santeuil*, was a cut above the bulk of the novels being produced at the time. He certainly knew that his friends and family considered him a dilettante, a talented dabbler, and that publishing a big serious novel would please and relieve them, his mother in particular, to whom he was so close. The temptation to shut his mind to any doubts he might have had about the project must have been enormous. And yet, without any of the panache of Stephen Dedalus/ the young Joyce refusing on her death-bed to carry out his mother's wishes, he simply abandoned it and turned to other things – his Ruskin translation, his critical essay on *Sainte-Beuve*. He did so, as Blanchot brings out so beautifully in his great essay on the subject, because something deep within him sensed that if he published it he would have ruined for ever his prospects of one day writing the book he felt he had it in himself to write even if he didn't as yet know how and certainly did not know if he ever would know how. The courage that must have taken is inconceivable. I certainly cannot conceive it, though I can acknowledge it. And I doubt if I could have done it.

(Compare Dedalus/Joyce and Proust here with Sartre and Beckett a few decades later. Sartre rejected the Nobel Prize for literature with a grand gesture and much publicity; Beckett accepted it and quietly fled to Morocco with his wife to escape the publicity, donating the money to charity.)

I have the feeling that there have been times when I have handed in novels to my publisher sensing that I had not got where I wanted with them but that this was the best I could do and leaving him to decide whether he thought it was good enough to publish, or accepting the views of friends who said they liked it. And certainly there have been times when I have shown work to friends who have not liked it and yet have gone ahead and published. On one memorable occasion a particularly exacting friend, and one to whom I show work for precisely that reason, rang up after she had read it to say: 'Gabriel, you won't like this, but I think you should put it in a drawer and forget it.' I put down the phone and went in and told my mother what had happened. 'What are you going to do?' she asked. 'Sleep on it,' I said. And the next day I told her: 'I've decided to ignore what she said.' Many years later I asked this friend if she'd changed her mind about the novel in the intervening time. She thought for a while and finally said: 'No.'

Yet there have been times when I have listened to advice and desisted from publishing. Admittedly only with short stories and essays. But with longer pieces of work I have usually not needed others to tell me something isn't working. I can sense it and try a different tack or drop the project altogether for a while, a month or two maybe, or possibly a year or two, or even a decade or two. If I find myself going back to it in my notebooks then I know it is something I need to have another go at. And sometimes that works and sometimes it doesn't. My metaphorical drawers are full of work that has fizzled out, come to nothing. Perhaps one day I will return to it and find that it can work after all.

On the other hand I know that sometimes the feeling one has on finishing a work is that what one has done is awful and yet when water has had time to flow under the bridge it starts to look not bad at all. Of course one will never know which impression was the right one.

I wish I worked like Thomas Mann, who wrote away steadily till a chapter was really finished and then moved on to the next one and did the same with that. My own procedure is much more hit and miss, which means that I have to get to the end of a book (perhaps that is why my books are so short), working without looking back, and then, if it feels as if there is something there (and if I've got to the end it usually means that there is), start again at the beginning and go right through it again, this time with the first draft in front of me, often copying, but then adding or taking away as I do so. And even after several drafts I am often not sure if the whole thing is worth anything at all.

But what all this is leading up to is the sheer pleasure of being able to sit down at my desk every morning and get back to what I had left off yesterday with the sense that this is good and it is taking me where I want to go. There is nothing like it, as Handke hints in *On Duration*. But this feeling can only be arrived at by finding a form, or perhaps what Eliot called an objective correlative, which allows me to discover as I write. There is no interest for me in thinking through a story and then giving it words. The form or the subject must be one that leads me, often like the protagonist, into areas I sensed I wanted to go into, even felt very strongly I wanted to go into, but could not have gone into without the Ariadne's thread of my fiction.

And this of course means that I must always accept the dark reverse of the pleasure, the joy even, I hinted at above: the sheer horror of feeling that there is 'something there' but there is no form for it, that there are no words for it, and seemingly no way to find a form, to find the words. So no daily sitting at the desk and writing. Because writing is not like training for a sporting event, where, whether one likes it or not, one has to get through the training and the reward will be there at the end. For some artists perhaps there is no distinction, but for me, who has done both, it is a gulf, despite the many similarities between the sheer joy of running well, swimming well and writing well. Instead, an empty day looms, which I can sometimes find ways to fill, but always with the knowledge, somewhere inside me, that this is no substitute for writing.

A strange way to live ones life. But, with the cards I've been dealt, my way.

25.6.2020

Heatwave. Too hot yesterday – even at 6.30 p.m., when we went up onto the Downs I felt the need for a hat and should have taken my sunglasses. But breezy and pleasant at the top, and this morning finished breakfast in the garden, it felt like Egypt in the early summer.

First anniversary of our wedding. What joy.

Everything more or less 'going back to normal' on 4 July – with no proper track and trace in place and daily news of huge parties in Manchester, London and other big cities, often ending in deaths, which the police seem incapable of breaking up. Clear that after the Cummings episode the public has simply gone its own way, ceased to pay much attention to the government or its now discredited medical advisers. So in a way more scary for us to think of emerging – at least till we see how things are doing, whether there are second spikes, etc. Parts of China and Germany back in lockdown and even New Zealand in a panic. So how can Britain be immune?

Zazie dans le métro

There are some books that have a greater influence on you than you realised at the time. *Zazie dans le métro* is one of them. I must have read it at Oxford, when I was toying desultorily with a B.Litt and wondering about the future. My copy is the old 1959 Livre de Poche edition with a great cover, cartoon-like Zazie, red tongue hanging out, arms and legs raised high in a dance of joy or rage, métro ticket (barred) for body, and on the back the parrot in his cage, red tail and head feathers, métro ticket (barred) for body, huge beak open and 'tu causes, tu causes…' emerging from it. Typically, no one is credited for the design.

I read it but it did not make much of an impression on me. What I was drawn to at the time was the work of Robbe-Grillet, Duras and Simon. Queneau's novel seemed amusing but lightweight. And yet when I was writing my first novel, *The Inventory*, it was not Robbe-Grillet, Duras and Simon I found myself suddenly thinking of, but Zazie. *The Inventory* took off when I let go and, having found a solid foundation, started to improvise. And in the course of the improvisation what gave me the courage to continue and to continue in the way I found myself going, was *Zazie*. I didn't re-read it, but I found – to my surprise – that it was there, waiting to help me.

What was it that was such a help? Simply the fact of knowing that Queneau could let himself go into the wildest fancies and the most 'unrealistic' uses of language and, somehow, he could keep us on his side. Zazie, for example, runs away from an unwelcome adult 'droit devant elle en zigzag' – she can't be both running straight ahead and zig-zagging, but we know just what Queneau means and just how Zazie feels. Or when the parrot, who goes by the glorious name of Leverdure and whose refrain has been 'tu causes, tu causes, c'est tout ce que tu sais faire', a marvellous indictment of what the humans in this book are doing, suddenly comes out with: 'Oui, nous ne comprenons pas le hinc de ce nunc, ni le quid de ce quod'. No one pays any attention. 'Négligeant l'intervention du pérroquet,' Queneau tells us, 'Gabriel répondit en ces terms a ses précédents interlocuteurs.'

I should have known. After all, I loved Charlie Chaplin and Buster Keaton, Laurel and Hardy, the Marx Brothers, and at the heart of all their films is the tenet that we lend a work of art our credence not because it seems plausible but because, for complex reasons, we have come to trust it not to let us down. And part of the contract, it seems to me, is that, however much the laws of plausibility are flouted, some of them have to remain in place. To do away with all of them leads to vacuity, to boredom. It's a matter of getting the balance just right, of pushing the boundaries of anarchy just far enough and no further. When, at the opening of one of the Marx Brothers films, we see a large silent room with several beds in it and an alarm clock suddenly goes off and in seconds the occupants of those beds have leapt out, shoved the beds up against the walls, and it looks for all the world as if we are now in a busy office – except for the fact that a slice of toast keeps popping out of the office typewriter and has to be hurriedly buried again. And in another of their films Chico stands against a wall and, on being asked: 'You, why are you standing there?' answers: 'I'm propping up the wall.' 'Scram!' the other says. Chico takes the hint and walks away and the wall falls down. Yet at once the episode of the wall is forgotten and the plot moves on. It had never struck me that I could or would even want to transpose all this to the pages of a novel, but suddenly in *The Inventory* that became a possibility and it was the memory of *Zazie* that gave me the confidence to go with my instinct and trust that all would be well.

In the following year, as I was rewriting the critical book I had begun to gestate as a graduate student and had worked on in bouts over my first years of teaching at Sussex, I added the parrot's theme tune as an epigraph to the chapter on Rabelais: 'Tu causes, tu causes, c'est tout ce que tu sais faire.' I had started working on Rabelais in the course of my B.Litt at Oxford and had gone for a while to the great Rabelais scholar at Christ Church, Alban Krailsheimer, who for years had been working on a book on Rabelais and the Franciscans. I had greatly enjoyed his lectures, which I found surprisingly full of humour (it was not in great supply in the Oxford of those years), but I discovered to my sorrow that he considered Rabelais above all a great Renaissance encyclopedist and felt (it was the orthodoxy of the time) that to see laughter and linguistic play as central to his work was somehow to belittle him. Later I discovered that (of course!) Queneau had been a great admirer of Rabelais, and for precisely that reason.

Zazie is best known for introducing the vernacular into the 'serious' novel. Walter Redfern, that fine scholar of French literature, even makes a Queneaesque pun to that effect in a delightful essay on parrots in Flaubert, Queneau and Beckett. One of the joke refrains of *Zazie* is Uncle (tonton) Gabriel's description to the tourists he shows round Paris that the Sainte Chapelle is 'ce joyau de l'art gothique', this jewel of Gothic art, and Redfern wittily describes *Zazie* as 'ce joyau de l'argotique', this jewel of *argot*, slang. Queneau delights in trying to reproduce vernacular speech rhythms and in forcing the reader to decipher the sounds behind the letters, as in the opening sentence of the novel: 'Doukipudonktan, se demanda Gabriel excédé' (*D'où qui pue donques tant?*, where the hell's this stink coming from?). And while this kind of joke phonetic transcription would be a struggle to decipher if perpetrated in any language, for the French reader it is much harder than for an English one, since with the establishment of the French Academy in the seventeenth century a far bigger gap was opened up in France between the literary and the vernacular than there has ever been in English, which has always resisted the notion of an Academy to regulate language. Proust and then Céline did much to bridge it, but it is ingrained in French culture and education and only now, with the advent perhaps of Francophone writing from Africa growing in popularity, is it beginning to disappear. Rabelais, of course, was writing before the advent of the Academy, but, as with Skelton and the Scots Chaucerians in the English canon, it took the modernist revolution (or perhaps it would be truer to say, where English literature is concerned, it took Pound) for this kind of writing to be fully appreciated. With Rabelais and Queneau, though, there is a difference. It is not just the 'earthiness' of the writing, the sheer delight in the local and the vernacular, that is on display but the awareness of the unbridgeable gap between the words out of which fiction is made and the reality it purports to present. As the epigraph, to *Zazie* (out of Aristotle) has it: *ho plasas eiphanisen*: 'He who created [it], [also] destroys [it].' That is, the artist invents at will and may destroy his invention at will. For Mallarmé, Kafka and the Hofmannsthal of the *Lord Chandos Letter* this was a dangerous discovery, a look into the abyss, because if the act of artistic creation is only this, a purely wilful and arbitrary thing, then what is the status or value of what has been thus created? For Rabelais and Queneau, as for the masters of silent film comedy (we should add Vigo's 1933 film, *Zéro de conduite*) it was a release of glorious laughter and anarchy, a blow struck at all pomp and stuffiness, as well as at obsessive self-aggrandisement.

It was good to discover this in myself in the course of writing *The Inventory*. From then on, I hope, at least in some works, laughter and absurdity have never been far from the surface, though it was only in *Infinity*, I think, that I finally managed to combine it with the darkness I found and loved in those other early mentors, Robbe-Grillet, Duras and Simon.

And now, as I think about it, it is no coincidence that my mother used to gobble up any new book by Queneau when she and my father were living in France in the 1930s, and that he was particularly dear to the friend and colleague who more than any other I feel understood what I was getting at in my work, George Craig. I have a copy of *Odile*, a little known early book of Queneau's that belonged to George and that his wife gave me after his death. Every page is covered in pencil marks and comments in George's characteristic elegant handwriting. I treasure it for everything it says about George but also as a sign of how books mark life as life marks books.

26.6.2020

Johnson's desperate need to have something 'positive' to announce led to the suddenly total easing of lockdown when a number of the Government's own tests for such easing had still not been met: the test-and-trace scheme is far from up and running, the P number is still hovering round 1, key medical advice is being ignored. Result: huge street parties with youths fuelled by drink fighting the police, the beaches swarming.

Yesterday hottest day of the year. Last two too hot for me but pleasant again today (around 21 degrees). Yet wonderful light on our walk from five to seven yesterday evening, and pleasure of dinner in the garden – reminded me again of Egypt, T of Israel.

What it must be like for those without gardens, cooped up in small flats – terrible – no wonder Government advice to 'use your commonsense' is equated with: Go out into the sun and enjoy yourselves.

Strange to be coming to an end of this. I don't think I've ever spent over 90 days sitting at my desk and writing every single day – not even when I was writing the Bible book.

Zoos

Like so many adults I recall the sheer pleasure of our visits to the zoo. Cairo Zoo on Gizeh island was one of the only green and open spaces in the city, made all the more exciting by having to trail through crowded streets from Bab el Luk station to get there. I remember walking with my mother and sometimes friends as well from one enclosure to another – the animals were often in large open spaces separated from visitors by moats as well as barriers. There were more species than one could possibly take in: zebras, giraffes, rhinos, black bears, sea lions, lions, tigers, elephants, cheetahs and gazelles, as well as flamingos, ibises, and many birds of prey, snakes and tortoises, and of course Nile crocodiles. There was an island with a tea-garden, not exactly Groppi but still good for an ice-cream or a coke.

In the years after we left Egypt and once I had a job and we acquired a car we would make a point of seeking out the zoo in whatever city Sacha and I stopped at on our visits to the Continent, and we must have seen dozens, though I only remember a fine one in Basle and a poor one in Rome. At some point, however, we simply stopped going. Was it that the zoos themselves had become more disappointing, or that we had begun to be aware of the misery even the best looked after wild animals must be experiencing in captivity? Whatever the reason, after a certain time we stopped automatically seeking out the zoo in whatever city we found ourselves in. Occasionally we would visit the botanical garden, and I recall an unbearably hot afternoon in Verona where the only shade we could find was in the botanical gardens, and then, with T, a delightful morning spent in the botanical gardens in Palermo. But zoos have more or less disappeared from my ken, and when passing Regents Park Zoo on foot or by car and hearing the screech of the birds, my heart fills not with joy but with sorrow. Children, I know, still find them exciting, but fortunately our grandchildren are still too young to ask to be taken.

27.6.2020

Rain, wind. Gloomy sense that this country, if not the rest of the world, is simply going to go back to what it was before the pandemic, even if there are more spikes or more waves. They have built another 20,000 or so deaths into their calculations but want only to get on with their wretched Brexit. Clear though that this was the world's last chance to do something fundamental about climate change before it was too late and it is going to blow it. Not very cheering in either the long or the short term. And all it would have taken was different people at the helm here and in the US, Russia and China.

I began this more than three months ago with Aachen and yesterday finished with Zoos. I had thought this was a chance to take stock and in a way it has been. But in another, of course, one can never 'take stock'. The only way to take stock, for me at any rate, is to write – to write fiction. And something is perhaps coming.

28.6.2020

Devastating summing-up of Johnson's first year in power and his handling of the pandemic in the *LRB* by Ferdinand Mount – once Mrs Thatcher's PPS, cousin of David Cameron, one-time editor of the *TLS*, a baronet of high intelligence (at Oxford, where he got a First in Greats, someone who knew him at the time told me he was touted as a future Prime Minister, but was felt to be too intelligent for that). Entitled 'Superman Falls to Earth' it is the deftest analysis of our Prime Minister and what drives him I have yet come across. 'It has been painful to watch the steadiness and sombre dignity of the first ministers of the devolved parliaments – notably Nicola Sturgeon -,' he writes, 'and then turn to the slapdash boosterism of Johnson and his associates, many of whom seem to have caught his feckless tone as well as his frightful virus. It is jarring to hear ministers claim they are "proud of our achievement" in the middle of a pandemic which has cost, so far, more than fifty thousand lives. The world's second highest death-rate per capita – wow, that's really something. Bolsanaro, Trump and Johnson these are men you wouldn't put in charge of containing an outbreak of acne.'

Labour, Mount says, left the NHS in reasonable shape, not perfect by any means but 'still meeting people's basic needs at a cost far below that of comparable health systems in Europe, let alone the US.' Then in 2012 came the disastrous Lansley reforms, cutting money and trying to centralise everything. 'The resulting confusion has been made evident at the daily press conferences given during the epidemic. Exactly what do these panjandrums flanking the pygmy minister of the day do... and which of them does what? We don't know and it's not always clear that they know either.' He traces this back to Thatcher's capping of the domestic rates in 1984 (which he confesses to have had 'a small but culpable hand in') and the abolition of the GLC and the Metropolitan Counties in 1986 ' 'What we have now,' he concludes this part of his essay, 'is a public health service that is simultaneously starved, fragmented and centralised.' The result can be seen in, among other things, the Care Homes *débacle* during the pandemic.

But even this does not quite explain how it is that the British Government, 'with all the expertise available to it, should have proved so spectacularly cack-handed.' 'Some leaders end up in their bunker,' he goes on. 'Trump has recently paid a trial visit to his. Johnson has been in one from the start.' The disaster to the economy and Britain's standing in the world that will ensue from the Brexit he is doggedly pursuing, he points out, 'will be the result of a freely chosen policy. We were not driven to the cliff edge by accident or incompetence... It was always the Brexiteers' destination of choice. It's a chilly place.'

Those infected with the Covid-19 virus across the world have now passed 10 million.

29.6.2020

Windy walk yesterday. In the field opposite Jonathan's house the barley just starting to turn copper though still predominantly green. The great waves sweeping the field as the wind gusted. To think that when we started the field was nothing but chalk and flint, then slowly the green shoots began to show – and now this. Another few weeks and the barley will be ripe.

Weather still very unsettled. Wind. Rain. Odd bursts of sunshine.

Finished Roussel's first book yesterday: *La Doublure*. Had never read any of his books right through before and a strange experience. Written in perfect alexandrines when Roussel was just twenty, it was in the writing of it that he felt the exaltation which stayed with him for the rest of his life and set him on the path to his strange career. Its total failure when he had imagined it would make his name and fame only contributed, it seems, to his subsequent shutting out of the world in the pursuance of his improbable dream.

Something precious is coming to an end. We are going up to London for the first time since T came down on 21 March, to see her mother and daughter and get a few things from the flat. And plans are afoot for us to drive to Wales to see Zoe and Sol. So, after a hundred days it is time to end this. I have enjoyed it. The excitement of having just one day to formulate a 'memory' or 'thought' (it has sometimes been difficult to separate the two) has been a joy some days, at others a task carried out through gritted teeth, but always, as the day's work gets done, leaving me with a pleasant sense of achievement. Not major, but still something. Whether I'll enjoy reading back through it remains to be seen.

Acknowledgements

More than any of my books this one was written for myself alone. But as it went on the old itch to get one's work read began to re-assert itself, and by the time I had finished I was quite keen to see how those who knew me well would react to it. The initial responses were gratifying, so I decided to show it to Michael Schmidt at Carcanet, who has been publishing me for more than thirty years.

My main constraint had been to write each mini-essay in one day and to keep this up for a hundred days. In the light of the responses to the finished work by Michael and the friends I showed it to, I went over it, cut out as much of the flab as I could as well as the obvious repetitions, and in one instance rewrote an entire piece, thus making it, I hope, a better book. I want therefore to thank Michael, John McAuliffe and Andrew Latimer at Carcanet for their unfailing care and courtesy. When I am sure they had better things to do Rosalind Belben, Stephen Mitchelmore, Tim and Judith Hyman, Liza Dimbleby, Dick Earle and Alison Bury read what turned out to be a fairly long book and were warm in their encouragement, even if they did not always agree with what I had written. Bernard Sharratt commented in extraordinary detail on just about every essay and many of the diary entries, leading to a vigorous exchange which could have resulted in a whole other book. Tamar was as usual both warm in her response and firm in her convictions, saving me from several *gaffes*, and in one instance getting me to rewrite. It's good to have such friends.

Index